a **PICASSO** *Bestiary*

a **PICASSO** *Bestiary*

by Neil Cox
and Deborah Povey

ACADEMY EDITIONS

Exhibition Acknowledgements

'Picasso is the heir to all great artists and, having suddenly awakened to life he sets out in a direction that none has taken before him ... he has vastly extended the realm of art in the most unexpected ways where surprises bob up like a toy rabbit beating a drum in the middle of the highway.' (Guillaume Apollinaire 1918)

Perhaps the greatest surprise is Picasso's unexpected appearance in the heart of Croydon. Our ability to mount this ambitious show has been due not only to the co-operation of the lenders but also to the foresight, commitment and vision of the London Borough of Croydon.

'Cock and Bull Stories: A Picasso Bestiary' is an exhibition created in the spirit of fun and childlike pleasure, combined with hidden mystery and meaning, which so often characterises Picasso's art. The exhibition offers the chance to discover a wealth of variety in Picasso's animal art by presenting works in diverse media and from all periods of his long and prolific career. In contrast to the many larger scale or 'blockbuster' shows of the last decade, we deliberately set out to make a thematic exhibition which was open to many different levels of response and which did not demand knowledge of the artist's life and work before it could be appreciated.

It is a great privilege for Croydon to be able to inaugurate a new museum and gallery with an exhibition of works by Pablo Picasso. When this exhibition was conceived it was never imagined that we would receive such favourable responses from so many people and institutions.

In particular, we would like to thank the following whose special efforts and contributions have made this show possible: Hélène Lassalle and Jeanne-Yvette Sudour, Musée Picasso, Paris; Nathalie Leleu, Musée National d'Art Moderne, Centre National d'Art et de Culture Georges Pompidou, Paris; Lionel Prejger, Paris; Quentin Laurens, Galerie Louise Leiris, Paris; Dr Helen Clifford, Ashmolean Museum; Dr Elizabeth Cowling, University of Edinburgh, Professor Christopher Green, Courtauld Institute; Christopher Brown and John Leighton, National Gallery, London; Sylvie Forrestier, Dominique Forest, Musée de Ceramique et d'Art Moderne, Vallauris; Maurice Fréchuret, Luc Deflandre, Musée Picasso, Antibes; Dana Josephson, Dr Bruce Barker-Benfield, Bodleian Library, Oxford; Nicholas Serota and Ruth Rattenbury, Tate Gallery, London; Evelyne Ferlay; Jan Krugier and Louisa Sellerin, Galerie Jan Krugier, Geneva; Christina Fassler and Doris Ammann, Thomas Ammann Fine Art Gallery, Zürich; Maria Teresa Ocaña, Museu Picasso, Barcelona; Brigitte Baer; Maia Widmaier-Picasso; Seiji Tanaka, Hakone Open Air Museum, Japan; and all the private lenders who graciously supported our show.

To conclude I would like to thank all the people who have worked closely together on this project from inception through to completion with unfailing energy and enthusiasm: Dr Neil Cox for devising and curating the show, Dr Deborah Povey for her invaluable contributions to both the book and the exhibition, Charles Ryder for his perceptive design skills and Alan Davidson for creating a lively and innovative computer interactive programme. Lastly, and most personally I would like to thank all the museum staff at Croydon for their constant support throughout the project.

Karen Mann, Exhibitions Officer, Croydon Museum Service

Book Acknowledgements

We would like to thank: Dawn Ades, Brian Connor, Elizabeth Cowling, Valerie Fraser, Rosy Hayward, Nicola Hodges, Tim Laughton, Carole Lyons, Sally MacDonald, Karen Mann, Gregory Mills, John Nash, Maureen Reid, Natasha Robertson, Annamarie Uhr-Delia, Peter Vergo, Caroline Wood, Barry Woodcock.

Neil Cox and Deborah Povey

COVER: Picasso, Detail of *Still-life with Cat and Lobster*, Mougins 23/10-1/11/62, oil on canvas, 130 x 162cm, Hakone Open-Air Museum, (Z.XX.356). © DACS 1995.

PAGE 2: Picasso with an owl in front of *Still-life with Owl and Three Urchins*, photograph by Michel Sima. Courtesy of Nicolas Taulelle, Selon Edition. © DACS 1995.

Published in Great Britain in 1995 by
ACADEMY EDITIONS an imprint of Academy Group Ltd,
 42 Leinster Gardens, London W2 3AN
member of VCH PUBLISHING GROUP

Distributed to the trade in the USA by
ST MARTIN'S PRESS 175 Fifth Avenue, New York, NY 10010

ISBN: 1 85490 401 9

Contents

PREFACE

It is a Bestiary: and those who know the name will have at least a rough definition of a Bestiary in their minds, as a sort of moralised Natural History illustrated with curious pictures. *(MRO James, 1928)*

This book is published to coincide with the exhibition 'Cock and Bull Stories: A Picasso Bestiary'. This exhibition was conceived as an anthology of animals, or a set of fables, which grouped a selection of Picasso's animal works by subject rather than chronologically. The focus was therefore less immediately on questions of style, or the place in the artist's development of particular works, and rather more on the meanings that might be discovered in them, or conjured by them. Picasso's pictures and sculptures invite us to tell stories about them, as Picasso himself liked to do. Telling stories, usually 'moralised stories', about animals, and making pictures to go with them, is a very old game. Usually we think that the stories came first. In this case, however, we begin with the 'curious pictures' and the pictures that came before them.

Our model is the mediaeval bestiary: a very luxurious 'book of beasts', produced by scribes and monastic painters for wealthy patrons. These scholars and artisans had to transmit the message of Christianity in their work, but they also had another job to do: to make a catalogue of the wonders of the animal kingdom, relying on existing knowledge and occasional fantasy. In this Picasso Bestiary, we perform comparable tasks: weaving stories of great or little significance around Picasso's represented animals and recording some, though by no means all, of the extensive knowledge that exists about them and their predecessors in the history of European art.

Throughout, the book does two things: it gives an account of some of the important animal symbolism in the visual art of Western Europe, and it discusses Picasso's depictions of the same animals. The book has been written in two 'voices', more or less independently. One deals with the pre-twentieth-century tradition, the other with Picasso. There has been no great determination to marry the two; rather, we hope the reader will be as excited as we were by the way a pattern emerges almost of its own accord. The greatest area of collaboration was in the choice of pictures, where often, though not always, deliberate visual resonances were sought.

The aim of this strategy is not to argue that all Picasso's works are deliberate copies of, or variations on, the earlier works described – although a few of them are – but rather to show how consistently certain long-established themes continue into his art. The book is concerned with the way that traditional symbolism persists, yet changes and adapts according to new demands and concerns. We have discovered that Picasso's depictions of animals both comply with tradition and deviate from it to fulfil more personal ends and ambitions. The juxtaposition of the traditional treatment of, say, the owl, with Picasso's represented owls reveals the degree to which he invests tradition with personal and contemporary significance; whilst Picasso's monsters reveal considerable departures from precedent. Most of all, we hope that the illustrations themselves catalogue the large number of extraordinary visual parallels, and question the wisdom of assuming that there are single specific models for Picasso's well tried and tested compositional formulae.

Each of the chapters is a discrete entity in its own right, and they may be read in order or according to the reader's own animal hierarchy. The Introduction sets out to provide a framework within which these individual chapters may be considered, by introducing the basic themes which have conditioned thought about, and representation of, animals throughout the centuries. In addition, it outlines the conceit, and the problems, of making a bestiary out of Picasso's animal art.

INTRODUCTION

Deep in the Palaeolithic caves of Lascaux in the Dordogne, in the so-called 'Shaft of the Dead Man', an anonymous artist painted an intriguing scene: a bison charges a man with an erect penis who falls backwards; his spear lies useless on the ground and below him is a bird on a stick – a sort of duck-decoy. The image is rich in narrative potential, but the story the artist was telling is no longer known.[1] What it does tell us, however, is that the earliest of western art was a meaningful art about animals which articulated a complex relationship between human and beast. Here and at numerous other sites throughout Europe, wild beasts rampage across ceilings and walls, sometimes being hunted by humans, less often, as here, overcoming their predators. Beasts are hunted for food and clothing, but the care and attention with which they are represented in these most inaccessible of places, indicates a respect for their vitality, vigour and beauty which transcends the practical necessities of a harsh life. Such considered and sustained re-enactment of the thrills and terrors of the chase may have served to commemorate a killing, whether of beast or man; or to prognostically safeguard the hunter and killer of a beast; or, perhaps, to conjure up, and appropriate, those animal qualities which were both feared and admired.[2] Occasionally, masked men with bestialised features, now known as 'sorcerers' are represented,[3] and in the cave at Montespan a life-size headless bear once had the skull of a real bear attached to it.[4] By such means, the reality of the animal, its power and essence, was appropriated for the act of representation, a totemic focus for ceremonies and rituals and a visualisation of the hopes, fears and desires of a people. The artist who conjured the image of the beast into being was a sorcerer – a magician of representation.[5]

Pablo Picasso, one of the most renowned and prolific artists of any century, lived a very different life in a very different culture from those unknown cave painters. Nevertheless, like many twentieth-century artists, he has been identified with such figures and the presumed magic purposes of their art.[6] One type of evidence for his own identification with them is in the large number of reported conversations with the artist. Here, for example, is the most stirring (if anthropologically uninformed) statement of Picasso's admiration for imagined 'primitive'

OPPOSITE: Anon. Palaeolithic, *Bison, fallen hunter and duck decoy*, Lascaux caves, 'Shaft of the Dead Man', 18,000-13/12,000 BC. Photo Hans Hinz.

ABOVE: *Adam Naming the Animals*, MS Ashmole 1511, Bestiary in Latin, early 13th-century, f. 9r. The Bodleian Library, Oxford.

artists, in this case for the makers of tribal masks which Picasso had seen in 1906 in the Trocadéro Museum in Paris:

> Those masks were not just pieces of sculpture like the rest. They were magic... These Negroes were intercessors – that's a word I've known in French ever since then. Against everything: against unknown, threatening spirits. I kept on staring at these fetishes. Then it came to me – I too was against everything. I too felt that everything was unknown, hostile! Everything! Not just this and that but everything, women, children, animals, smoking, playing ... all these fetishes were for the same thing. They were weapons. To help people not to be ruled by spirits any more, to be independent. Tools. If you give spirits a shape, you break free from them.[7]

Picasso's art – and in particular that which features animals – often self-consciously invokes this understanding of art and the artist as magical, ritualistic and potent. Giving a 'shape' (rather making a 'work of art') is thus presented as if it were a totemic practice, an insurance against an alien or demonic natural order. Indeed, this fantastic primordial sense of picturing made an important appearance – along with animal subjects – when Picasso wanted to address a terrible event. In his most famous work, *Guernica*, painted in 1937 as a response to the German bombing of civilians in a Spanish town, human suffering is articulated around the looming presence of a bull and the last agonies of an impaled horse. Like the cave painters, Picasso has worked on a mural (literally 'wall') scale, and his creatures appear dreamlike against a mute ground. Yet whereas we imagine the cave artist to have made his works in the context of some kind of ritual, Picasso's *Guernica* is a political allegory. It therefore relies on the tendency of its public to see the represented animals not as manifestations of some god, but to interpret them, even with their totemic aura, as symbolic of very human actions and emotions. Picasso emphasised this transfer of responsibility from painter to public:

> This bull is a bull and this horse is a horse. There's a sort of bird, too, a chicken or a pigeon. I don't remember exactly what it is, on a table. And this chicken is a chicken. Sure, they're symbols. But it isn't up to the painter to create the symbols; otherwise, it would be better if he wrote them out in so many words instead of painting them. The public who look at the picture must see in the horse and the bull symbols which they interpret as they understand them. There are some animals. These are animals, massacred animals. That's all as far as I'm concerned. It's up the public to see what it wants to see.[8]

In this book we explore the history of western depictions of animals alongside those of Picasso, in order to uncover the sort of past which made it possible for *Guernica*'s public to see a bull as fascism, or a dying horse as the people of Spain; or the public of other bull pictures to find in the features of the animal an image of 'darkness and brutality'.[9] In the context of this history, as one might expect, Picasso's denial of responsibility for the symbolic character of his animal pictures is not always entirely credible.

The Forces of Nature and the Battle for the Soul

The Palaeolithic caves exemplify the beginnings and the essence of human representation of animals. It is probably here that we would find the root of the oral tradition which engendered the rich tapestry of myth and religion, legend and folklore, fables and proverbs which manipulated and appropriated the qualities and characteristics of animals to human design.[10] The harnessing of bestial 'magic' in the stone cathedrals of the caves, marked the beginning of a long process of assimilation in which sometimes for good, sometimes for bad, humans were considered in terms of their animal counterparts and vice versa. In all aspects of life, sacred or profane, mystical or merely practical, animals have had their part to play in the fulfilment of human needs, and have been represented by artists in commensurate fashion. In the individual chapters that follow, it will be seen that those themes which occur and recur throughout the history of animal representation are ultimately reducible to those most fundamental of human concerns: birth, sex, food and death – those concerns which, in short, humans share with animals. Unlike animals, however, humans have articulated these most basic constituents of animate being through ritualised activity – which seeks to engage with those forces which create and regulate life and death. Whether these forces are called Nature or God or by some other name, human endeavour is directed towards ends which animals cannot fathom, that is, towards the future and to a certainty in the rejuvenating properties of sacrificial death.

As one very important book has shown, fertility, procreation, death and renewal inform the essence of ritual and religious sensibility in all cultures and all ages.[11] It is to these concerns that, in one way or another, human attitudes towards nature in general and animals in particular, have been addressed, conditioned by a fundamental desire to create order out of chaos, control out of subjection. Through the domestication of some animals and the development of agriculture, humans asserted their authority over the world and their ability to shape it to their own design. In this respect humans had

Picasso, *Guernica*, May-June 1937, oil on canvas, 349 x 777cm, Museo Nacional de Arte Reina Sofia, Madrid. On permanent loan from the Museo del Prado (Z.IX.65). © DACS 1995.

Albrecht Dürer, *Adam and Eve*, 1504, engraving, 25.2 x 19.4cm, British Museum, London. Copyright British Museum.

affinities, it was thought, with those higher authorities which rule the natural world. Yet humans also shared with the beasts dangerous drives and desires. These 'natural' passions and urges had continually to be moderated and checked by that one faculty animals were seen to lack – that of reason. These ideas achieved their most structured form in classical cosmographies such as Plato's *Timaeus* and the many mediaeval works it inspired. These writings on the nature of the cosmos were founded on the notion of essential correspondence between microcosm and macrocosm. At stake was harmony in nature and the cosmos, and within the human body and soul, but it must always have been abundantly clear that nature, and humans, fell short of this ideal. Only in a distant golden age did universal harmony reign.

This vision of a lost but ultimately recoverable state of being has coloured attitudes to animals, however transformed they may superficially appear, to the present day. In antique thought it was represented by The Golden Age; in Judaeo-Christian Theology, Paradise. In the former, it was Orpheus who charmed the animals with the sweetness of his music. To early Christian artists, however Orpheus represented the Messiah whose coming would fulfil Isaiah's prophecy that: 'the wolf shall dwell with the lamb and the leopard shall lie down with the kid'.[12] From the image of Orpheus were derived early representations of a youthful, beardless Christ as a shepherd, also lulling his flock by playing on a lyre. In the Old Testament, this role was fulfilled by Adam.[13]

Made in the image of God, Adam was given dominion over the earth and all living things. To Adam was also given the task of naming the animals. Adam and Eve lived in harmony with all natural things, with everything in its place. With the Fall, a triumph of sensuality (represented by Eve) over reason (Adam), this equilibrium was destroyed, a moment commemorated in Dürer's engraving *Adam and Eve*. In one important interpretation of this picture, before Adam bit the apple offered him by Eve, his internal equilibrium was perfectly balanced, mirrored by the calm coexistence of the creatures in Eden. The animals, though, 'were mortal and vicious from the start' and ruled by the predominance of one or the other humours 'sanguine', 'phlegmatic', 'choleric' or 'melancholic'. With the Fall, man became contaminated, like the beasts, with the humours, which would continually rage war within him, bringing vice and disease.[14] The orchestration of the Fall through the agency of Eve has been responsible for much of the inherent misogyny of animal representation apparent in the following chapters. Similar thinking also gave moral urgency to the perception of animals as essentially sensual and sexual beings: what we today term 'Freudian' symbolism is probably the oldest and certainly the most basic symbolism of all. Although most animals were simultaneously subject to positive interpretation, generally the emphasis is on those base and bestial instincts which humans share, but which must be moderated and subordinated to reasoned activity.

Thus animals so often represent the senses or the vices, and those men and women who have succumbed to them. This is the spirit in which, in the margins of mediaeval manuscripts, animals and man cavort in a topsy-turvy and bestial world. In some of these marginalia, animals freely and unselfconsciously copulate (see p23), unlike humans who are ever conscious of the shame of the act.[15] In other manuscripts, animals perform human actions and rituals, even the most sacred and solemn: conducting the Mass, for example, or a funeral (see p27, above left). Even though the image reproduced here is a humorous one, it is nevertheless 'unnatural'. Elsewhere, strange hybrid monsters abound, often combining human and animal form. This destruction of equilibrium both around and inside humanity, was restorable only by Christ, the new Adam. Orpheus had failed to lead Eurydice out of the Underworld, but Christ would lead the soul out of limbo. With the coming of the millennium, wild animals would once more live in harmony with humanity.[16]

Meanwhile, humans had to make sense of the post-lapsarian world, to learn lessons from those beasts whose actions so often mirrored humanity's own. From observation of the animal kingdom, humans could understand their own viciousness; they could also discern that, even in their bestiality, animals could also exemplify the nature and workings of divinity. This task was undertaken by the mediaeval bestiary, a Book of Beasts, the format of which this Picasso Bestiary emulates. In the opening pages of the bestiary, or at the beginning of the section dealing with domestic animals, was often placed the image of *Adam Naming the Animals*, giving an indication of the objective of the book: to categorise and explain the nature of beasts. To name something is to order it, to give it a designated place within a system of thought and in the bestiary, to make sense of the struggle between the human and the animal, reason and the senses. If the message of the bestiary were heeded, equilibrium could be restored to our topsy-turvy world.

The Book of Beasts

The bestiary is a moralising encyclopaedia of animals which became particularly popular in the twelfth and thirteenth centuries in England (and, to a lesser extent, in France) where with the Psalter and Apocalypse it was one of the leading picture books.[17] These often sumptuously illuminated productions collected together belief both pagan and Christian, factual and symbolic, concerning animals. They aimed to elucidate the function of beasts within God's divine schema and to focus the reader's attention on the moral and spiritual lessons that could be learned from their real or imagined characters and habits. Thus the beasts are not arranged alphabetically but according to importance. Often, the lion, king of beasts and likened to Christ, came first. Importantly, the bestiary perpetuated certain fundamental beliefs about animals – beliefs which have either survived, or have been challenged, over the centuries.

Usually written in Latin,[18] the bestiary descends from Greek manuscripts of the *Physiologus* (meaning the 'Naturalist'), which probably dates from the second century AD and possibly originated in Alexandria, and which itself gathered together animal lore from diverse classical and Christian sources.[19] The *Physiologus* was translated into Latin in about the eighth century when it was geared to the concerns of a largely ascetic, cloistered audience. It appears that sometime in the twelfth century, the task was undertaken of revising its contents according to the demands of a burgeoning lay and clerical clientele anxious to reconcile spiritual truth with the realities of everyday existence.[20] Thus the bestiary functions as an important mediator between pagan and Christian thought, between religious and mystical concerns and those of practical morality and ethics.

Doubtless, the popularity of the bestiary in the Middle Ages was largely due to the number and quality of its illustrations, a selection of which are provided throughout this book. It will be noticed that some of the bestiary illustrations are quite 'realistic', others are decidedly fanciful, absurd even. It has to be remembered, however, that especially for the more unusual animals (and those, such as the monsters which no-one had ever seen), the artist had to rely on hearsay and precedent for his models. There is a direct line in bestiary illustration which can be followed back to the earliest illustrated *Physiologus*,[21] and a number of bestiaries have punched outlines suggesting that they were used for tracing.[22] Besides, the nature of the material gives little occasion for marked derivation.[23] It is likely, too, that pattern books could have been employed.[24] Where there was no pictorial precedent to follow (eg when the number of bestiary chapters increased from about forty to over a hundred), other sources had to be plundered. It has been suggested, for example, that certain of the animals on gold grounds in so-called Second Family Bestiaries were inspired by designs on Eastern carpets, which would account for their rather stiff and schematic heraldic appearance.[25]

Almost as bizarre as the illustrations are some of the bestiary anecdotes which have been liberally used in the chapters that follow. Both seem less odd once we remember that the bestiary is not so much a natural history as a history of nature, and a compendium of belief. Thus it mattered little whether this or that anecdote was true, or even whether the reader did or did not believe it to be so, the importance lay in the moral that could be expressed by it. Thus pagan and Christian sources were brought to the purpose of edification, in the belief that, by learning about the world and its inhabitants, we can also learn something of the nature of God and ourselves. All material existence, being created by God, was a mirror of the divine will,[26] and even the pagan myths, gods and goddesses had their place:[27] these, together with the events of the Old Testament prefigured, it was thought, those of the New.[28] Everything, in short, was part of the schema; there was not one event, person, animal or thing whose existence and function had not been preordained and which did not fit into the pattern of the grand design. Great lessons could be learned from the observation of nature, a process akin to passing through the carved portals of those Romanesque and Gothic churches and cathedrals such as Saint-Pierre at Aulnay-de-Saintonge, with its *Carnival of Animals*, where irreverently bestial monsters committing all sorts of profanities are represented[29] or those of Saint-Denis and Chartres, which are decorated with the labours of the months and the signs of the zodiac.[30] Often subsumed within a decorative scheme that also included sacred personages and episodes from biblical history, they contextualise the mysteries to be experienced within the church: attention to the world provided a gateway to the divine.

Natural and Unnatural History

Predictably, the format and lore of the bestiary could itself be accommodated to a variety of purposes, notably a cynical reworking of the courtly tradition of love allegory: Richard de Fournival's *Bestiaire d'amour*, written in the middle of the thirteenth century and probably the most popular of all the French bestiaries.[31] By appropriating the form of the bestiary for an anguished petition to his female object of desire, and speaking to the woman not with the voice of reason, as the bestiary purports to do, but through the senses, Richard perpetuated the belief that women (like the beasts) were incapable of listening to the voice of reason.[32] As the individual chapters of our study indicate, this basic thinking has permeated representations of women and animals throughout the centuries. Alongside the anthropocentric and misogynistic world-view represented by the bestiary, however, there

Anon. French, *Carnival of Animals*, South Transept Portal, Church of Saint-Pierre, Aulnay-de-Saintonge, France, 12th century. Photo by Janetta Rebold Benton. Courtesy Abbeville Press, New York.

African Scene, from *Description de l'Afrique* by Olfert Dapper, 1686. By permission of The British Library.

had always been naturalists, artists and traditions of representation which delighted in animals for their own sake. Aristotle, for instance, had scrutinised the natural world with an objective curiosity that 'had achieved an astonishing maturity' and several of the works chosen to illustrate this book indicate a concern that the tiniest details of the natural world are depicted with scrupulous honesty.[33] Some Renaissance artists, notably Pisanello, Leonardo and Dürer, made superb studies from life. These were exceptions, though, to the rule and the bestiary tradition did not have to compete with the more rational world of science until the seventeenth century.[34] With the advent of the printed book, a new wave of zoology had begun, heralded by Conrad Gessner's monumental *Historia animalum* published in Zurich 1551-87, but this taste for scientific enquiry coexisted with, rather than supplanted, older ways of thinking about animals. Edward Topsell's *The Historie of Foure-footed Beasts*, published in 1607, though largely indebted to Gessner, is 'one of the most notorious, most popular, most scientifically worthless, most plagiarised and most fascinating of all books purporting to deal with the animal kingdom'.[35] Nevertheless it has to be said that it is no more so than the mediaeval bestiary. Other seventeenth-century works display an equal amount of fancy dressed up as fact. The *African Scene* from Olfert Dapper's 1686 *Description de l'Afrique* would clearly flout even the most rudimentary trades description act. Dapper had never visited Africa[36] and the giant tulip in the foreground raises suspicions that his grasp of the reality of his own surroundings was no less tenuous.

Against this mood of enlightened progress, it is worth remembering the extent to which the fable and myth which formed the origins of bestiary lore persisted in proverbs, adages and other forms of popular culture which have always had their own active life independent of the bestiary and which lay outside the remit of natural history proper. One of the most self-conscious usages of this lore, and one of the vehicles which ensured the perpetuation of the old traditions, was that product of the great humanist revival of the sixteenth century, the emblem book. Inspired by the claimed 'rediscovery' in the early fifteenth century of a book known as the *Hieroglyphica of Horapollo*, a 'handbook' of the pictorial symbolism of Egyptian hieroglyphics,[37] later devisers and compilers of emblems endeavoured to give a new and intriguing twist to a well-known saying or proverb through a witty combination of motto, image and verse. Frequently they made new and ingenious use of bestiary lore, often, like Richard de Fournival had, to the purposes of articulating the mechanics and fortunes of love and desire. Emblem books were particularly popular in the Dutch

Republic in the seventeenth century.[38] It was also in seventeenth-century Holland that the moralising scene of everyday life and the still-life flourished. These are given some prominence here because not only are certain animals well represented, but also the popular wit and wisdom which inform their representation demonstrate the persistence of old ways of seeing the world to which the demands and requirements of science are an irrelevance.

It was only in the eighteenth century, that Natural History became recognisable as today's scientific discipline. A glance at the two pictures of dromedaries reproduced here serves as illustration. That from Topsell's *The Historie of Foure-footed Beasts* is evidently a product of not quite accurate visual recollection, but in Thomas Bewick's wood engraving from the 1792 *General History of Quadrupeds*, especial care has been taken to place the animal in its native desert surroundings – evidence of a new humility in the representation of animals.[39] Even so, the distinction between dispassionate observation and didactic method was not always so clear cut.[40] Carl Linnaeus, who must take the credit for establishing the classification system still in use today, 'mingled his zoological descriptions with moral and aesthetic judgements; the versions put out by his English editors and adaptors were particularly free in their use of terms such as "loathsome" or "disgusting"'.[41] The Comte de Buffon's *Histoire Naturelle*, though highly influential on many seriously scientific works, nevertheless contains much that is spurious and opinionated.[42] Of course, numerous works of genuine natural history were published in the eighteenth and nineteenth centuries and some, for example Audobon's *Birds of America* (1827-38), have yet to be surpassed in quality, comprehensiveness and perceptiveness. But these are not the concern of this book. Interpretation, not level of exactitude, is the subject of our enquiry and most of the works of art that we have chosen to illustrate this bestiary are those in which animals exist within a far broader based system of social and intellectual endeavour, filtered through the temperament and desires, wit and ingenuity of the artist.

Our decision to embrace these concerns in our enquiry into Picasso's representations of animals, and to develop it throughout a discussion of the history of animal representation, has not been undertaken without some misgivings. Personal considerations so often condition Picasso's most conventional interpretations of animals; sometimes his vision of animal forms is so much the product of his own thoughts and desires that no precedent should be sought for it. Nevertheless, in his work there is often an apparent vacillation and tension between emotion and structure, chaos and order, the idyllic and the

ABOVE: *Dromedary* from *The Historie of Foure-footed Beasts* by Edward Topsell, London, 1607, Bodleian (M.3.14 Th.). The Bodleian Library, Oxford.

BELOW: Thomas Bewick, *Dromedary* from *General History of Quadrupeds* by Thomas Bewick, 1792, wood engraving. By permission of The British Library.

brutal, the ideal and the painfully real. In these dichotomies we see an engagement with those most fundamental and enduring of human concerns: the struggle for reconciliation, a striving for harmony and, above all attempting to make sense of the natural world, manipulating it for human benefit. In this respect it is telling that Picasso identified himself with the artist Orpheus, the god of classical myth who charmed the animals, beguiling and taming them with the sweet music of his lyre.

A Picasso Bestiary?

Unsurprisingly, Picasso, a twentieth-century artist, never illustrated a bestiary as such. He came closest to doing so in 1907 when doodling illustrations for a volume of poems by his friend Guillaume Apollinaire entitled *Le bestiaire ou cortège d'Orphée*. On this sheet we find a array of creatures: horse, bull, owl, cockerel, flamingo, penguin, dog, squirrel, and grasshopper – the challenge being to draw all of them with a single line. Unfortunately, Picasso's elegant drawings were usurped by Raoul Dufy's woodcuts (see opposite) when the poems were eventually published in 1911, even though Picasso seems to have annotated one of Apollinaire's autograph manuscripts of the poems with drawings.[43] In a sense, however, Dufy's nostalgic woodcuts are closer to the symbolist spirit of Apollinaire's poems – which draw out traditionally spiritual meanings from the animal subjects – than Picasso's fresh and playful sketches. Although Picasso had probably seen Apollinaire's poems by the time he made this sheet of drawings, and certainly knew them once he had a manuscript, he seems to have made little attempt to 'illustrate' them.

Just as Picasso never made a bestiary, so he never really illustrated a natural history – at least not according to the rules of scientific interest or perfect naturalism which we might expect of a Stubbs or an Audubon. Once again, though, Picasso produced a bastardised version, and this time it was published. By the thirties Picasso was well established as a print and book artist, and so early in 1936, at the suggestion of Ambroise Vollard, Picasso began to make a suite of thirty-two sugarlift aquatint prints (for example see p36) for an album to illustrate some selections from Georges Louis le Clerc, Comte de Buffon's *Histoire Naturelle*.[44] Once again, however, the story is not simple. Picasso produced one or two prints a day, each one usually evolving through two states, in the atelier of Roger Lacourière. For a joke, Picasso left out the cat until Vollard, a cat-lover, was forced to ask him to produce it (see p104, above left). Yet Vollard, who was killed in a car accident in 1939, never saw the project to its completion. Vollard's watermarked paper and the rights to the project were acquired by Martin

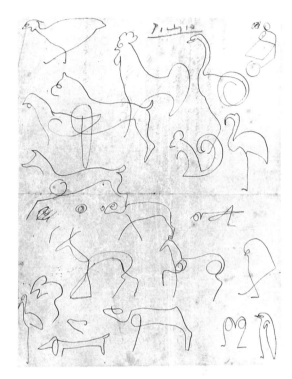

OPPOSITE: Raoul Dufy, *Le Boeuf* from *Le bestiaire ou cortège d'Orphée* by Apollinaire, woodcut, RV 29.323. Roger-Viollet.

ABOVE: Picasso, Studies for illustration of *Le bestiaire ou cortège d'Orphée* by Apollinaire, 1907, ink on paper, 26 x 20.7cm, Musée Picasso. [MP 1989-1]. © Photo RMN. © DACS 1995.

Fabiani who published the book in the occupied Paris of 1942. There were considerable discrepancies between the existing prints and the only abridged Buffon text that could be found by Madame Lacourière.[45]

The relative naturalism of the Buffon prints is a rare exception in Picasso's oeuvre. There are some early drawings showing a genuine interest in accuracy, but on the whole, unlike Leonardo da Vinci, Dürer or Stubbs, Picasso stuck to the aim of invention rather than documentation. Even in the Buffon suite, Picasso enjoys characterising some of the animals with anthropomorphic traits. In fact this is not out of keeping with the tone of Buffon's text (which, as has been suggested above, is not as scientific as we might at first imagine). In all but the last of the nine chapters of this book (there are no 'Monsters' in an enlightened natural history), a print from the Buffon suite will appear.

So is it gratuitous to talk of a Picasso Bestiary? The phrase has cropped up over the years in writings on the artist, being taken most seriously in a rare little book by a vet, Guy Cumont.[46] There are two reasons why the notion of making a bestiary out of Picasso's work has merit. Firstly, there is the consistency with which certain animals recur in the works, encouraging the experiment of categorising them not by date but by animal. Secondly, there is the tenor of Picasso's representations, which has some of the symbolic, allegoric, and moralising interest which was central to the bestiary. Roland Penrose suggests that:

> There are certain animals and birds whose behaviour and appearance make them appropriate symbols of human passions, but in his desire to use this vital link with antiquity, Picasso did not limit himself to oversimplified conventional interpretations, nor did he arbitrarily draw parallels between their actions and moral issues in the manner of La Fontaine. By encouraging a sense of ambiguity he left the spectator the liberty of choosing his own interpretation.[47]

To some extent this is true, but by creating a Picasso bestiary, the arbitrary feel of Picasso's symbols is tempered. The degree of fit between the allegorical tradition and Picasso's animal works is surprisingly greater than Penrose's comment would imply.

An extreme example of such a resonance is in a schoolboy drawing now in the Museu Picasso in Barcelona. In a textbook on Rhetoric and Poetics, the twelve or thirteen year old Picasso had drawn his own marginalia: a male and female donkey copulating, accompanied by a lewd verse:

Without so much as a how-d'ye-do
The She-Ass lifts her tail

OPPOSITE: *Copulating Animals*, MS lat. 16169, Albert the Great: *De animalibus*, 14th century, French, f. 84v. © photograph Bibliothèque Nationale, Paris.

ABOVE: Picasso, *The Donkey and the She-Ass*, La Coruña 1891, pencil on paper, 20.7 x 13cm, Museu Picasso, Barcelona, (MPB 110.927, p178). © DACS 1995.

Without so much as a by-your-leave
The Donkey drives in his nail.[48]

The fact that the pubescent boy unconsciously produced something remarkably similar – and in a similar spirit – to manuscript marginalia reveals something important: the past is not only digested through channels of which one is conscious as an adult, but creeps into us even before we can recognise it. This is a concrete example of the way in which our childhood, filled with nursery rhymes, superstitions, and fairytales, trains us in long established animal iconographies.

Which animals are a part of this Picasso Bestiary, and why? Just as the medieval bestiary ranked its animals in order of importance, so the first few creatures we include are easy to guess. The key to the meaning of *Guernica* has always been thought to lie in the figures of two animals: a bull and a horse, which occupy the centre and left hand parts of the vast canvas.[49] We have already heard that when Picasso was asked about the symbolism of these creatures, ten years after the picture was finished, he drew attention to another, a bird of some sort, which can be seen next to the bull's head. In terms of sheer number, these three creatures: the bull, the horse, the pigeon or dove, outstrip all others in the artist's work. Their interest to Picasso goes back to his childhood – to his father don José's love of the bullfight, to which he often took his son, and amateur success as a painter of pigeons and doves. In *The Bullfight and Six Studies of Doves*, a drawing made in 1892 when Picasso was eleven, the two paternal loves are combined. John Richardson has recently suggested that the rather fluent row of pigeons along the top are either by or direct copies from don José.[50] Whatever the case we find here the beginnings of the fascination which leads to the ordering of the first three animal types in this bestiary: the bull, the horse, and birds. The bull and horse figure for Picasso are those animals most capable of showing in their mortal confrontation great drama. Only the Minotaur (and perhaps the cat) can serve similar functions. This sense of emotional drama is reflected in the quintessential Spanishness which Picasso saw in the bullfight:

For we Spanish, it's Mass in the morning, the bullfight in the afternoon, the brothel in the evening. And where do all three end? In sadness.[51]

The first creature in Picasso's bestiary, the bull, is a double one, since the artist's strong tendency to identify with it and its plight in the ring sees it sometimes transformed into a Minotaur, the mythical half-man half-bull, imprisoned in the labyrinth. The overlap is clear when we realise that Picasso's Minotaur is often to be seen with a wounded horse. Thus, the Minotaurs appear in the final chapter, a reprise of the most human and humourless themes of Picasso's bestiary. Alongside this tragic monster, however, are some sprightly fauns and lusty satyrs, whose animal urges cause them little guilt. As for the birds, they occupy both a sacred and profane position in the order: the dove for example being symbolic of peace but also a creature of lust.

Beyond Picasso's childhood acquaintance with the three opening beasts, some of the ensuing creatures in the book: cats and dogs; the sheep, the ram, the goat; and the monkey are all animals familiar to Picasso in his studio or household. There are certainly identifiable pets in some works, and their importance to Picasso is considered below. Apart from those animals destined to occupy the first places in Picasso's Bestiary, and those which enter as pets and familiars, there are also some which occur very often as decorative motifs and only occasionally, but no less emphatically in major works of considerable atmosphere. These are the 'Watery Creatures' of the sixth chapter. Here, and in the chapter on 'Insects', we are dealing with categories of living creature whose interest to Picasso is at least as much due to previous works of art as to the creatures themselves. Certain artists figure as especially important for Picasso's animal art, and provide models for works which are quite closely emulated. These include amongst others Velázquez, Goya, Chardin, Géricault, Courbet and Manet. There are other cases of compositions where one cannot be sure of a direct response on Picasso's part, but where the similarities between an earlier standard composition and his own is striking and illuminating; for example, Thomas Gainsborough's *The Painter's Daughters Chasing Butterflies* and Picasso's *The Butterfly Hunter*. Finally, there are clear cases, such as the *Octopus Plate*, where Picasso represents a creature in a style of decoration which belongs to another time and culture.

Marginalia – Animals not in A *Picasso Bestiary*

There are very few insects in Picasso's work, but enough major pieces (three) and attractive drawings to make them worthy of inclusion. One animal fails to enter the pages of this bestiary, however, whose absence is somewhat surprising. This is the pig. Pigs, like bulls, horses, sheep, goats, cats, dogs, and birds, would normally feature in a mediaeval bestiary as domestic creatures. If there are any animals a reader might be interested in, it would surely be those in the backyard. Yet Picasso, in spite of the fact that pigs are a very significant form of domestic livestock in his native Spain, and also in rural France, failed to dignify the pig with his art. There are a few, a very few exceptions, and both of those presented here are burlesques. Around 1917, when Picasso was designing the set and costumes

Picasso, *Child in a Sailorsuit with a Butterfly Net [The Butterfly Hunter]*, 2/4/38, oil on canvas, 122 x 86cm, Museum of Modern Art, New York. © DACS 1995.

for a ballet called *Parade* with a libretto by Jean Cocteau, music by Eric Satie, and choreography by Massine, he produced an abortive *Study for a Manager and a Pig*. For a while Picasso planned to mount the managers on horses, or in this case a pig.[52] Eventually, the horse became a separate character and the managers large walking cubist constructions in *Study for the American Manager and the Horse's Head*. The pig in French culture has similar (undeserved) connotations of greed and filth as it does in English. Whether Picasso saw the French or the American manager as more deserving of this ignominy is difficult to tell from the surviving drawings.[53] In either case, the manager in question seems a victim of the rite of the carnival, where those in a position of high office or social rank are mocked and made low. A similar spirit of inversion and charade is present in a very strange sequence of drawings from 1952 showing animals in a funeral procession. The pallbearers in this procession are marching pigs (see opposite), whilst the horses become camels. The similarity between this bit of buffoonery and a marginal illustration in a bestiary of a dog's funeral attended by rabbits (see opposite) is again quite striking.[54]

Another kind of animal altogether, but which also fails to enter Picasso's ark, is the elephant. Exotic creatures are extremely rare in Picasso, whereas they formed an important and colourful part of the mediaeval bestiary. A strange and exceptional drawing from 1905, entitled *The Elephant Trainer*, shows the keeper of a (rather fittingly white) elephant. This magician, showing his miniature charge in the palm of his hand, is perhaps based on one of the Cirque Médrano acts so admired by Picasso and his friends, Guillaume Apollinaire and Max Jacob, and often represented in the so-called 'rose period'. If Picasso's representation of an elephant per se is almost unheard of, his way of doing so here is entirely in character: Picasso often delights in inversions of scale. Nevertheless, lions, tigers, giraffes, peacocks, lizards; all these glorious subjects for the painter hardly appear at all in Picasso's huge oeuvre. Perhaps it is not so fanciful, then, to order his works into the nine animal chapters that follow, and to see how his career is accompanied by a retinue of quite specific natural muses.

Picasso made a great show of his animal companions, and there exist numerous references to his ability to charm them, like a modern-day Orpheus.[55] Picasso himself cherished the image of himself in this role, as the very first words of his first prose-poem, written on the 18th April 1935, clearly show: 'If I were to go outside the wild beasts would come and eat from my hand...'[56] These words express a momentary fantasy. A *Picasso Bestiary* compiled out of work from so many years and different situations, could not always be so idyllic.

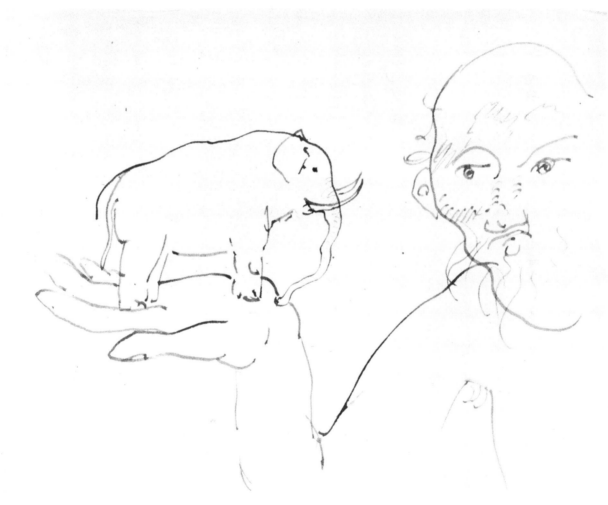

Picasso, *The Elephant Trainer*, 1905, China ink on paper,
30 x 41.5cm, Picasso Estate, (Inv828; Z.XXII.191). Courtesy
of Musée Picasso, Paris. © DACS 1995.

THE BULL

You, the lone matador.
Picassian pink and gold.
Pablo Ruiz Picasso, the bull.
And me: the picador.[1]

Within the spirit of the mediaeval bestiary, which classified animals according to their symbolic importance, we begin this Book of Beasts with the bull. For Picasso, the bull held a particular fascination and although birds outnumber it in his own bestiary, it has to take precedence here for the complexity of its symbolism and the dynamic vigour of its representation. Picasso's bulls are rarely oxen – rarely domesticated tillers of soil – but nearly always dangerous and sexualised creatures ruefully under the dominion of human beings.[2] This tension between power and helplessness underpins the nuances of Picasso's identification of the bull with suffering of a most noble kind and, ultimately, with death. But even the most personal meditations and self-reflections are invoked and epitomised by the very public spectacle of the bullfight. For Picasso, the bullfight engendered special relationships between the horse, the matador, the picador, the Minotaur and, of course, the artist himself. As we shall see, the ritualistic dimension of the bullfight mediates Picasso's own assimilation and reworking of the bull's ancient status in myth and religion as both sacrificial victim and giver of life. For in his work the vestigial survival in the bullfight of centuries of mystical metamorphoses of the virile power of the bull is given fresh urgency and meaning.

In most religions, and in most eras, the bull has been an emblem of kingship, worshipped almost universally for its powerful fighting ability and fertilising power.[3] It has thus been intimately associated with creation, birth, death and renewal, a distinction which has earned it, with goats and sheep, the dubious honour of being one of the animals most frequently sacrificed in supplication to higher authorities. It was, for example, one of the many animals in the guise of which Dionysos, one of the ancient deities of vegetation, was commonly depicted, notably at his marriage, 'a piece of sympathetic or mimetic magic intended to promote the fertility of men, animals and crops'.[4] A bull was commonly slaughtered in rites to the god, its flesh being eaten raw or buried in the fields 'to

OPPOSITE: Picasso, detail of *Bull's Head and Artist's Palette*, 10/2/38, oil and ink on canvas, 72.5 x 92cm. Collection Marina Picasso (Inv 12844). Courtesy Galerie Jan Krugier, Geneva. © DACS 1995.

ABOVE: *Boar, Ox, Bull*, MS Harley 3244, Bestiary in Latin, c1255, f. 47. By permission of The British Library.

Anon. Roman, *Mithraic Altar*, AD 2, San Clemente, Rome.
Courtesy of Collegio San Clemente, Rome.

convey to the fruits of the earth the quickening influence of the god of vegetation.'[5] As Dionysos could also be a personification of the sun which ripens these crops, an intrinsic link was forged between the bull, the sun, and their mutual fruitfulness.[6]

This mystical identification with cosmic energy and the fruitfulness of the earth informs the bull's sacrificial significance, a principle enshrined in the ancient cult of Mithras, which enjoyed especial popularity in the early years of the Christian religion and with which, indeed, it shared certain ritualistic similarities. In both, the consumption of bread and wine in lieu of blood and flesh was a regular ceremonial component, but it is also probable that the followers of Mithras did drink of the 'holy beverage'[7] which issued from a freshly slaughtered bull, sacrificed in honour of their god, bearer of the world's salvation: life and fertility.[8] Their altars, such as that from the Temple of Mithras in San Clemente, Rome, represent the moment of the world's creation when Mithras plunged his sword into the spinal cord of the bull on the orders of the sun-god Apollo, seen in the guise of a raven, to release the blood of this most vital of creatures. From the bull's blood issued all life on earth.[9] Occasionally, three stalks of corns are depicted on the end of the tail of the bull or issue from its wound, possibly representing the bull's incarnation as the corn-spirit, a measure of the fertilising power of its blood.[10]

Although in the Christian Mass, the symbolically consumed flesh and blood is that of Christ, it shares a common aim with Mithraism and all those other religions in which the King or an animal substitute was ritually killed, that of renewal and rebirth through the death of the sacrificial victim.[11] As discussed in the Introduction, recognition of this congruence would not have been deemed blasphemous or irreverent to even the most fervently pious theologian, but, rather, would have provided further proof of the perfection of God's design of and for the world. Importantly, though, Christ's sacrifice on the Cross was seen as not only supplanting, but rendering redundant and unnecessary, all animal sacrifice. In historical terms this marks an important culmination of the ritual slaughter of animals.[12] The Old Testament is full of gruesomely detailed descriptions of the ritual slaughter of bulls and other animals, for example in Exodus XIX, but it was a practice denounced most vehemently by Isaiah, whose utterances were considered by biblical exegetes to prefigure the events of the New Testament:

> To what purpose is the multitude of your sacrifices unto me? saith the Lord: I am full of the burnt offerings of rams, and the fat of fed beasts; and I delight not in the blood of bullocks, or of lambs, nor of the goats.[13]

As Hebrews explains, Christ was the one true sacrificial victim:

Neither by the blood of goats and calves, but by his own blood he [Christ the high Priest] entered in once into the holy place, having obtained eternal redemption for us. For if the blood of bulls and of goats and the ashes of an heifer sprinkling the unclean, sanctifieth to the purifying of the flesh: how much more shall the blood of Christ, who through the eternal Spirit offered himself without spot to God, purge your conscience from dead works to serve the living God.[14]

Christ was, in effect, the sacrificial bull, an equation perpetuated by the bestiary. Although the section on the bullock is usually illustrated by a lone creature (see p29) one at least depicts a kneeling priest holding a tiny bullock in his hands by an altar.[15] As one text explains: 'bullocks were always sacrificed to Jove by the Gentiles' later stating 'The bull is Christ'.[16] The Son, to reiterate the message of Hebrews, had offered himself to his Father as the supreme and ultimate sacrificial bull, just as the ancients had offered the bull to their own supreme god.

Characteristically, the bestiary also acknowledges that, despite this exalted identification, 'Bulls have both a good and evil significance', notably that they are 'the princes of this world, tossing the common people on the horns of their pride'.[17] This ambivalence characterises later representations of the bull such as Pieter Aertsen's *The Butcher's Shop*, a painting which takes as its subject carnage and carnality, but which, too, reiterates the Christian dimension of sacrifice discussed so far.[18] Immediately striking the eye is the sheer profusion of gruesomely dismembered limbs of animals and the various products which ensure that no part of the animal went to waste. Most arresting, though, is the image of an entire bull- or ox-head staring at the viewer. The very subject both repels and fascinates. As in Picasso's animal heads and skulls which are discussed below and in subsequent chapters, there is an uneasy relationship between the awfulness of what the painting depicts, and the delight to be had in the skilfulness and artistry of its representation.

Nevertheless, this tension makes the animal head such an effective medium for contemplation, for meditating on the pathos of a once proud and virile creature reduced to slabs of meat. In *The Butcher's Shop*, these *Vanitas* implications contextualise the background detail. To the right hangs a flayed carcass and beyond men and women make merry in an interior. Their debauchery is announced by the discarded mussel shells, conceivably symbols of the female genitalia, scattered on the floor near the young man filling an earthenware pot with water.[19] To the left, the Holy Family is depicted, dispensing charity to the poor and needy on the flight to Egypt.

ABOVE: Picasso, *Still-life with Bull's Head*, Cannes 25/5-9/6/58, oil on canvas, 162.5 x 130cm, Musée Picasso, Paris (MP.213; Z.XVII.237). © Photo RMN. © DACS 1995.

BELOW: Pieter Aertsen, *The Butcher's Shop*, 1551, oil on panel, 124 x 129cm, Universitäta Kunstammlung, Uppsala. Courtesy of the Art Collections of the University of Uppsala.

In other representations, for example Pieter Bruegel the Elder's engraved *Series of the Seven Virtues*, a flayed animal, its innards, flesh and skin being preserved against the leanness of the coming months is held up as an exemplar of prudence.[20] But in Bruegel's print, as here, the sheer abundance of food being preserved negates the virtue of the action, and in Aertsen's picture is to be contrasted with the Holy Family's simple act of charity. There is a marked distinction between the carnality and fecundity which is so manifest before the spectator's eyes, and the spiritual interpretation offered by the small detail. But both the charitable act and the flayed animal may also function as a prefiguration and evocation of the Eucharist, a commemoration of the sacrifice of Christ, as he hung, like a flayed ox, on the Cross, a comparison which had been made unambiguously in, for example, the thirteenth-century *Bible moralisée*.[21] Even in the seventeenth century, it was believed that meat-eating was a consequence of the Fall, and the death of brute animals could be made a paradigm of Christ's atonement.[22] The multivalence of these interlocking levels of meaning is, furthermore, given additional focus by the carousing company, which is so evocative of those many Dutch representations of the Prodigal Son, squandering his inheritance in the tavern. As Kenneth Craig notes:

> Since Tertullian the parable has been explained as an allegory of God's forgiveness to sinners, with the Prodigal Son said to represent either the Gentiles or backsliding Christians. In this scheme, the killing of the fatted calf at the joyous return of the Son is the symbolic equivalent of the sacrifice of Christ on the cross ... St Jerome said flatly, 'The fatted calf, which is sacrificed for the safety of penitents, is the Saviour Himself, on whose flesh we feed, whose blood we drink daily,'[23]

– a notion which was perpetuated in bestiary lore:

> Augustine, the holy father, when he discusses the symbols of the Evangelists, calls the Lord himself a calf, who offers himself as a sacrifice for the salvation of the rest ... Christ is the calf in the Gospel: 'Bring hither the fatted calf and kill it' [Luke 15:23].[24]

All, or only some, of these meanings may have been recognised in Aertsen's painting by his audience. Nevertheless, it demonstrates the variousness of Christian and moral interpretations of the sacrificial bull, their redefinition and re-orientation of the primeval spirit of pagan practice. In some works, for example, The Master of the Procession of the Ram's *The Procession of the Fatted Ox* (which was owned by Picasso) Dionysiac and Bacchanalian festivity is deliberately recalled. However, rather than documenting the persistence of the old

Master of the Procession of the Ram, *The Procession of the Fatted Ox*, 108 x 166cm, Musée Picasso, Paris. © Photo RMN.

rites in a peasant community, its intended meaning was possibly closer to the moral message offered by an emblem depicting a similar scene from Jacob Cats' *Sinne- en Minnebeelden*. In the words of the 1627 English version:

> What helpes a little Joy? certaine,
> When after pleasure, followeth paine.
> When as you see this stall-fed oxe, thus deckt with flowers grene:
> Then thinke you see the joy of those, that in their wreake and teene
> Doe tryumph in lasciviouse lust: who for a moments pleasure
> In dauncinge, musicque, wyne and myrth, doe make thereof a treasure:
> But soone this pleasinge pastyme endes, which many bringes to thrall;
> such sweete beginninges often are powdred with bitter gall
> Let this ox your example bee, least that you prove like rodd
> His body soone was butchered, his flesh was roast and sodd.

This painfully unpoetic verse conveys less a message of salvation, than an invitation to think upon the futility of worldly pleasure. Nevertheless, by contemplating this proud creature, and thinking on its eventual fate, one may at the very least learn moderation in one's own life.

These latter images also demonstrate the extent to which oxen, if not bulls, have been subject to domination by humans, even as their strength and virility were admired. In purely practical terms, cattle of all kinds have been exploited for their meat, and have been subject to a rigorous programme of selective breeding which, by the eighteenth and nineteenth centuries, had produced varieties of most monstrous shape and proportion. In England, journeymen artists depicted in careful, but naive fashion, portraits of prize bulls (and cows and sheep) for their proud owners. The gross anatomical exaggerations of paintings such as James Clark's *The Thorney Prize Ox* seem ludicrous to us today, but as Thomas Bewick observed in his *Memoires*:

> Many of these animals were during this rage for fat cattle, fed up to as greight a weight and bulk as it was possible for feeding to make them; but this was not enough; they were to be figured monstrously fat before the owners of them could be pleased. Painters were found who were quite subservient to this guidance, and nothing else would satisfy.[25]

In short, the bull (and artists) was considered fully domesticated and completely subject to human control. Yet in one area, at least, its power is still celebrated and vestiges of the old rituals remain: in the bullfight. The persistence and ritualistic content of the bullfight points to ancient religious

ABOVE: James Clark, *The Thorney Prize Ox*, 1858, oil on canvas, 56 x 66cm, Museum of English Rural Life, Reading. Courtesy of University of Reading, Rural History Centre.

CENTRE: Picasso, *The Bull*, second state, 12/12/45, lithograph, 32.6 x 44.5cm, Musée Picasso, Paris (MP 3333). © Photo RMN. © DACS 1995.

BELOW: Picasso, *The Bull*, tenth state, 10/1/46, lithograph, 32.6 x 44.5cm, Musée Picasso, Paris (MP 3341). © Photo RMN. © DACS 1995.

orgies,[26] possibly a survival of the Cretan biennial festival in which a live bull was torn to pieces by humans with their teeth, a re-enactment of Dionysos' dismemberment at the hands of the Titans.[27] Certainly, in ancient Crete, home of the Minotaur, and other parts of the eastern Mediterranean, bull-games formed an important part of worship. Their vigour and spirit is captured in a tiny statuette of a *Bull and Acrobat*. It is unclear, though, whether these rituals were as dangerous or bloodthirsty as we might think. Aelian noted that:

> It seems that a special characteristic of the bull is its docility, once it has been tamed and from being savage becomes gentle … And you will even see a Bull bearing a woman on its back or standing erect on its hind legs while it supports with ease the entire range of its body on some object or another. And I have even seen men dancing on the backs of Bulls, and the same men motionless there also and standing unlodged.[28]

It has also been observed that Cretan representations of the bull-games appear to celebrate a form of ritual play which lacks the war-like element found in hunting scenes and related subjects in the closely related art of Mycenean Greece.[29] Nevertheless, whatever the precise form and function of these rituals, it is clear that the bull and acrobats played a game of chance and skill, the might and fury of the one being pitted against the agility and quick-wittedness of the other. It is also evident that they were performed to celebrate and revere this mightiest of creatures. Much the same spirit continues in the modern bullfight, captured by Goya in his *Tauromachia* series and Manet who, in 1865, wrote to Zacharie Astruc, explaining his fascination with these 'games' (see p37):

> … the outstanding sight is the bullfight. I saw a magnificent one, and when I get back to Paris I plan to put a quick impression on canvas; the colourful crowd, and the dramatic aspects as well, the picador and horse overturned, with the bull's horns ploughing into them and the horde of *chulos* trying to draw the furious beast away.[30]

The bullfight was, of course, immensely important to Picasso. The play of domination and subjugation, grandeur and pathos which characterises his pictures of bulls and their Cretan cousin the Minotaur, is essentially a product of that almost religious intensity of the rituals of the ring. The bull, in fact if not in name, is still sacrificial victim. We can also be certain that whenever Picasso identifies himself with the bull it is not the miserably subjected creature created by the livestock specialist, but the dangerous *Spanish* bull – a formidable combatant resisting defeat.

OPPOSITE: Picasso, *Bullfight: Death of the Torero*, Boisgeloup 19/9/33, oil on wood panel, 31 x 40cm, Musée Picasso (MP 145; Z.VIII.214). © Photo RMN. © DACS 1995.

ABOVE: Anon. Cretan, *Bull and Acrobat*, bronze, 16 BC, height 11.1cm, British Museum, London. Copyright British Museum.

The Bull is illustrated twice in the prints for Buffon's *Histoire Naturelle*. Once as *Le Taureau*, [*The Bull*], and once as *Le Toro Espagnol*, [*The Spanish Bull*]. When the publisher of the book, Martin Fabiani, eventually came to match the existing prints which Picasso had made with some excerpts from the naturalist's text, it was found that in the Buffon edition the publisher was working from, the only text was for the Ox and the Bull. Thus Picasso's print which he had subtitled *Le Taureau* [*The Bull*] became *Le Boeuf* [*The Ox*], and *Le Toro Espagnol* became francised as *Le Taureau*. This and other problems of matching necessitated the omission of Picasso's hand-scratched subtitles from the book plates.

Many of the characteristics of Picasso's *Le Toro Espagnol* are recurrent features in the artist's representations of this animal: the charging appearance, the eyes staring proudly from the erect head, the boldly swinging testicles. In this case the bull seems to be emerging from the darkness of the *toril* [bullpen] where it has been kept for several calming hours, into the Plaza or bullring ready to fight the matador. The swirling dust at its feet reminds us of the thunder of its hooves, and the high position of its head indicates danger. Another bull, this time in charcoal and from 1934, steams into the arena of the page in the same mood (see overleaf, above). Here, however, Picasso stylises the body with elegant sweeps of black, and renders its face as if it were the grinning mask of fate. This apparition of a bull has between its horns the faint echo of a screaming horse.

The Buffon print and the charcoal drawing reflect two possibilities which are ever present for Picasso, two avenues in representation – naturalism and abstraction – which capture at one level the strange attraction and repulsion of this creature. Two works in Picasso's own collection, a small Iberian bronze bull[31] and *The Procession of the Fatted Ox* reflect this dualism. The former an archaic token of mystical respect, perhaps an offering to a divinity of sorts; the latter a painted profanity in the face of the old mystery of the bull, whose now familiar appearance speaks volumes for its fate – castrated and reared for food and labour – in rural domestication. What was once a rite giving meaning to the world is now a riskless *Wine Feast* (the alternative title of *The Procession of the Fatted Ox*) before a hearty meal. Picasso complained about this picture when it belonged to his dealer Kahnweiler:

> The Le Nains – they're peasants. Look at the raised foot of this peasant. Compare it with the Zurbaráns in Grenoble Museum … Look at any of the French painters and you find the same thing. Even with the greatest … you find awkwardness. Not with the Spaniards, nor with the Italians of course; with the Italians the slickness is revolting.

OPPOSITE: Picasso, *The Spanish Bull* [*Le Toro Espagnol*], Spring 1936, sugar lift aquatint, 36 x 28cm, Victoria & Albert Museum, London (B 331). Photo © Victoria & Albert Museum. © DACS 1995.

ABOVE: Édouard Manet, *Bullfight*, 1865-66, oil on canvas, 90 x 110cm, Musée d'Orsay, Paris. © Photo RMN.

ABOVE: Picasso, *Bull*, 10/7/34, charcoal on paper, 35 x 51cm, Picasso Estate (Inv 3805). Courtesy of Musée Picasso, Paris. © DACS 1995.

BELOW: Picasso, *Head of a Bull*, Boisgeloup 1931-32, bronze (unique cast), 35 x 55 x 53cm, (MP 296; S.127 (II)). © Photo RMN. © DACS 1995.

Basically the French are all peasants.[32]

Picasso speaks here of national differences in styles in painting, but the peasant style is representing in this case a peasant universe, where the strange power of the Spaniard Zurbarán, or of the dignity of the bull in the bullfight, is unthinkable. Despite, or perhaps because of, his complaints, Picasso bought this peasant painting from Kahnweiler.

In 1945 Picasso paid tribute to his icon by stripping it away from appearance to essence, from naturalism to abstraction in a sequence of eleven lithographic prints of *The Bull* of which the second and tenth are reproduced here (see p33 centre and below respectively).[33] The artist transforms a hulking, bellowing leathery mass into a precise inventory of elements: horns, eyes, bulk, four legs, tail, testicles and penis. Lithography depends on the fact that oil and water do not mix. A stone slab is wetted, and drawn upon with a greasy crayon. When an oil based ink is applied, it takes to the crayoned areas, but is repelled by the wet unmarked parts of the surface. Thus the drawing made by the artist is printed (reversed, like a mirror image). Picasso sometimes cut into the stone in order to get properly white areas where there was no drawing. *The Bull* series was made using such a scraping technique and the lithographic ink applied with brush and pen. Thus, at one level, the bull is simply a pretext for a demonstration of invention and daring. On the other, it is the bull which is worthy of the treatment, which calls for it, amongst all the possible subjects at Picasso's disposal. Indeed, it is often in turning to animals that Picasso enters into these performances which are not simply against nature (abstract), but also at times with it (naturalistic), as if the living creature, like no simple *thing*, summons above all else a tribute of skill from the image-maker. The artist recalls the diversity and vitality of the natural world which inspired the painters of Altamira and Lascaux and the mosaicists of the Roman Empire.[34]

The same swing, from more naturalistic representation to daring abstraction seems at first glance to characterise two sculptures of the *Head of a Bull*. In 1942, Picasso infamously combined a bicycle seat and handlebars to make a bull's head. Picasso talked about this paradigmatic work of assemblage on numerous occasions, and in different versions, of which the following is an entertaining example:

One day I took the seat and the handlebars. I put one on top of the other and I made a bull's head. Well and good. But what I should have done was to throw away the bull's head. Throw it in the street, in the stream, anyway, but throw it away. Then a worker would have passed by. He'd have picked it up. And he'd have found that, perhaps, he could make a bicycle seat and handlebars with that bull's head. And he'd have done it... That would have been magnificent. That's the gift of metamorphosis.[35]

In conversation with Brassaï, Picasso pointed out that although the bronze casting of the piece gave it more coherence, losing sight of the component parts and their quotidian origin would diminish its interest. Picasso understood that the interest of this work depends upon our seeing the bull and the bicycle parts all at once, and thus sensing a permanent 'metamorphosis', an unstable identity in the thing. This is the magic, the craft, with which Picasso paid his tribute to the bull. To see this famous work as an abstraction would thus be a mistake, since it is in fact the simple realism of the piece, its success as a bull's head, that makes for its effect.

The earlier work was also cast in bronze, this time from an original modelled in plaster in the Château at Boisgeloup to the north of Paris. The plaster can be seen perched on a bench in a photograph taken by Brassaï in 1932, where it is menaced by another plaster, this time of a bird.[36] As many other photographs show, Picasso was in the habit of making jokey and improvised groupings of sculptures in this way, both in his studio and at home. In this case, the juxtaposition is one that has both a natural basis in the birds which pick at the ticks on grazing cattle, and perhaps a symbolic one, for the juxtaposition of bird and bull is known in Mithraic altars (see p30).

There is another marked difference in these two works. The 1932 head is clearly a piece designed to sit on a flat surface, as if cut from the animal for the purposes of the cook. The almost jolly vivacity of the head conflicts with this impression. The assemblage, however, is obviously for hanging on a wall, in imitation of the bull's heads found in bars and Bullfight Museums all over Spain.[37] Such heads are those of bulls renowned for causing terror in the bullring. Metamorphosed into sculptures by the taxidermist, they remind the aficionados of great deeds, but they also secretly echo ancient Mediterranean cult objects.[38]

Thus a consideration of the bull as a single subject in Picasso's art leads inevitably to that of the corrida, the Bullfight proper. Many of us are familiar with the gaudy and festive dimensions of the bullfight, and their counterparts in costume, music and poster art. In the same way that Picasso's bulls are sometimes wittily abstracted from naturalism, and at other times vividly rooted in it, so his art of the bullfight covers a range of possibilities from decoration to psychological depth.

In the early fifties, Picasso often decorated terracotta plates with bullfight scenes.[39] He particularly enjoyed playing illusionistic games with the shape of the plate, rendering the

bullring as if seen from a seat deep in the shade (*sombra*) and looking into the sun (*sol*). Sunlight and shade form the two areas of seating in the bullring (and also the name of a Spanish drink). Bullfights are staged in the afternoon, when the heat can be unbearable, and so those who can afford the seats enter by the door marked 'Sombra'. The blacker side of the ring is the colour of the bull himself, whilst those seated in the sun are allied to the *Traje de Luces*, the immensely coloured and embroidered 'suit of lights' of the Matador.

In the drawing *Bull on a Branch*, of 1956, Picasso represented a mystical bull in miniature climbing a branch, turned to a black silhouette by the burgeoning eye of the sun. This blackness is well documented in photographs not only of the bull itself, but of its cast shadow as it stands on the hot sand of the ring. The association of the bull and the sun, enshrined in the seating arrangements of the bullfight, and brought out in Picasso's drawing, takes us back to the distant cults of archaic Europe:

As between the sun and the shadow

Between the matador and the bull there is a nameless god.[40]

The struggle of the Matador is that of light against dark, of technique against force, of wisdom against nature. Yet the actors are not firmly to be placed on one or other side of the ring:

The shadowy heart of the matador

burns like a luminous flame.

And that of the bull

which is the pure light of fire

extinguishes itself like the gloomy night.[41]

Thus, what seemed at first a struggle of good and evil, turns out to be more of an exchange of elusive roles – not without risk – between matador and bull.

Picasso's earliest representations of the bullfight were childhood scenes. As a young independent artist, the bullfight was a subject for scene painting in the style of Manet (see p37). We could say that sun and shade in these works were pure. Yet it was in the twenties, ushered in with the notable achievement of the *Dying Horse* (1917, now in the Museu Picasso, Barcelona), that Picasso discovered the potential of the bullfight to represent the complexity of the inner world, the dramatic life of desires, and the forces of malevolence. In the year 1930, Picasso was honoured in the 'dissident' Surrealist periodical *Documents* by his friend the writer Georges Bataille, who published a text linking the obsessive effect of the midday sun to the god Mithras, and thus the bull.[42] In this text, entitled 'Rotten Sun', Bataille claims that the idea of the sun is one of serenity and spiritual elevation. But this is merely an idea of beauty. Once looked at, the burning and unbearable light of the sun is a source of madness, and becomes horribly ugly:

> In mythology, the scrutinised sun is identified with a man who slays a bull (Mithra) …: in other words, with the man who looks along with the slain bull… The Mithraic cult of the sun led to a very widespread religious practice: people stripped in a kind of pit that was covered with a wooden scaffold, on which a priest slashed the throat of a bull; thus they were suddenly doused with hot blood, to the accompaniment of the bull's boisterous struggle and bellowing – a simple way of reaping the moral benefits of the blinding sun. Of course the bull himself is also an image of the sun, but only with its throat slit. The same goes for the cock, whose horrible and particularly solar cry always approximates the screams of slaughter… All this leads one to say that the summit of elevation is in practice confused with a sudden fall of unheard-of violence…[43]

Picasso's great works on the theme of the bullfight from the mid-thirties are in this way emphatically divided in their loyalties. We cannot approach these works in the hope that one or other participant will resolve into good or evil, light or dark, man or woman.

Picasso's *Bullfight: Death of the Torero* was painted in Boisgeloup on the 19th September 1933. This small painting, in its intricate enlacement of bull, horse and matador, is a visual statement of the interdependency of the sun and shade in the bullfight, and in the rite of passage which it preserves. The incident is known technically as a *cogida* (goring/tossing) and Picasso frequently depicted it, although rarely with a view to giving an accurate or technical impression. In order to appreciate the liberties taken, it is worth pausing to outline the basic shape of a typical fight.

A bullfight consists of three tiers or *tercio*, which correspond to unmarked concentric circles in the ring itself. These are: the goading; the banderillas; the death. Prior to the entrance of the bull the matador and his team (*cuadrilla*) parade to the accompaniment of a frenetic and gaudy paso doble. On the arrival of the bull, banderilleros run the bull around, so as to gauge its temperament and the place in the ring which it is drawn to (its *querencia*). The picadors, mounted on armoured horses, commence work on the bull, forcing a lance (*pica*) into its hump three times in order both to both weaken and anger it. Then banderilleros, specialist matadors now armed with banderillas, insert these small harpoons into the hump, further weakening the bull and drawing its blood. The matador then performs his *faena* with the bull, a courtship with the cape which is the focus of great attention amongst connoisseurs of elegance and nerve.

Finally the matador executes the bull cleanly or otherwise, by inserting a long épée (the *estoc*) into its heart through the spine. If the matador has impressed with his efforts, he may be awarded one or both ears of the bull, and/or its tail.

The *cogida* of Picasso's painting is, then, a dangerous accident in which the matador finds him or herself hooked on the horn of the bull, and then thrown to the ground or more rarely in the air. The *cogida* is often fatal. Picasso's depiction of it here revolves around the highly improbable event of the matador being borne along on the back of the bull, and the conjunction of this matador, almost always on foot,[44] with the horse. As Antonio Saura has pointed out,[45] the combination of torero and horse borne aloft on the back of a rampant bull is highly improbable given the fact that the torero never rides a horse, and most *cogidas* result in the torero being pitched into the air or dragged along like a rag doll. Despite being an avid fan of the event, Picasso's painted bullfights are partly idealised creations: the bull is rarely, as he would be in reality, covered in blood.

Picasso's preoccupation with the *cogida* and the *pica* (or goading of the bull) is like that of late Roman sculptors with Laocöon, or Rubens with scenes of the hunt and equestriana: the pictorial problems of capturing such dynamic movement are immense. Picasso's greatest models in making paintings, drawings and prints of the bullfight were Manet and Goya. Yet it was Goya's dark prints on the theme, for example *Tauromaquia 32*, which were most important when Picasso moved away from the festive interpretation of the bullfight, and towards these grave incidents. The *cogida* is one of the three most terrible moments possible in the bullfight (the others being the *pica* and the *estocade* or killing of the bull). It is, in its way, a disastrous version of the bull-riding which is probably at the origins of the whole affair (see p35). It is the event which inspires many of the *cante jondo* of Andalusia, flamenco ballads of lament for the great matadors, and of course Goya's print commemorating the death of Pepe Illo (1754-1801), a part of his *Tauromaquia*.[46] It is equally clear that the subject is loaded with expressive content for Picasso. In particular, the twenties and thirties saw a series of deaths in the ring which captured the imagination of artists, writers and poets as well as flamenco singers. Joselito died on the 16th May 1920, at Tavalera de la Reina, and Manuel Granero on 22nd May 1922, in Madrid. These deaths brought Picasso to produce his first *Death of The Torero* paintings.[47] But it was another fatal accident which produced a remarkable cultural tribute to a bullfighter, the Andalusian poet Lorca's 'Lament for Ignacío Sánchez Mejías'. This poem can provide us with a resonant evocation of many of Picasso's most harrowing depictions of the bullfight.

Sanchez Mejías (1891-1934) was a famous but atypical bullfighter who also wrote poetry and enjoyed flamenco. He made a late comeback to the bullfight, and was attacked by a bull at Manzanares on 11th August 1934. The bull succeeded in knocking him to the ground and goring him persistently. Witnesses apparently recalled the trail of blood which the Matador left behind him as he was taken to the hospital. Finally, after much agony, Sanchez Mejías died of gangrene two days later in Madrid. The poet Lorca 'was nearby and followed his progress on the radio, but he could not face visiting him, and … he refused to see his body'.[48]

This event, which prompted such a great poem, came after a number of paintings by Picasso on the theme of the bullfight in the first six months of 1934, and especially in July. Although Picasso did not turn to the subject as a result of the death of Sanchez Mejías, there is no doubt that in retrospect it gives an added poignancy to these works. Indeed, on 22nd July 1934, a few weeks before the event, Picasso seems to have anticipated the refrain of Lorca's poem in a grisly painting of the Picador torturing the bull (see overleaf):

> At five in the afternoon.
> Ah, terrible five in the afternoon!
> It was five by all the clocks!
> The shadow of five in the afternoon.[49]

Most of the paintings done before the death of Sanchez Mejías are of the bull/horse couple alone, where the bull exacts gruesome penalty from the horse. In the *Horse and Bull* of the 21st January 1934, for example, a bull very like the victim in *Bullfight*, of the same year, feasts quite improbably on the entrails of the shrieking horse. The archaic and ritual look of the bullring is exaggerated. The same motif, with a vivid bull but fading horse, marks a pencil drawing of 24th July 1934, *Bull and Horse*. The 16th July brought the bull another victory, this time as the impaler of the fleeing horse, *Bull and Horse*. The grimace of the bull in this highly elaborated pen drawing echoes the terrible contentment of the bull in Lorca's poem:

> The bull alone was glad of heart
> at five in the afternoon.
> [...]
> The bull roared through his forehead now
> at five in the afternoon.[50]

Picasso visited Spain in August 1934, and doubtless learnt of the death of the Matador, and then returned to the theme in September once back in France. Yet in these later works, Picasso tended to focus not on the matador, or the horse, or the Picador as victims, but to continue his study of the bull, and its

ABOVE: Picasso, *Horse and Bull*, 21/1/34, oil on canvas, 65 x 54cm, Picasso Estate (Inv 12677; Z.VIII.225). Courtesy of Musée Picasso, Paris. © DACS 1995.

BELOW: Picasso, *Bull and Horse*, Boisgeloup, 16/7/34, pen and china ink on paper, 12 x 25.5cm, Klaus Hegewisch Collection, Hamburg, (Z.VIII.211). Courtesy of Klaus Hegewisch. © DACS 1995.

Picasso, *Bullfight*, 22/7/34, oil on canvas, 54 x 73cm, Fundación Colección Thyssen-Bornemisza, Madrid, 1994 (Z.VIII.219). © DACS 1995.

suffering in the *pica*, which he had begun in *Bullfight*. Thus in a characteristic inversion, the bull, in reality now responsible for the death of the hero, stands for the suffering hero in Picasso's works of later 1934. Once again, the clear black and white character of the bullfight begins to blur, and what was evil becomes good. This recasting of the bull as a heroic sacrificial victim does have some basis in the bestiary tradition which saw the figure of Christ in the bull, but it would be pointless to insist on a precise single meaning of this kind. Picasso's concentrated period of work on the Bullfight in the thirties leads to a dreamlike interplay of situations, characters, and meanings. Among these is the spirit of the gored matador, who has at last shared in the agony of the bull.

Three types of incident from the bullfight have been explored – the clash of horse and bull, the tossing of the matador into the air (*cogida*), and the goading of the bull (*pica*). These are only equalled for drama and danger by the final execution of the bull, a moment comparatively rare in Picasso's work.[51] In Picasso's writings, however, this moment is given a special significance as one of great self-knowledge:

> Little Girl II: Only the eye of the bull that dies in the arena sees.
> Little Girl I: It sees itself.[52]

This mysticism carries over into the last category of work to be considered: the numerous paintings and drawings of a still-life with a bull's head. Clearly, in attributing a revelation of the self to the dying bull, Picasso recalls the *Vanitas* tradition in part I: meditation on the flayed ox brings together consciousness of death and of the sacrifice of Christ. But for Picasso it is not the carcass but the detached head of the bull which summons up the most harrowing self-analysis. Once again we might recall its iconic status in Spain. The bull's head made from bicycle parts may have been assembled as a tribute to Picasso's Spanish friend, sculpture technician and sculptor in his own right, Julio Gonzalez.[53] Certainly Picasso seems to have painted two still-life works featuring a bull's head in tribute to Gonzalez on the 5th and 6th April 1942.[54]

The death of a close Spanish friend found its image in these paintings, as had that of Sanchez Mejías in Lorca's poem:

> The bull does not know you,
> nor the fig tree,
> nor the horses nor the ants of your house,
> the child does not know you, nor does the afternoon,
> because you have died for ever.[55]

The poem was with bitter irony to become a lasting lament for Lorca's own death: he was shot by Franco's men on the 18th or 19th August 1936 in a village near Granada.

In the accelerating pace of the Spanish Civil War, it was the bombing of Guernica that received Picasso's most public response. After its appearance in the Paris International Exhibition of 1937, the huge canvas of *Guernica* toured several countries, ending up in the United States. Yet the enormous public attention it attracted had done little to avert the decline of the Spanish Republic. Picasso apparently suffered a severe bout of sciatica in late 1938,[56] and in this combination of personal and political despair, Picasso undertook a series of paintings featuring a bull's head, a physical and metaphysical meditation on art and death. The dramatic and mysterious *grisaille* painting, *Bull's Head and Artist's Palette*, is the last in the sequence of five (see overleaf).[57] All of the paintings in the series have roughly the same composition. They feature an artist's palette and brushes on the left or at the centre of the picture, and the bust/head of a minotaur (in two of the canvasses) or of a bull (in the remaining three) on the left. In the four pungently coloured paintings which preceded *Bull's Head and Artist's Palette*, the palette rests on an open book, next to a candlestick holding a lighted candle.

How can we interpret these recurring elements? Firstly, Picasso never used a palette. Indeed, there is an amusing photograph by Brassaï of him mocking the style of academic painting which he associated with it.[58] On the other hand, a frequently repeated anecdote suggests that the palette may have personal significance. Picasso's father, don José, was an amateur pigeon painter of some small merit. His confidence was apparently not great and his personality deeply affected by the early death of a daughter. One evening in La Coruña in 1895, when Picasso was fourteen:

> ... don José asked his son to help him finish the painting of a pigeon that had been giving him trouble. His eyesight was no longer sharp enough for the intricate bits, he said, so he chopped off the claws, nailed them to a board and set Pablo to paint them. When don José returned from his evening stroll, he found the claws had been painted with such skill that then and there he handed over his palette brushes and paints to his prodigy of a son. He declared that he would never paint again.[59]

This story is certainly exaggerated if not entirely invented, but what matters is that Picasso may have believed it. In any case, the juxtaposition of palette and book echoes many a still-life painting of the artist's studio. The palette and brushes are at one level clear metonyms for the artist himself.[60]

Secondly, the candle, in addition to its obvious symbolic traditions in still-life painting – of divine light but also perhaps of the 'rotten sun' tending towards oblivion – has weight when

Picasso, *Bull and Horse*, Boisgeloup, 24/7/34, pencil on paper, 26 x 34.5cm, Klaus Hegewisch Collection, Hamburg, (Z.VIII.217). Courtesy of Klaus Hegewisch. © DACS 1995.

we recall that *Guernica* features a woman holding a lamp next to a bright sun/electric light in the upper centre.[61]

The candle disappears in the last painting, as does the book, as does colour, leaving only the vividly drawn bull's head to dominate a grim corner of a cramped room. Some commentators on the painting have pointed to the way in which the head, with its alarmed expression, seems to float above the table cloth. The head itself partly suggests a hollow mask, of the type which might be worn by an actor playing the Minotaur, and in his oscillation between the head of a bull and that of the Minotaur, Picasso once again, and perhaps deliberately, echoes Lorca:

> Now the well-born Ignacio lies on the stone.
> It is finished; what is happening? Look at him:
> death has covered him with pale sulphurs,
> and placed on him a dark minotaur's head.[62]

One is left asking, at the end, who was this bull, that matador, this picador? Which of them is Picasso? Many writers on Picasso offer answers to this question, many of them apparently from Picasso's own lips, or incontestably picked up from his writings. Unsurprisingly, the answers don't add: Picasso is the matador;[63] Picasso wanted to be a picador;[64] Picasso is the bull.[65] In this painting, especially harrowing for its ascetic colour, buffed surface and sparse composition, Picasso brings the unstable principle of the play of *Sol y Sombra* to bear on his struggle to paint the idea of death. The identification with the matador is strong here, but it only addresses death if we accept the matador's understanding or even love for the bull, by turns his executioner and victim. Picasso was able to use this strange relationship as a way of thinking about painting itself:

> Just imagine that you're in the middle of the ring. You've got your easel and your white canvas, and you've got to paint it, while the whole world is there watching you. Go to it, the moment has come, you've got to start on your canvas, you've got to do it. Imagine that, [Picasso] said. Nothing could be more appalling: ten or fifteen thousand people are there, watching you. If you make the least mistake, you die.[66]

Like the bullfight itself, the symbolism of the bull in Picasso is under constant transformation from poles of absolute terror and pity, and is usually a mix of both. Picasso had several personal reasons to honour the bull: for its special significance in Spain, and thus as a token of his own Spanishness; for its virility; and for its tragic destiny in the bullfight. All of these points have their roots in the tradition which we have explored, where the bull was represented in connection with worship and sacrifice, or as an object of meditation in the face of death. Only the fatted ox, the castrated bull, finds no reflection or continuation in Picasso's art.

Most pointed of all, and owing to his involvement with Bataille and other intellectuals in the Surrealist circle, Picasso embraced the deeper meanings of the conjunction of Bull and Sun. In another painting of 1958 (see p31, above), painted 'with four letter words', there is a double reflection of the sun in the window.[67] It has been argued that this painting reflects the left-wing Picasso's anxiety over the contemporary uprising in Algeria which had led to the resurgence of de Gaulle, and also that the rich (French) colours of this piece, and the flowers, reflect a more optimistic mood alongside the sombre skull.[68] Our exploration of the meanings of the bull as a motif, and of the bull's skull, would tend to suggest that even if the painter were inspired to anger by these events, the painting itself can only speak in the most poetic terms of an ancient sense of tragedy:

> The ear of the bull at the window
> Of the wild house where the wounded sun
> An interior sun goes to earth
>
> Curtains of waking the walls of the room
> Have vanquished sleep.[69]

Picasso, *Bull's Head and Artist's Palette*, 10/2/38, oil and ink on canvas, 72.5 x 92cm. Collection Marina Picasso (Inv 12844). Courtesy Galerie Jan Krugier, Geneva.
© DACS 1995.

THE HORSE AND THE DONKEY

One of the strongest lines of association in Picasso's Bestiary is that between the horse and the bull. Without doubt the link is firmly based in the bullfight. However, whereas Picasso's depiction of the bull is in some degree almost always informed by the bullfight, there is more variation in representations of the horse, and its relatives the mule and the donkey. These variations reflect not only the diversity of contexts in which Picasso may have encountered the horse, but also the strong, and equally varied, position which this animal occupied in the pictorial tradition.

From the gallant knight on his white palfrey, to the king on his stallion, from the stocky workhorse, to the elegant lady's mount, the horse has usually been represented as an extension of its owner, an appendage announcing social and economic status – an emblem of lifestyle. This is perhaps why, of all the creatures in the bestiary, the horse is subject to the least mystical and moral reflection. Indeed, the bestiary is remarkably practical on matters equine, concentrating mainly on the physical characteristics of the horse, useful when choosing one's animal, and its behaviour in harness or on the battlefield.[1] Thus although at first sight the bestiary illustration reproduced here represents a quartet of wild, charging horses, its main purpose is to demonstrate the harmonious teamwork that earned the horse its name:

> Horses get their Latin name 'equi' because when they are harnessed in a team of four, they are equally matched, in equal size, and with equal stride.[2]

Because these horses are not harnessed or saddled, the inference is that they possess these qualities naturally, the onus being on their owner to match them carefully in order to maximise their performance. Even the inevitable comparison with the four horses of the Apocalypse from Revelations VI:1-8 could elicit a prosaic response from the pseudo-Denis who interpreted these bearers of war, famine, pestilence and death as a symbol of obedience and docility.[3] That is, for all the destruction these horses wreak, they nevertheless do so efficiently. This teamwork amongst their own kind, is matched by the horse's relationship with its owner. In the other bestiary illustration reproduced overleaf, there is careful symmetry in the way the artist has depicted two saddled horses fighting, mirroring the hand-to-hand combat of their masters. This

OPPOSITE: Picasso, detail of *Woman with a Veil*, China ink and watercolour, 6/5/36, 25.5 x 34cm, Picasso Estate (Inv 3817). Courtesy of Musée Picasso, Paris. © DACS 1995.

ABOVE: *Horses*, MS Bodley 764, Bestiary in Latin, c1250, f. 46r. The Bodleian Library, Oxford.

demonstrates their loyalty, matched only by the dog: the bestiary relates stories of horses which would only suffer their master to ride them and would shed tears on his death in battle:

> They are dejected when beaten and delight in winning. Some of them can scent out enemies in battle so well that they try to bite them.[4]

This viewpoint was also taken in the seventeenth century by Topsell who deemed the horse 'the most noble and necessary creature of all foure-footed beasts' and devoted to it no fewer than 153 pages, generally covering practical topics ranging from the ideal terrain for riding, the diet of horses and their life span, to handling and breaking in horses and riding them to war.[5] In this pre-industrial age, therefore, consideration of the horse in the 'natural' histories has much of the tone of the instruction manual about it, inevitably for a creature that performed many of the tasks that today are carried out by machines. Nevertheless, the horse was elsewhere considered a proud creature (by Aristotle – because of its dislike of losing)[6] and, like so many other beasts, an embodiment of sensuality, a free spirit, difficult to restrain and, thus, yet another player in the *Psychomachia*, that is, the battle for the soul. Far from being the obedient and compliant creature of the bestiary and 'natural' histories *always* willingly subject to human command, the horse was seen to have an inbuilt wild streak which allied its being to the forces of nature. This conception of the horse not only has been responsible for some of the more interesting and compelling aspects of horse lore and representation, but also appears to be a more fruitful source for shedding light on the paradoxes presented by Picasso's many horses – creatures which suffer the terrors and indignities of the bullfight and the circus, yet which are credited with a natural energy that transcends their abject situation.

Like most of the creatures we consider in this Picasso Bestiary, the horse could symbolise the senses and sensuality in general[7] and riding was, in the Middle Ages (and still is in many languages), a barely-concealed euphemism for sexual intercourse.[8] Like the bull, the horse was considered a most virile creature, as even the bestiary notes in passing:

> We also find it noted that a horse called Opus went on copulating to the age of forty. The virility of horses is extinguished when their manes are cut.[9]

This account may appear quaint, naive even, but when we consider the Old Testament account of Samson, whose strength resided in his hair, it becomes clear that the bestiarist was not merely repeating an isolated titbit of animal lore, but was yet again articulating a deeply-held belief originating in ancient ritual. As Rowland points out: 'The head with its glorious mane

OPPOSITE: *Horses*, MS Royal 12F xiii, Bestiary in French, c1230, f. 42v. By permission of The British Library.

and upstanding ears was the quintessence of the phallic animal,'[10] thus to cut a horse's mane is effectively to castrate it, to deprive it of its manhood, just as Samson lost his strength when his hair was shorn by Delilah.

Today the phallic horse-head survives divested of all its original significance as a child's entirely innocuous plaything: the hobbyhorse. Originally, though, in Scandinavian religious processions a hobby horse represented Odin, the horse-god, and its name reflects its function: 'hob' is a variant of 'Rob' which, in Cornwall, still means 'phallus'. Originally, Robin Hood and Robin Goodfellow were not the heroes later immortalised in countless feature films, but ithyphallic gods.[11] In Shakespeare's time, 'hobbyhorse' designated a loose woman, a lustful person, a prostitute.[12] Perhaps Israhel von Meckenem was drawing on this tradition in his engraving of *Children Playing* in which a small boy, naked like his companions, gleefully rides a hobby-horse. Like Pieter Bruegel the Elder's painting *Children's Games*, now in the Kunsthistorisches Museum, Vienna,[13] Israhel's picture may have been intended as a skit on the folly of adult behaviour, perhaps related to allegories or proverbs.[14] Artists have always been fascinated by the tension between innocence and knowing, mature childhood and childish adulthood, whether this be expressed in religious, moral or social terms or for the purposes of titillation – see the examples of Greuze and Fragonard reproduced in Chapters Three and Four of this book. In Picasso's paintings of children and animals reproduced in Chapters Three and Six we find both innocence (*Child Holding a Dove*) and knowing glee (*Boy with a Crayfish*).

Characteristically, this sexual aspect of the horse could also be appropriated to the act of creation and to creativity. Paradigmatic of this principle was the winged horse of myth, Pegasus, who has been splendidly captured on the antique vase reproduced on p62. Picasso, as we shall see, frequently associated the winged horse with death but, as already noted, from death comes renewal and Pegasus though born out of death, was the source for poets of divine inspiration.[15] His name means 'springs of water'[16] and the Hippocrene spring, sacred to the Muses on Mount Helikon in Boeotia, which watered the fertile ground of the Muses' home, with its 'spangled lawns with all their countless flowers',[17] was created from rock struck by his moon-shaped hoof. Here the horse could conceivably signify the female creative principle for, in folklore, the horse's 'leg and foot symbolise the male generative organ, and the curved shoe the female organ'.[18] The erotic significance of feet and shoes is widespread; water too has played an extensive part in the symbolism and ritual of creation and birth, due to a perceived equivalence between uterine fluid, urine and

OPPOSITE, ABOVE LEFT: Israhel van Meckenem, *Children Playing*, engraving, 10.9 x 13.9cm, Albertina, Vienna, Inv 1244, 1926. Courtesy of Albertina, Vienna.

OPPOSITE, ABOVE RIGHT: Anon., *Christ on a Donkey*, late 16th century, polychrome wood, Musée d'Unterlinden, Colmar. © Musée d'Unterlinden, Colmar.

OPPOSITE, BELOW LEFT: Diego Velázquez, *Baltasar Carlos on Horseback*, 1635, oil on canvas, 209 x 173cm, Museo del Prado, Madrid. All Rights Reserved © Museo del Prado, Madrid.

OPPOSITE, BELOW RIGHT: Picasso, *Boy with a Horse on Wheels*, Vallauris, 9/6/49, oil on canvas, 130 x 96cm. Collection Marina Picasso (Inv 13190; Z.XV.145). Courtesy Galerie Jan Krugier, Geneva. © DACS 1995.

ABOVE: Paolo Uccello, *Niccolo Mauruzi da Tolentino at the Battle of San Romano*, early 1450s, oil on panel, 183 × 319.5cm, National Gallery, London. Reproduced by courtesy of the Trustees, The National Gallery, London.

CENTRE: Picasso, *Sport of Pages*, Vallauris 24/2/51, oil on wood, 54 × 65cm, Musée Picasso, Paris (MP 204; Z.XV.184). © Photo RMN. © DACS 1995.

BELOW: Jean Louis André Théodore Géricault, *Race of Wild Horses at Rome*, 1817, paper on canvas, 45 × 60cm, Musée du Louvre, Paris. © Photo RMN.

OPPOSITE, ABOVE: George Stubbs, *Horse attacked by a Lion*, oil on panel, 24.1 × 28.2cm, Tate Gallery, London.

OPPOSITE, CENTRE: Picasso, *Woman with a Veil*, China ink and watercolour, 6/5/36, 25.5 × 34cm, Picasso Estate (Inv 3817). Courtesy of Musée Picasso, Paris. © DACS 1995.

semen.[19] Thus like the bird, in particular the dove as discussed in Chapter Three, the winged horse was a source of inspiration, of life-giving spirit. In a woodcut of 1507, the German humanist Conrad Celtes, created his own 'pagan' Trinity in which the place of God the Father blessing Christ was taken by Jupiter hovering over his son Apollo, and Pegasus was substituted for the dove, the Holy Ghost – the spirit moving across the waters.[20]

For all this, the horse was nevertheless subject to that universal rule that the senses must be ruled by reason, and it was a commonplace of classical times that the horse and rider were equatable with body and soul – when the rider loses control, that is, fails to subdue his passions, he is thrown.[21] In art, the dignified strength of the horse often predicates that of cultivated and powerful men, an association responsible for the continued popularity of the royal or noble equestrian statue or portrait. Much more could be suggested by evidence of the ability to control a spirited steed than just good horsemanship. In Uccello's *Niccolo Mauruzi da Tolentino at the Battle of San Romano* the exaggerated perspective of bodies and lances on the ground, which creates order out of the chaos of battle, offsets (and is offset by) the two-dimensionality of the rearing horses, endowing them with a heraldic quality commensurate with the nobility of their riders who are so manifestly in control, both of their horse and of their faculties. Similar intentions inform the series of five equestrian paintings commissioned from Velázquez in the second half of the 1630s for the Hall of Realms, focal point of the Palace of the Buen Retiro.[22] One of these, reproduced on p52, below left, *Baltasar Carlos on Horseback*, appropriates a distinctly 'grown up' type of portraiture to a painting of a small boy, the aim being to invoke ideas such as rulership and the education of the prince.[23] The smallness of stature of the boy and his pony is at odds with the grandeur of the representation and its authoritative associations. But the picture is prognostic of the child's destiny and proof of the validity of his inheritance. He is assured as a horseman, and in control of his small steed, prefiguring his future dominion of the great Habsburg empire.

A different interpretation of the relationship between man and horse is offered by Ingres' study for the imperious centurion in his *The Martyrdom of Saint Symphorien*. Many of the great number of studies for this picture are derived from antique models.[24] This, and the protracted process by which Ingres constructed his painting may hint at an important dimension of its meaning – an attitude to antique models that was evidently so important for Picasso in his own *Boy Leading a Horse* discussed more fully below. In Ingres' sketch, the man wears no clothes, the horse no saddle; man and beast coexist in an unforced harmony and because of the incomplete state of the sketch, appear, like the centaur, to be of one body. It is a melancholic evocation of a Golden Age but in the finished painting this pre-lapsarian mood has disappeared, hidden beneath the trappings of so-called civilisation.

Such quiet communion with nature is dramatically denied by George Stubbs in his *Horse attacked by a Lion*. In this struggle to the death, the wild beauty and dignity of the untamed horse is undiminished by its terror and pain, a worthy prefiguration of Picasso's representations of decidedly non-pathetic victims in the bullring. Yet, no less than Ingres' studies, this vision of life in the raw was itself inspired by antique sculpture rather than the amalgam of direct observation and imagination we might expect.[25] It has been suggested that far from being produced out of a spirit of sympathy or involvement, the painting, repeated often by Stubbs,[26] was 'influenced no less than other subjects by his intellectual objectivity and emotional restraint', that is, that same curiosity which manifested itself in his famous *Anatomy of the Horse* published in 1766.[27] Géricault, on the other hand, the great horse-painter of the succeeding century, appears to have been motivated in his *Race of Wild Horses at Rome* by a more empathic, 'romantic' engagement with his subject. This picture represents the Race of the Barberi horses, an event which Géricault witnessed in 1817 and like Ingres, he produced a number of studies for the picture, inspired by the statuesque forms of antique nudes.[28] His aim, however, was to retain the spirit, not just the form, of the antique. These annual games were 'a rude survival of the animal games of antiquity',[29] thus it was appropriate that rather than setting his scene in the present, the action takes place in the distant past, not a Golden Age, but one in which a great civilisation is falling into ruins. In this context the wild horses may be considered as symbols of the might of nature struggling against the control of man, a struggle that later would absorb Picasso in paintings such as *The Circus Horse*.

In contrast, Géricault's *The Derby at Epsom*, is a conformist and stereotypical representation, in which the galloping horses are represented with that 'rocking-horse' motion typical of eighteenth- and nineteenth-century English hunting and sporting prints. In the late nineteenth century, Eadwaerd Muybridge's photography demonstrated the various stages of movement which constitute the horse's gallop and exposed the absurdity of these representations. Yet Géricault's studies for the *Wild Horses* demonstrate that some fifty years prior to Muybridge's work, he was perfectly capable of accurately rendering these different stages.[30] It has been conjectured however, that Géricault

PREVIOUS PAGE, BELOW: Jean Auguste Dominique Ingres, *The Martrydom of Saint Symphorien* study, black chalk on paper, 54.8 x 41.3cm, Nelson-Atkins Museum of Art, Kansas City, Missouri (Purchase: Nelson Trust) 33-1401.

OPPOSITE: Picasso, *Boy Leading a Horse*, early 1906, oil on canvas, 220.6 x 131.2cm, The Museum of Modern Art, New York. The William S Paley Collection, (Z.I.264). Photo © 1994 The Museum of Modern Art, New York. © DACS 1995.

ABOVE: Picasso, *Circus Horse*, 1937, ink and pastel on paper, 29 x 43cm, Berggruen Collection, on loan to the National Gallery, London (Z.IX.83). Reproduced by courtesy of the Trustees, The National Gallery, London. © DACS 1995.

produced this work according to the tastes of the English horse dealer MA Elmore, perhaps as deliberate pastiche or parody.[31] Also, in contrast to the race of wild Roman horses, in the *Derby at Epsom* control is all, and the skill of the rider, as much as the strength and speed of the horse, will determine the outcome of the race. This is a picture of an English subject, the 'Sport of Kings', painted in an appropriately restrained and 'civilised' English manner.

The admiration evident throughout this range of horse lore and representation for this most noble and beautiful of beasts, was not, however, extended to its humble cousin, the donkey. The horse was valued for its virility, but the donkey was denigrated for being a randy, lustful creature. Even so, it was not a proud horse, a mount fit for a king, that was chosen to carry the king of kings to his fate at Jerusalem, but a humble ass. A polychrome statue of Christ on the donkey in Colmar, though intended for use in religious processions, has all the character of a toy horse. (see p52, above right). It is evocative therefore of the belief that foolishness and childishness, more than the proud posturing of adulthood, were the qualities the good Christian should emulate. As Paul exhorted:

> Let no man among you seemeth to become wise in this world, let him become a fool, that he may be wise. For the wisdom of this world is foolishness with God ... We are fools for Christ's sake.[32]

Jean Louis André Théodore Géricault, *The Derby at Epsom*, 1821, oil on canvas, 92 x 123cm, Musée du Louvre, Paris. © Photo RMN.

The most important situation for the Picassian horse is in the bullring. The darkness of the *toril* from which *The Spanish Bull* emerges in the Buffon prints seems to carry over to *The Horse*. This alert and wild horse is slightly startled, and is the pure white of Pegasus. Picasso has used the device of crowding this horse into the limits of the print, a device which both bestows grandeur and heightens the tension. However, one shouldn't overplay the possibility that this horse is awaiting a bull since there seem to be considerable similarities between Buffon's text and Picasso's print, as if the artist may on this occasion have done his homework. Despite his emphasis on the relationship between horse and man, the Comte de Buffon is at pains to evoke the poetic beauty, elegance and grace of this sublime creature:

> The finest conquest that man ever made was of this proud and fiery animal…
>
> The horse seems to wish to set itself above its condition as a quadruped by raising its head. In this noble attitude it looks at man face to face: its eyes are wide open and alive; its ears are well set and of a good size… [33]

As with the bull, Picasso takes liberties with the horse he knew from the corrida. Those employed in bullfights were usually old nags, mares of poorer quality. Picasso's horses are sleek and refined, an idealisation which lays the basis for the tragedy which surrounds them. This idealisation might be thought to extend to the nakedness of the horse, which in the modern bullfight is heavily protected. Such an impression is not quite correct, however, since before the 'Belmonte' reforms were instituted in 1928, which made the *peto* (a caparison or suit of padded armour for the picador's horse) compulsory, the exposed horse frequently left the ring eviscerated and dying. The ignoble gracelessness of the picador's horse gave rise to the grotesque pleasure which the public took in the goring and disembowelling of the mare. The horses often continued to run from the bull whilst trailing their guts behind them: the offending viscera were quickly gathered up or covered with straw. Ernest Hemingway and the Surrealist writer and anthropologist Michel Leiris both attest to the burlesque qualities of this event, which precedes the high tragedy of the death of the bull at the hands of the torero. [34] The closest Picasso came to gloating over the horse's predicament was perhaps in a pencil drawing of 15th April 1935, *Minotaur and Horse*, showing the horse confronted this time by a Minotaur wearing the sort of sailor's shirt beloved of Picasso himself. [35] The bizarre expression on the horse's face seems to owe something to the emergent form of animated cartoons. The neighing of a horse, where it flares its nostrils, distends its upper and unfurls the

ABOVE: Picasso, *The Horse*, [*le cheval*], Spring 1936, sugar lift aquatint, 36 x 28cm, Victoria & Albert Museum, London (B 328). Photo © Victoria & Albert Museum. © DACS 1995.

BELOW: Picasso, *Minotaur and Horse*, Boisgeloup 15/4/ 35, pencil on paper, 17.5 x 25.5cm, Musée Picasso, Paris, (MP 1144; Z.VIII.244). © Photo RMN. © DACS 1995.

lower lip exposing deep seated teeth, is in itself a moment which, if caught in the wrong way, can seem to caricature the normal dignity of the creature. The contrast between this hideous, sometimes comic horse, and the elegant whiteness of Pegasus is one to which we will return.

All such humour disappears in Picasso's representations of the horse paralysed with agony as its innards drop onto the sand. Picasso was reputedly opposed to the Belmonte reform, not because of any sadistic attachment to black comedy, but rather because of the loss of sublime drama and mortal danger which the reform inevitably brought about.[36] Nevertheless, Picasso's continuing devotion to the pre-1928 nakedness of the horse may also reflect a kind of 'good old days' nostalgia:

> I must have been ten years old when my father took me to see El Lagartijo fight. I remember his hair was white, snow white. In those days bullfighters didn't retire so young as they do now. Well the bulls were different then too, huge – and they charged the horses as much as twenty times. And the horses dropped like flies, their guts everywhere. Horrible! Those days were different, and so was the bullfight...[37]

In *Woman with a Veil* of 1936 one can find no trace of nostalgia. This quite extraordinary composition shows a staggering horse, with the penetrating stare of a last agony, unleashing its intestines onto a boarded stage. As it falls, a voluptuous and naked woman, apparently climbing onto the horse's back, casts her funereal veil over it. Behind this couple, a strange curtain of wave forms gives way on the far right to the faces of a paying crowd at the edge of this ring. Perhaps the waves in the background are a reference to Poseidon, the god of horses as well as the sea in Greek mythology? Yet the enigmatic qualities of the scene rule out simple solutions to the puzzle which the scene presents. In many ways, Picasso's own poetic prose of the same period is more helpful in providing a basis for the visual imagery. On the 5th May 1936, the day before this drawing was made, Picasso wrote:

> ... and the veil covered in shit of the very ceremonious costume of the young bride cut into sausage slices and served like stag and the registration fees and the costs of the boleros the *Gitanes* matches and one thing leading to another and fear of the flame taken from the hair by the teeth of the horse's shadow belly open behind the shutters in the lukewarm of weak sun sprinkle on the air of flute of the corner of the mirror seated under the olive tree of the white curtain of the evening this Tuesday 5th of the month of May of this year at five to seven.[38]

Other references to the disembowelled horse contain similar morbid personal imagery, often linking it to the presence of a curtain – raised by its suffering – or a young girl.[39] The association of the horse with a young girl, or with the female in general, does of course have its basis for Picasso in the fact that the picador's horse is usually a mare.[40] Much more significant in terms of Picasso's inscription of imagined male and female forces into the corrida, however, is that elegance, purity, defencelessness and suffering which Picasso bestows upon his horses, and which is set against the lack of control, blackness, destructive power of the bull. The link between these idealised aspects of the horse and projected ideas of the woman is clearly shown in Picasso's representations of the *Bullfight: Death of the Female Torero*. In this first painting of the subject, produced two weeks before *Bullfight: Death of the Torero*, a naked female is tossed in the *cogida* along with her mount. The mounted female matador was not a complete fiction, although her semi-nakedness is, since women matadors found more opportunities in the bullfight when working on horseback (as *rejoneadors*) than as matadors proper. Once again the incident occurs in the darker side of the ring. The horse, although recently described as a mare,[41] is neither female nor a gelding. This underscores the nature of Picasso's method: the female side of the bullfight is not necessarily occupied only by identifiable females, but rather it imposes a (far from surprising or sophisticated) model of 'femininity' upon those who enter into it. From time to time, this side can be seen in the female matador and the horse, even the male horse, to be sure; but it also touches at times on the male matador and the bull (or – later in this book – the Minotaur) himself. The bullfight, with its courtship, risk, physicality, play of power, was used as a metaphor for eroticism long before Picasso discovered it as such. The *Faena* (the ballet of matador and bull) and the phallic penetration of the bull's horn into the side of the horse, were both eminently suited to eroticisation. Picasso's numerous works exploring the dynamic coupling of the bull and the horse, or including the matador, are inevitably partly to be seen in this context.

In the previous chapter, we saw how the bull could acquire for Picasso a mystical character through its association with ancient rites and cults. This is no less the case for the horse, whose importance and mythological credentials reach at least as far back in Indo-European cultures. Whereas the Mithraic sacrifice was conducted under the sign of the 'rotten sun',[42] the horse was often connected to the night or even death (as in the 'pale rider' of the Apocalypse).[43] The colour of the horse in question – especially its blackness or whiteness – was especially important to its meaning, its black or white magic.

One of Picasso's horses is connected with the moon.[44] At Juan-les-Pins on the 5th September 1930, Picasso took a

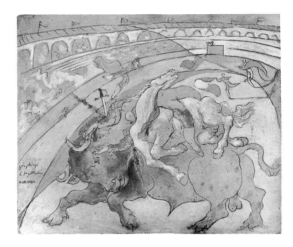

Picasso, *Bullfight: Death of the Female Torero*, Boisgeloup 6/9/33, oil and crayon on wood, 21.7 x 27cm, Musée Picasso, Paris (MP 144; Z.VIII.138). © Photo RMN. © DACS 1995.

ABOVE: Picasso, *Horse Lying Down*, Juan-les-Pins 5/9/30, Indian ink on a postcard of the moon, 8.8 x 14cm, Musée Picasso, Paris (MP 1034). © Photo RMN. © DACS 1995.

CENTRE: Picasso, *Curtain for the Ballet* Parade, 1917, distemper on canvas, 1060 x 1725cm, Musée National d'Art Moderne, Paris (Z.II*.851). Courtesy of the Centre Georges Pompidou. © DACS 1995.

BELOW: Anon. Greek: *Proitos, Bellerophon and Pegasos*, Apulian, early 4th century BC, red-figure stamnos, Museum of Fine Arts, Boston (00.349). HL Pierce Fund. Courtesy Museum of Fine Arts, Boston.

postcard showing a photograph of the moon, obscured the title 'The Moon after the First Quarter' and inked onto it the forms of a tightly curled horse, to create *Horse Lying Down*. The card, probably part of a collecting set from a chocolate box or something of that sort,[45] carried a short text on the back describing the play of shadow and light on the surface of the satellite. Picasso uses the surface textures of the moon to evoke in particular the rougher or more complex surfaces of the horse's head and legs. The large open deserts on the other hand become a piebald coat. This horse emerges through the manipulation of light and dark. It is neither black nor white, but made, like the moon, of both:

> ... to the moon [the Greeks] ascribe two horsses, one blacke and another white ... and the Moone which for the most part is hidde and covered with earth, both encreasing and decreasing, they had the same reason to signifie her shadowed part by a black horse, and her bright part by a white one.[46]

The aura of magic and serenity born out of darkness relates to the idea of the white winged-Pegasus with its moon-shaped hoof, born out of the death throes of the Gorgon Medusa, who was herself sired by the 'black-maned' horse-god, Poseidon. Just as assigning an identity to the bull, or sexuality to the horse is difficult, we find that the symbolic good or evil of the figure of the horse varies in a dialectic of light and shade.

Picasso's writings regularly refer to dying horses as winged (see *The Winged Horse*, p190), but he rarely depicts a Pegasus as such.[47] In the drop curtain for the ballet *Parade*, Picasso included a pseudo-Pegasus amongst a crowd of circus performers and figures from the Commedia dell'Arte. The white horse, licking at its foal, may have false wings, as a girth of some sort is clearly visible. On its back stands the ubiquitous girl, also winged, who pursues a monkey climbing a ladder. There are plenty of ambiguities in this scene, which probably continues a tradition of *trompe-l'oeil* games in theatrical curtain design.

This curtain was before the audience as they listened to the overture in the Théâtre de Châtelet in Paris on the 17th May 1917. It seemed to assure them of an evening of sentiment and tender celebration tinged with magic. However, as the curtain rose:

> The music changed; sounds 'like an inspired village band' accompanied by the noises of dynamos, sirens, express trains, ... and other outrageous dins broke on the ears of the startled audience... They announced, together with rhythmic stamping like 'an organised accident', the entry of the gigantic ten foot figures of the 'managers' ... The third manager was a horse. Its head held high on a long

wrinkled neck had the fierceness of an African mask. Two dancers hidden inside the body pranced about the stage with perfect realism…[48]

Picasso's drawings for the head of this 'pantomime' horse, for example *Study for the American Manager and the Horse's Head*, show how carefully he worked to produce a kind of grimacing death's head in black and white. The contrast between the pseudo-Pegasus of the curtain and this grotesque and comic figure could not be more pronounced. In one way the contrast reminds us of the possibilities of abstraction and naturalism between which Picasso's bulls seem to oscillate. The grimace of the horse seems to be more than simply the product of abstraction, however, and by no means simply a token of fright as it is in the confrontation of horse and Minotaur. This anthropomorphic grimace gives expression to the more ridiculous, mischievous or even satanic side of the horse. Picasso persists in his representations with this strange characterisation of what is normally taken to be a noble creature.

The oscillations in Picasso's depictions of the horse are echoed in an essay by his friend Georges Bataille on the subject of 'The Academic Horse', published in *Documents* in 1929.[49] As he had in 'Rotten Sun', Bataille pointed to a contrast between classical elevated conception and its pagan and abased version. The 'academic horse', well-proportioned, proving the worth of ideal beauty, is that of the sculptors of ancient Greece and Rome.[50] It reflects the aspirations of classical philosophy to unity with an ideal nature, expunged of all accident and ugliness. For Bataille, it is unthinkable that such a culture could have chosen a spider or hippopotamus as its emblematic creature.

The ambitious young Picasso attempted to modernise the 'academic horse' in 1906 with *Boy Leading a Horse*. In this painting, reminiscent of Ingres' study for *The Martyrdom of Saint Symphorien*, Picasso gives the academician's typical attention to the essence of the figures, stripping them and the landscape bare.[51] The absence of any halter for the horse has often been plausibly taken to prove that the pairing of boy and horse is intended to be emblematic of the harmony of 'man and nature' or even of 'the artist and nature'.[52] We may wonder whether or not this is the case for Picasso, or whether the absence of the halter simply reflects a pictorial convention (which may in any case owe its existence to a desire to see the 'essential' relations between figures). What is clear nevertheless is that this rose-tinted academic horse is of a very different kind to that represented in an ostensibly similar composition, *Circus Horse* of 1937. The ungainly beast in this wash and pen drawing, with its black shadow and distorted features, is firmly

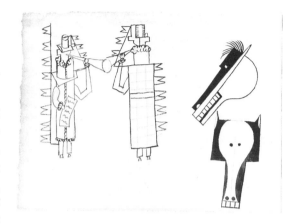

ABOVE: Picasso, *Study for the American Manager and the Horse's Head*, 1916-17, gouache and pencil on paper, 20.5 x 28cm, Musée Picasso, Paris (MP 1598; Z.II*.956). © DACS 1995.

BELOW: Picasso, *Little Girl with a Horse and Doll*, 22/1/38, oil on canvas, 73 x 60cm, Picasso Estate (Inv 12834; Z.IX.101). Courtesy of Musée Picasso, Paris. © DACS 1995.

gripped by its master. The faces of the crowd which peer into the ring are equally frightening – except of course for that in the top left, of the ever-present 'young girl'.

In the gap between *Boy Leading a Horse* and *Circus Horse* we have what Bataille calls the 'dislocation of the classical horse'.[53] According to Bataille, those peoples, like the Gauls, who lived in the imperial shadow of Greece and Rome, made similarly hideous versions of the academic horse on their coinage. Bataille detects in the stylistic difference between classical and 'barbarous' civilizations an inability and an unwillingness to live according to the 'ideal' and accept its taboos (against for example blood, comedy, all that is hideous and frenetic disorder).

Unlike his predecessors in the classical tradition, the bestiary, and in the equestrian portrait, Picasso often conjured up a rather frightening and anti-academic horse where his subject was war or combat. In 1951, he painted a strange *Sport of Pages* showing a grinning horse, an armoured knight, and three pages in attendance. The flippant decoration of this painting took on a more sinister appearance in the light of Picasso's inclusion of black horses towing a chariot of death in the large *War* panel of the following year.[54] A white winged horse pulls the plough in the companion panel, *Peace*.[55] In *Head of a Horse*, of 3rd and 4th November 1962, the horse is painted as in a portrait, and the dagger clutched by its rider is reminiscent of the one held out in defiance thirty years earlier by a maquette made for the cover of *Minotaure* (see p188). This horse is in fact inspired by a subject – the 'Rape of the Sabine Women' – depicted by two important classicising painters, David and Poussin.[56] Clearly, this horse is not merely a dumb animal, although the thoughts which might be ascribed to it are debatable – is it an aggressor or a victim? Picasso's 'Sabine' works were preparatory for a final major work destined for the *Salon de Mai* of 1963, where a roughshod horse plays a prominent role.[57] This left-wing exhibition, organised by Picasso's friend Edouard Pignon, took as its theme in that year variations on Delacroix' *Entry of the Crusaders into Constantinople*, a theme which Picasso ignored. According to some scholars, Picasso chose the less triumphalist 'Sabine' theme in response to the worsening political situation in Cuba in 1962, a response which has also rather improbably been seen in the *Still-life with Cat and Lobster*.[58] As a communist sympathiser, Picasso opposed the imperialist posturing of the United States during the crisis, and dreaded the possibility of yet another war. Unlike many of his predecessors in the representation of horses, Picasso seems to have been less interested in, or perhaps sanguine about the military horse. Even the horses he regularly depicted from the bullfight – which ostensibly have an aggressive role – are unsaddled and often more independent of human direction than one would expect. A reported encounter of 1940 indicates Picasso's unease at the sight of military horses:

> A little while before we reached Royan, we met groups of horses going in the opposite direction, and these attracted the attention of Picasso. They were horses requisitioned by the army; they went in twos or threes; a man on foot leading each pair or each group holding all the reins in one hand, arm raised. The downtrodden look of these animals made an impression on Picasso.[59]

Two forms of horse, not quite horses, remain to be discussed as important in Picasso's work. The first is the donkey or ass, the second the *toy* horse.

The ass is not often represented by Picasso. In the Buffon prints, the ass, like the horse, matches the text well. For the Comte de Buffon, the ass is a fine creature ill-appreciated and poorly treated by man. Its merits, from a human point of view, lie in its combination of humility, durability and economy.[60] In its youth it is jolly, but a working life soon removes this spirit. Picasso painted *Donkey*, showing a hard-working beast of burden in the burning heat of Malaga on a family holiday in the summer of 1896. In this exercise in capturing the look of the afternoon sun on the landscape, Picasso nevertheless found interest in the dumb patience of the ass. Perhaps this ass was his own mode of transport into the *plein-air* around the town, and thus merited a portrait? A complementary tension clearly exists between the sublime, ambitious and intelligent craft of the painter, and the servitude of the once grand, now humble beast, traditional mount of religious figures (see p52, above right). In a famous statement on the horse, Picasso underlined this contrast:

> Work is a necessity for man.
> A horse does not go between the shafts of its own accord.
> Man invented the alarm clock.[61]

Square Tile with Donkey and Flute Player, 1961 and *Donkey/Ass*, 1940, are two other works on the theme of the ass which show its more pagan side. As Buffon pointed out, when tormented, the ass will give a kind of mocking grin by pulling back its lips. However, Picasso's bizarre grinning ass seems closer to the very pagan, anti-academic, graceless form which Bataille discussed, than to a naturalistic observation. The mediaeval *Feast of the Ass* was an event of great licentiousness, which may relate to the fact that the ass has an oversized penis. Thus the ass had been a priapic symbol in ancient times, a thought which carries over into modern Spanish.[62] Similarly, the braying and highly excited ass charmed into erection by pastoral pipes is probably a topic of amusement for Picasso. The ass had in ancient

ABOVE: Picasso, *Donkey*, Malaga, c1896, oil on canvas, 28.5 x 37cm, Museu Picasso, Barcelona (MPB 110.933). © DACS 1995.

BELOW: Picasso, *Donkey/Ass*, 1940, ink on paper, 13.5 x 21cm, Picasso Estate (Inv 4112; Z.X.554). Courtesy of Musée Picasso, Paris. © DACS 1995.

thinking been associated with the lyre, harmony and the birth of music, but in later Christian thinking the ass was compared to a: '… singer of burlesque perpetrating barbarities on music'.[63] The flute-player recurs in a number of drawings and paintings of sheep and goats during the last few years of Picasso's work, for example *Man with a Lamb, Watermelon Eater and Flautist* of 1967, no doubt partly for his clear phallic potential.

At the other extreme of innocence and experience, the last two works to be considered concern the childhood toy horse, and two of Picasso's own children. Maya is the daughter of Marie-Thérèse Walter, born on 5th September 1935, and protected from the public eye during her infancy. In what is therefore a very private portrait entitled *Little Girl with a Horse and Doll*, of 22nd January 1938, she clutches a male doll to her chest and a toy horse to her lap. This painting is companion to another now in the Musée Picasso, where the horse is missing and the doll is clearly female. Picasso's highly developed vocabulary for bringing all the features of the human head into an almost tactile order, but without loss of a sense of realism, is given an additional meaning in rendering the childish cramped frills and fat fingers. The naked horse, returns us to the predominantly female identity of this animal in Picasso's Bestiary, but here with complete innocence.

Having made an ambitious academic painting of a *Boy Leading a Horse* in 1906, and the dramatic *Circus Horse* in 1937, Picasso returned ironically to the composition on several occasions over the years, with the elegant horse now transformed into a hobby horse or a horse on wheels. In *Boy with a Horse on Wheels*[64] of 1949, Picasso relishes imitating a childish vision of the world, showing Claude, then aged two (born 15th May 1947), towing his comical horse about the room.[65] As a reflection on Picasso's earlier and more pretentious works of human and horse companionship, the diminution of the horse to fit the boy reminds us of Balthasar Carlos on his pony, posing as a grown up horseman in *Balthasar Carlos on Horseback*, and the pathos and humour of the children at play in van Meckenem's engraving *Children Playing*.

The tender or comic theme of the child with the animal is one to which we will return in the next chapter.

Picasso, *Square Tile with Donkey and Flute Player*, 27/2/
61, faience, engobe painting beneath glaze, 25.5 x
25.5cm, Ludwig Collection, Aachen. © DACS 1995.

BIRDS

Everyone wants to understand art. Why not try to understand the song of a bird?[1]

There are more birds in Picasso's work than any other type of animal. Moreover, their meanings seem closer to the norms of the tradition than those of animals in some other chapters of this Picasso Bestiary. The range of *specific* birds consistently represented by Picasso is, however, surprisingly small. Again and again we find the dove, the pigeon, the owl and the cock are the main subjects. Birds elicited from Picasso some of his most lyrical works, and one real owl in particular impressed him enough to become the subject of a string of paintings – and anecdotes. As with the horse and the bull different birds are treated as possessing human sexuality, either male or female, and are sometimes taken to represent the artist in some way; but as with the bull, birds are also simply *living things*, decorative 'nature' *par excellence*, with which Picasso seeks in happier moments to ally himself – an Orpheus of playful creativity.

This small range of birds chosen for representation by Picasso, is also well represented in literature, lore and pictorial representation in which we can see often surprising affinities with Picasso's own attitude towards these feathered creatures. Undoubtedly, as we shall see below, the dove was for Picasso of supreme importance, provoking from him associations with peace and hope that are not far removed from the earliest Christian practice. In the bestiary, 'columba' is 'a simple bird, free of gall, which looks lovingly at its mate', and is likened to the preacher who is 'free from rage and bitterness'.[2] It was equatable with 'spirit', with the Holy Ghost, and in the oldest versions of the *Physiologus* the account opens with the words of John I:32 in which the descent of the spirit of God is described as 'like a dove'.[3] In this capacity the dove is most often seen in Annunciation scenes, descending on the Virgin. In some representations it also descends, as visual evocation of divine inspiration, on saints, notably Jerome who ardently defended Mary's perpetual virginity and whose translation of the Bible into the Latin Vulgate made the word of God incarnate, as the Holy Ghost made Christ incarnate in the body of the Virgin.[4] Nevertheless, its representation in the bestiary is usually disappointingly dull (merely a single, drab bird) and were it not for the accompanying text, it would be difficult to identify.

OPPOSITE: Picasso, detail of *Woman with a Cock*, Paris 15/2/38, oil on canvas, 142 x 120cm, Private Collection, Kunsthaus Zürich (Z.IX.109). © DACS 1995.

ABOVE: *Turtle Dove*, MS Ashmole 1511, Bestiary in Latin, early13th century, f. 44r. The Bodleian Library, Oxford.

In MS Bodley 764, however, two doves are charmingly represented looking lovingly at each other in an elaborately constructed home, an image that is not dissimilar to that sometimes accompanying the turtledove ('turtur') who when widowed, 'refuses any new match, and will not dissolve the oaths and bonds that tie her to her dead mate.'[5] For this reason she is usually represented with her mate, either billing and cooing[6] or copulating,[7] illustrative of 'the chastity which it pledged at its first mating'.[8] In MS Ashmole 1511 (see previous page), the turtledove is incorporated into a cross, where we would expect to see the crucified Christ,[9] or even 'columba', to designate Christ in his capacity as the bridegroom of the *Song of Songs*.[10] But as Theobaldus' *Physiologus* relates:

> … as the Turtledove once united to one mate is always at his side, so any faithful soul, one linked to its Spouse, namely Christ in Baptism, always sought to remain at His side in well-doing day and night, so that from Christ it should never be separated by sinning mortally.[11]

This interpretation is very close to those exegetical convolutions that considered the *Song of Songs* as a spiritual allegory, thereby justifying the inclusion of this most erotic of love poems in the biblical canon. It is also symptomatic of the ambivalence that designated birds in general and doves in particular as creatures both spiritual and sexual. It has been suggested, for instance, that the image of the dove descending on the Virgin was itself a spiritualisation of the sexual act: the winged bird was a giver of life, and perhaps, originally, the image was intended to perpetuate the old equation of birds with phalli to signify the conception and Incarnation of Christ.[12]

Comparable concerns coalesce many years later in Greuze's *Girl with Doves* which ostensibly perpetuates the image of the dove as exemplar of purity and innocence, but at the same time contradicts it with the doe-eyed, knowing and inviting look of the girl at the viewer. This tension between innocence and sensuality (evocative more of Venus, whose attribute is the turtle dove) is simperingly sentimental and archly erotic. Nevertheless, the dove generally represents a tender sexuality that, as in the *Song of Songs*, is contextualised by the gentleness and wholeness of the relationship between true lovers.

The cock, by contrast, represented strident, robust and straightforward sex, about which more will be said below. Equally the cock was renowned for its voice, its crowing, and it is this characteristic which forms the basis of bestiary description and interpretation, over and above its usefulness as a domestic fowl. For this reason, no more complex image was deemed necessary than a lone cock often, as in the example illustrated here, in the process of crowing.[13] The cock was

Cock, MS I.i.4.26, Bestiary, in Latin, mid 12th century, f. 42v. University Library, Cambridge.

admired for its timekeeping[14] and its call was, according to the bestiary:

> ...a pleasant thing of a night, and not only pleasant but useful. It is nice to have it about the place. It wakes the sleeping, it forewarns the anxious, it consoles the traveller by bearing witness to the passage of time with tuneful notes. At the cock's crowing the robber leaves his wiles, the morning star himself wakes up and shines upon the day. At his singing the frightened sailor lays aside his cares and the tempest often moderates, waking up from last night's storm.[15]

The call of this 'gladsom byrd, the deys messenger'[16] heralded the optimism of a fresh beginning at the start of each new day, rousing the faithful to prayer. In the New Testament, as Christ predicted, Peter denied Christ thrice before cockcrow, afterwards being filled with remorse. To the bestiarist, this too signified hope, the expurgation of sin and the return of the light of faith.[17] For this reason, the cock also became a symbol of the Passion.[18] But although cockcrow was '... the voyce ryght of the byrd of blys',[19] its heralding of Peter's grave deed perpetuated, or perhaps encouraged, the widely-held belief that cockcrow presaged ill omen. For lovers, cockcrow brought its own sorrows, for with the coming of dawn they must part,[20] but for Richard de Fournival, both twilight and daybreak, when the cock sings most frequently, 'signify the love where one has neither complete confidence not complete despair'.[21] Midnight 'signifies totally despairing love' and the hopeful lover must, like the cock, sing louder and more forcefully.[22]

Richard's identification with the cock, and his decision to open *Le Bestiaire d'amour* with it rather than the regal lion, would have been rather shocking, particularly considering the traditional association of the cock with castration.[23] But it also sets the tone of the book – cynical and misogynistic, but also sexually assertive.[24] Cockcrow was considered a sign of the bird's masculinity,[25] and perhaps when the anonymous female respondent to Richard's *Bestiaire* wrote that she understood, through his exposition of the nature of the cock, that he had 'spoken penetrating words' to her,[26] she was signalling that she also understood his sexual intent. For the cock was, as in today's English slang, most commonly a vulgar symbol for the penis.[27] Famously, this equation is most explicit in the English verse 'I have a gentle cock':

> I have a gentle cock,
> Croweth me day:
> He doth me risen erly
> My matins for to say
> [...]

ABOVE: Picasso, *Child Holding a Dove*, Paris, Autumn 1901, oil on canvas, 73 x 54cm, anonymous loan to the National Gallery, London (Z.I.83). Reproduced by courtesy of the Trustees, The National Gallery, London. © DACS 1995.

BELOW: Jean-Baptiste Greuze, *Girl with Doves ('L'Innocence tenant deux pigeons')*, Salon 1800, oil on panel, 70 x 58.8cm, Wallace Collection, London.

His eynen arn of cristal,
loken all in aumber:
And every night he percheth him
In mine lady's chaumber.'[28]

Visually, one of the most graphic illustrations of the pun, is Bonaventura Genelli's print *Who will buy Love-Gods?* of c1875, a robust version of equally obscene antique models and a parody of Joseph-Marie Vien's prettified and sentimentally Neoclassical *Cupid-Seller* of 1763 (Fontainebleau, Musée Nationale).[29] Between the antique models and these late nineteenth-century representations, numerous painters, notably in the Netherlands, produced pictures that played on the eroticism of the 'cock' and which as our reproductions demonstrate, share remarkable affinities of form and, perhaps, content, with Picasso's representations. In Gerard Dou's *Woman holding a Cock at her Window*, a painting which, like Abraham van Beyeren's discussed below, Picasso may have seen in the Louvre,[30] a woman holds a dead cock out of a window with one hand, her other clasping a shiny metal bucket. The juxtaposition is visually echoed, and its erotic suggestiveness reinforced, by the open tankard lying on its side on the window sill, next to a snuffed-out candle. Hanging by the side of the window is a birdcage. Numerous bawdy lyrics of the period play on the erotic possibilities of open vessels and 'scouring' them[31] thus the candle may in this context, be considered a phallic symbol.[32] The offering of dead birds (not necessarily cocks) could signal a sexual proposition,[33] a visual evocation of the vulgar possibilities of *vogelen* (literally, 'to bird', that is, copulate), *vogel* ('bird', ie penis) and *vogelaar* ('bird catcher', ie procurer or lover).[34] Libido, for instance, is sometimes represented as a pair of copulating birds perched on a lady's fingers.[35] But in Dou's painting such lewdness is at odds with the woman's apparently respectable appearance and demeanour, evidence that the meaning of such pictures is not necessarily simple. Well-scoured vessels could also be seen as evidence of cleanliness, whether physical or spiritual, following Matthew XXIII:25ff.[36] However, could it be that only the outside of this pot, the side on show to the viewer, is shiny?[37]

Nevertheless, the rather thoughtful demeanour of the woman, the dead bird and the presence of the candle may have encouraged some viewers to detect a *Vanitas* aspect to the painting like that offered by some relatively uncomplicated and simply designed game pieces such as Abraham van Beyeren's *Still-life with Turkey*. Game pieces were especially popular in Holland from the mid-seventeenth century and in an age when hunting was the preserve of the nobility and other high-rankers granted the privilege, they conferred a vicarious prestige on the

OPPOSITE, ABOVE: Picasso, *Woman with a Cock*, Paris 15/2/38, oil on canvas, 142 x 120cm, Private Collection, Kunsthaus, Zürich (Z.IX.109). © DACS 1995.

OPPOSITE, BELOW: Picasso, *Untitled* (Serenading Man, Naked Woman, and Owl), 11/5/70 (IV), etching, 27.5 x 35cm, Galerie Louise Leiris, Paris (B 1901). © DACS 1995.

ABOVE: Gerrit Dou, *Woman holding a Cock at her Window* ('*La Ménagère hollandaise*'), 1650, oil on panel, 26.5 x 20.5cm, Musée du Louvre, Paris. © Photo RMN.

BELOW: Bonaventura Genelli, *Who will buy Love-Gods* ('*Wer kauft Liebesgötter'?*), c1875, location unknown.

ABOVE: Picasso, *Woman with a Green Hairbun and a Bird on her Shoulder*, 14/1/70, oil on canvas, 100 x 81cm, Picasso Estate (Inv 13670). Courtesy of Musée Picasso, Paris. © DACS 1995.

BELOW: Jean-Baptiste Greuze, *Girl with a Dead Canary*, 1765, oil on canvas, 52 x 45.7cm, National Gallery of Scotland, Edinburgh.

household in which they were displayed.[38] The game piece was, therefore, an item announcing the importance of its owner, and like any other object of conspicuous display, was susceptible to *Vanitas* interpretation. Although any dead game bird would suffice to make the point, it is appropriate that in van Beyeren's picture a turkey, symbol of envy, has been chosen, and particularly apt that the mortar and pestle also included is inscribed with the familiar words from Ecclesiastes: '*Vanitas vanitatum*' – Vanity of Vanities.[39]

The suggestiveness of dead birds, whether as *Vanitas* or erotic symbol, or a mixture of the two, was perpetuated in eighteenth-century France by, above all, Greuze. His contemporary viewers, no less than Dou's, understood that a bird in a cage indicated virtuousness, intact virginity; an empty cage, the bird whether absent or perched on top, would have invoked the sense of the common saying 'the bird has flown', ie, virginity is lost.[40] For this reason, artists such as Carlo Crivelli frequently included a bird in a cage in their Annunication scenes to signify the *virgo intacto*.[41] In Greuze's *Innocence*, the girl has taken her doves out of their cage perhaps slyly indicating that she still holds (but only just) her virtue in her hands.

The same artist's *Girl with a Dead Canary* may be understood simply as a sentimental representation of grieving over a lost, much-loved pet. On the other hand, the girl's deshabille alone indicates that her distress is caused by something much more consequential. Diderot, in *Les Salons* of 1765,[42] enthused over the painting (*Délicieux! délicieux*) and weaved an elaborate story around it, conjecturing the arrival of a handsome young beaux who, while the girl's mother was out, seduced her. He opined that the subject of this 'poem' was so 'delicate' that many would not be able to understand its true import.[43] The Goncourts, however, understood perfectly well – better, perhaps, than Diderot, what these paintings signified:

> … what sort of woman comes to life beneath the touch of the painter of 'La Cruche cassé', 'L'Oiseau mort' and 'Le miroir brisée'? A beautiful creature with defenceless eyes, her lips shining with a moist light, her gaze liquid, abstracted, and yet lively and very much on the lookout beneath the lowered lids. It is Parisian innocence in the eighteenth century, an easy innocence lingering on the brink of defeat … Greuze has no other purity to bestow upon the young girl, whose features he repeats so often, except the purity of a smile, of youth, of fragility and of tears … the painter offered her to an aging world, offered her to the exhausted appetites of the eighteenth century, as a perverted child might be offered to an old man to awaken his senses.[44]

The image may perhaps be considered an illustration of Aristotle's 'omne animalum post coitus triste est' – after coitus all animals are sad.

The owl, too, was occasionally represented as sexually symbolic,[45] but more commonly it elicited fear, loathing and ridicule. To the ancient Greeks, the owl was the attribute of Pallas Athene (Minerva), Goddess of wisdom, and often represented the goddess herself,[46] the 'owl-eyed maiden':[47] like the wise person the owl, a bird which flies by night, can see through darkness. The owl's nocturnal habits did, however, earn it a far more prevalent reputation as a creature of evil, and harbinger of doom. In the Old Testament, the owl's habitat is the desert, the realm of dragons;[48] Ovid writes of 'A loathsome bird, ill omen for mankind, a skulking screech-owl, sorrow's harbinger'.[49] Numerous sources through Chaucer and Shakespeare to the present day, testify to the owl's essentially evil nature.[50] The bestiary was no exception, and took, by and large, its cue from the Old Testament, singling out the screech-owl for particular censure.[51] 'Ulula' is so called because of its mourning and lamentation, its imitation of weeping and groaning, which 'signifies the wailing of sinners in hell...'.[52] It is:

> ... a bird associated with death, burdened with feathers but bound by a heavy laziness, hovering around graves by day and night and living in caves ... an image of all those who yield to the sluggishness of sin and flee the light of justice. Hence it is counted amongst the unclean creatures in Leviticus. The screech-owl is the symbol of all sinners.[53]

Additional lessons could be learned from direct observation. When an owl appears in daytime, it is mobbed by other birds, for which reason it was often used by bird-catchers as a decoy. Although representation of this scene in the margins of manuscripts need not necessarily be symbolic,[54] in the bestiary (see p85, below) this phenomenon signified the recognition, in broad daylight, of the sinner who, caught in flagrante delicto 'becomes an object of mockery for the righteous ... [who] ... hate the carnal deeds of the sinner and curse his excesses.'[55]

In an anonymous Dutch or German *Vanitas* although the owl, perched on a skull, is quite clearly represented as an agent of death, perhaps here it has also been credited with something of its former status as an attribute of wisdom (see overleaf, below). The snuffed-out candle is a reminder of mortality, of the brevity and fragility of life; the fly is a small remnant of the putrefaction that has stripped bone of flesh. But the candle is also a source of light, a symbol of knowledge and of faith: a brief spark still remains of this candle's flame, which may yet be rekindled by a soft breath. The opening words of Ecclesiastes, 'Vanity of vanities; all is vanity' are explicitly invoked by

ABOVE: Picasso, *Still-life with an Owl and Three Urchins*, 6/11/46, oil on wood, 81.5 x 79cm, Musée Picasso, Antibes, (Z.XIV.255). © DACS 1995.

BELOW: Anon. Dutch or German, *Vanitas*, 17th century, oil on panel, 54.2 x 40.4cm, Coll. Granville, Musée des Beaux-Arts, Dijon.

OPPOSITE, ABOVE: Heinrich Khunrath, *Amphiteatrum sapientiae aeternae*, 1602: vignette 'Wat helffen fakeln licht oder brillen...'. By permission of The British Library.

OPPOSITE, BELOW: Francisco José de Goya y Lucientes, *Caprichos 75*, ¿No hay quien nos desate (Is there no one to untie [annul] us?), 21.5 x 15cm, etching and burnished aquatint, Trustees of the British Museum. Copyright British Museum.

Vanitas pictures such as this, which invite the viewer to think on the vain achievements and pleasures of life, rendered nought by death. But on the piece of paper below the skull and owl, the '*Cogita mori*' – think on death – written there is offset by the proverbial '*Finis coronat opus*' – the end crowns the work.[56] Negative thoughts of death are sublimated by the announcement that a god-fearing existence on earth is crowned by eternal life,[57] and the owl here is a reminder that to think on death is the ultimate wisdom. What is most striking about this picture, is the contrast between the large, round, seeing eyes of the owl and the skull's empty sockets, inviting the viewer to meditate on the meaning of life and death; good and evil; the wise man whose 'eyes are in his head' and the fool that 'walketh in darkness'.[58]

As this *Vanitas* demonstrates, the relationship between wisdom and folly was by no means simple and by the Middle Ages, if not before, the owl was more commonly a symbol of folly and stupidity. Because it shuns daylight, it became a living illustration of the proverb 'there are none so blind as those who won't see', alternatively expressed in the saying 'blind as an owl.'[59] Conversely, the folk-fool Til Ulenspieghel ('Howleglasse' – owl-glass) embodied the belief that the natural fool, though potentially subversive, could see through what conventionally passes for wisdom to the simple, plain truth.[60] His emblem, with which he is depicted on the title page of most editions,[61] is an owl and a mirror (which can both reveal and deceive).[62] In the seventeenth century, the owl was much more commonly depicted with candle and spectacles, both instruments of seeing. As in the vignette from Heinrich Khunruth's *Amphiteatrum sapientiae aeternae*, an alchemical treatise, this illustrated the proverb 'what use are torches, light or eyeglasses, if people will not see'.[63] The general tenor of the proverb and its illustration was applicable in a wide variety of contexts. In Gabriel Rollenhagen's *Nucleus emblematum...* (Utrecht, 1613), the bespectacled owl, which can see neither by the bright light of the sun nor by candle and torches, symbolises the man who is blind in the face of belief.[64] In the background of the print the owl is mobbed, as decoy, by the other birds. In Jan Steen's *After the Drinking Party* (see Chapter Four), a print on the wall depicting an owl, a candle and spectacles, bearing a variant on the familiar motto[65] reinforces the fact that this drunken couple is 'zo beschonken als een uil' – as drunk as an owl,[66] that is, blind drunk. Unwittingly, though, Khunruth's choice of vignette points the finger back at himself, with a delicious double irony. Presumably, he intended it to address those unbelievers who failed to see that alchemy was the way to the truth. The majority, however, who considered alchemists deluded, if not mad, would have deemed the proverb and its illustration more fittingly directed at the alchemists.[67] Steen apparently introduced the motif into one of his paintings of an alchemist.[68] Who, according to whom, was the greater fool?

In the majority of cases, these 'foolish owls' moderate the seriousness of the moral with a fair amount of good-humour. In Goya's *Caprichos* no 75, however, the owl is a demonic and predatory presence, symbol of most pernicious folly as it presses down on a couple struggling to free themselves from the rope that binds them together, a dead tree the symbol of their destroyed and destructive relationship. ¿No hay quien nos desate? (Is there no one to untie [annul] us) is their plea, inscribed on the print. But the presence of the owl, in its antiquated spectacles, signifying 'outmoded custom, the weight of convention, or religious dogma that would not permit divorce' ensures that their impassioned plea is in vain, and their imprisonment dissoluble only with death.[69]

WAS HELFFEN FAKELN LICHT
ODER BRILN,
SO DIE LEVT NICHT SEHEN
WOLLEN.

¿No hay quien nos desate?

More than with any other creature in our bestiary, a spirit of artistic harmony with nature is most often evident in Picasso's depictions of pigeons and doves, where he made some of his greatest efforts to paint like his lifelong rival and later friend, Henri Matisse. *The Perched Pigeons* (*Landscape with Pigeons*) is part of a larger series, and relates to an earlier sub-series of the *Las Meninas* variations.[70] It is like Matisse not just in terms of its colour but also its subject – the view from the 'bourgeois' painter's Mediterranean studio. The perch itself was indeed placed in the window of the third-floor studio of Picasso's villa at La Californie, as can be seen from an exterior photograph by Edward Quinn.[71] There are a mix of birds in evidence here, ruddy pigeons and pure white doves – whose whiteness is not merely bare canvas, which can be seen on the right, but the purest pigment. The bay at Cannes is seen at night, when Picasso often worked, speckled with the light of houses and street lamps. This is a painting preoccupied with balance: of the vast blue and the piercing spots of yellow, of the perch with the tree, and of the perching birds themselves. Imagery connected with pigeons and doves in Picasso's writings often tends toward the same sense of luxuriant equanimity:

> ... celestial blue the milk of sweet almonds of the flight of pigeons... [72]

Matisse spent much of his career struggling with a self-imposed demand to paint every work from scratch: with virgin eye, brain and hand.[73] To tease out rather than impose the way of painting appropriate to his room-with-a-view, or model, or whatever. In this way Matisse hoped to reinvigorate the traditional means of painting, to free it from academic torpor. In spite, or perhaps because, of this ambition, Matisse sometimes tended towards a formula for a fashionable and artificially prudish beauty in modern painting. Unsurprisingly, it would seem that in his art Picasso reacted with wild swings of mood to Matisse, sometimes sarcastically adding carnal lust to nudes that Matisse would have preserved in the Garden of Eden, and at other times highly impressed by his drawings and trying to outdo the balancing act of sensitivity and formula in his paintings. *The Perched Pigeons* are in the latter category, and for some years Picasso softened in this and other works to the sentimental and aesthetically charming side of Matisse after the latter's death in 1954. Picasso was very distressed by the loss of this fellow-traveller of 'modern art'. Thus it was fitting that in paintings of pigeons and doves the Matissean side of Picasso was brought out, because both painters shared an affection for them. In the late forties, Matisse gave Picasso four white Milanese Pigeons, one of which was, by misinterpretation as a dove, to be the subject of a lithograph to become synonymous with the World

Peace Congress of 1950.[74]

Louis Aragon, the former Surrealist poet and now luminary of the French Communist Party, chose the lithograph (dated 9th January 1949) of the pigeon or 'dove' from a portfolio. In a matter of days the poster itself, with its dove of peace was all over Paris advertising the event at the Salle Pleyel. Picasso's fourth child was born to Françoise Gilot during the Peace Congress, and thus earned the Spanish name *Paloma*, meaning 'dove'. Picasso's affiliation to the Communist Party in 1944 had some effect on his choice of subjects in the ensuing years, but his drawings and prints of doves between 1949 and 1951 provided the only real opportunity for collaboration in the then politically significant cause of 'World Peace'. Following Aragon's choice of the lithograph, Picasso produced three more prints which were used for posters: showing a couple with a dove, a dove in flight, and a dove against a rainbow.[75] In September 1951, he produced a lithograph for his last collaboration with Eluard on the book *Le Visage de la Paix*.[76] A preparatory drawing, *The Face of Peace*, shows how Picasso integrated a classicising woman's face into the breast of the bird, shown triumphant with its wings outstretched (the subject was later turned into a medallion by the goldsmith François Hugo). This heraldic invention is one of the clearest examples of Picasso exploiting a long established simple piece of animal symbolism deriving from Noah's dove sent out from the ark, with the express aim of conveying a political message. It was nevertheless with irony that Picasso watched his pictures of doves act in the cause of peace: those real doves he kept in his houses and studios were often caged because – despite their angelic appearance – they were possessed of a vicious streak![77]

The other major characteristics of doves, their fidelity and amorousness, are both attested to by Buffon and represented in Picasso's work.[78] In one text Picasso connects his mistress Marie-Thérèse Walter with a song entitled 'My Dove' and the opening of a cage 'like a flower'.[79] In *Woman with a Green Hairbun and a Bird on her Shoulder* and a number of very late paintings, a naked woman appears with a dove, and sometimes the bird sits between a naked couple.[80] Picasso frequently commented on the unbridled lust of the birds he kept. Two turtledoves eventually revealed themselves to be male, despite their constant copulation:

> Everyone speaks so well of animals' [Picasso] said. 'Nature in its purest state, and all that. What nonsense! Just look at those two turtledoves: as wholeheartedly pederast as any two bad boys.[81]

The nakedness of the woman in the painting implies sensual interest in the bird, so it is also worth remembering the slang

Picasso, *The Face of Peace*, Vallauris, September 1951, pencil on paper, 51 x 66cm, Musée Picasso, Paris (MP 1416). © Photo RMN. © DACS 1995.

connotations of 'bird' when we look at it.

Earlier representations of a figure with a dove seem to conjure not so much with the sexual connotations of the bird, but its reputation for fidelity. As we saw in the Introduction, Picasso had personal reasons for finding the subject of pigeons and doves a touching one, and this must be especially so in the case of paintings of children with doves. Sabartés recalls Picasso one day recounting how his father:

> ... painted an immense canvas representing a dovecote decorated with pigeons on their perches.' ... When [Picasso] spoke, he seemed to count these birds so dear to his father, as if he could see them in his mind's eye. There it was, the dovecote of his childhood illusions...[82]

The *Child Holding a Dove* of 1901 is at one level deeply indebted to the paternal association which existed for Picasso between the subject of the dove and childhood. Perhaps, as some writers have suggested, the particularly withdrawn and pitiable look of this girl-child reflects Picasso's enduring sense of loss over the death of his little sister Conchita in 1895, at the age of seven.[83] Painted during Picasso's transition from *belle époque* gaiety to the sombre isolation of malnourished and listless figures in the 'blue period', this child is the fragile innocence that Greuze never intended to paint in his *Girl with Doves*, and *Girl with a Dead Canary*. Indeed, the firm grasp of the girl on the dove suggests that unlike the pseudo-innocence of Greuze's painting, this child genuinely treasures a world which she will soon be forced by the bitterness of poverty to release.

An entirely different, more boisterous and amusing composition of 1943 repeats the theme of *Child with Doves*. This bald, fat boy is probably inspired by the child of Inès Sassier,[84] Picasso's maid for many years. Picasso obviously derived immense pleasure from the juxtaposition of the 'googly' eyes of the boy and the bird on the chair, the boy seemingly parodying the painter's work with his rattle. The low viewpoint may reflect Picasso's interest in a child's way of coming at the world.[85]

That there is remarkable consistency in Picasso's representations of doves can be seen if one turns from the painted dove alongside the boy to the famous ceramic birds made in Vallauris in 1953. Doves like this one (see opposite, above) modelled with great spontaneity in wet clay, have prompted more 'Orpheus' stories about Picasso. According to Parmelin, the creation of such a dove silenced a film crew shooting Picasso at work in 1954.[86] Penrose recounts the formation of these birds:

> Taking a vase which had just been thrown by Aga, [the Ramiés'] chief potter, Picasso began to mould it in his

fingers. He first pinched the neck so that the body of the vase was resistant to his touch like a balloon, then with a few dexterous twists and squeezes he transformed the utilitarian object into a dove, light, fragile and breathing life. 'You see', he would say, 'to make a dove you must first wring its neck.[87]

This is a very neat expression of the paradoxical nature of Picasso's highly transformative way of working. It has the same black humour as a joke which was shared amongst Picasso's close friends during the period when Picasso's doves were icons of 'World Peace' and brought him rather paradoxical and ambivalent recognition from many quarters. According to Parmelin, the gang amused themselves by sadistically imagining the dove of peace served-up with green peas.[88] As it happened, some years later Picasso returned a casserole, having eaten the pigeon pâté which it had contained, to Monsieur Tiola via Lionel Prejger. When Prejger opened the lid, there was a cardboard pigeon on a bed of peas, and underneath a serving cloth.[89] As usual, nothing so ostensibly sacred as the paternal pigeon was immune from the oven. Picasso had never learned anything: '... but to love things and to eat them alive.'[90]

Turning from the dove and pigeon to the cock, there is again considerable consonance between traditional cock symbolism and Picasso's work.[91] The virility, pride and covetousness of the cock over his hens was perhaps an ironic element of Picasso's interest in this bird, but its defiant presence is at least as important for its heraldic connection with the French nation, rather in the way that a bear can stand for Russia or a dragon for Wales. After the ballet 'Parade', but still very much impressed by the ideas and the aesthetic of the French poet and nationalist Jean Cocteau, Picasso had drawn some elegant cockerels in 1918 as the end of the First World War approached. The gesture was repeated in the Spring of 1945 with several drawings of a crowing cock, distinguished with the Cross of Lorraine or on a tricolour background.[92] In the Buffon prints the strutting cockerel, although executed before the war commenced, must have taken on some of the same significance in 1942. Buffon's own description of the bird which accompanied Picasso's print emphasises its spirit:

> A good cock is one which has fire in its eyes, in its strut, freedom in its movements, and proportions which tell of strength.[93]

According to Buffon, the cock sings indifferent to the hour of day or night. This seems to fly in the face of the symbolism attached to the supposedly timely crowing of the cock. In March 1938 Picasso produced some marvellous charcoal and pastel drawings of the shrieking cock, which are partly icons

ABOVE: Picasso, *Dove*, Vallauris, 14/10/53, ceramic, 15 x 21 x 13cm, MAM Ceret Coll., Musée d'Art Moderne, Ceret. © DACS 1995.

BELOW: Picasso, *Terrine: Pigeon with Peas*, Cannes 8/3/61, mixed media, 7.4 x 19.5 x 12.9cm, Private Collection, Paris (S.577A). Courtesy of Lionel Prejger. © DACS 1995.

of this moment of ill-omen for Europe, and partly attempts to translate the piercing, even harrowing morning sound into form:

> [Picasso] was doing a large charcoal drawing of a terrifically dramatic rooster. 'Roosters', he said, 'we always have roosters, but like everything else in life we must discover them … Roosters have always been seen but seldom so well as in American weather vanes.[94]

Some of the aesthetic of the weather vane, the emphatic silhouette, is evident in the sculpture which Picasso modelled in plaster in 1932 at Boisgeloup, and which was subsequently cast in bronze as *The Cock*. This cock, exhibited in the Liberation Salon in Paris in 1944, was also destined to become a symbol of France.[95] At the time of its creation, however, it was closely related to tumescent plaster heads of a woman normally thought of as Marie-Thérèse Walter. These heads, with their widely acknowledged sexual connotations, can be seen to give birth quite logically to a cock! Yet this cockerel is not in the act of triumphant crowing as has recently been suggested.[96] It may be preening itself, although the gesture seems to have become mournful, reminding us again that *after coitus all animals are sad*! One other problem posed by this bustling bird is that it changes its personality quite radically from one well-organised side where its eye is open, to the other, more complex and confusing, where it is closed. Once again the shift from sunlight to shade may be present in the life of this animal. In a text of Christmas Eve 1935 Picasso connects the killing of the cock with the hour of midnight; in another of 20th May 1940 we read 'songs of midday cocks disordered agitations of the petrified sky'.[97]

As with Picasso's beloved bull, the pride, sexual prowess and grandeur of the cock all come to nothing at the time of slaughter.[98] *Woman with a Cock* of 1938, is an alarming painting which changes the meaning of the crowing of the cock entirely. Here the sound we must imagine recalls the solar cry of the cock in Bataille's 'Rotten Sun'.[99] The scene depicts a bulky farmer's wife on a tiled kitchen floor. She has trussed the cockerel on her lap and has a firm grip on its wings. She has a knife at her side and a bowl in hand, ready to catch the blood from the cock's throat. Picasso's work seems to have none of the humour of Dou's *Woman holding a Cock at her Window*, nor does it suggest the same sexual sub-text: there is ample opportunity to see this as a not very subtle image of the Freudian 'castration complex' rather than a suggestion of dalliance. Yet to leave the painting at this level is to underplay it, as can be seen if we turn to the image of the slaughtered cock in Picasso's writings:

… the bitter price of her virtue and making wine of her life the flea[100] skewers the heart of the cock with exposed throat and lemon squeezer the indifference of its black destiny lights the table laid at lunchtime…[101]

This is of course also a classical *memento mori* image, of the recently slaughtered or hunted bird destined for the dinner table. *Dead Cock and Jar* is a version of the scene Picasso had described, where the slashed throat of the cock is clearly visible, and its plucked, ragged, splayed body is echoed, mourned and threatened all at once by the simple *sol y sombra* shape of the ceramic pot on the table behind it. The sunlight and shade of the pot give us the basic vocabulary of this grisaille ('in grey') painting – notice how the forms of the cock are at some points drawn in black on white (eg the tail) and at others delimited as white against black (eg in the wings). This creature is, as we have seen, another which changes its meaning and situation from midday to midnight.

Unfortunately, Picasso's favourite midnight bird, did not feature in the Buffon prints. This may be because the owl did not really rise to prominence in Picasso's work until the late forties. *Matt Owl*, a replica of a ceramic plate decorated by Picasso in 1947, shows us the owl in its glum state surrounded by stars. Owls must be amongst the most perplexing beasts in terms of their symbolism: as we have seen their meanings range across all possible extremes. In the plate, the notion of the wise owl (of Minerva) comes in for some sarcasm, and we seem to be confronted instead with a true if risible harbinger of doom. It is worth remembering that Picasso himself was something of a night-owl when it came to painting.

Erotic owl symbolism occurs only a few times, mostly in late works. One hilarious print of the 11th May 1970 (see p72, below) shows an enthusiastic Flamenco singer charming or being charmed by the most bizarre contortionist. In the French language, one word for owl (*la chouette*) is rich in obscene connotations, and perhaps Picasso had these in mind, as much as Goya's print, *Caprichos* no 75, when he improvised the scene.[102]

However, Picasso became something of an owl *aficionado* for a time, and made some major paintings on the subject, because a real owl found its way into his care. This pet owl was christened UBU, partly out of assonance with another French word for owl, 'hibou', and partly after the obnoxious hero of Alfred Jarry's play Ubu Roi. Jarry was himself a hero of Picasso, and Jarry had lived for a time in an apartment – which he called in his only-half-joking manner 'Dead Man's Calvary' – decorated with religious objects and shared with owls (see p76, below).[103] The story of *l'hibou* Ubu is told by Françoise Gilot among many others:

Picasso, *Matt Owl*, 1955, rectangular dish: authentic replica white earthenware clay, decoration in engobes engraved by knife, glaze underside, black, white, blue, 32 x 39cm, Musée de la Ville de Vallauris (AR 284; R 726). © DACS 1995.

While Pablo was still working at the Musée d'Antibes, [Michel] Sima had come to us one day with a little owl he had found in the corner of the museum. One of his claws had been injured. We bandaged it and gradually it healed. We bought a cage for him and when we returned to Paris we brought him back with us and put him in the kitchen with the canaries, the pigeons, the turtledoves. We were very nice to him but he only glared at us. Any time we went into the kitchen, the canaries chirped, the pigeons cooed and the turtledoves laughed but the owl remained stolidly silent or, at best, snorted. He smelled awful and ate nothing but mice.[104]

The photographer and sculptor Sima found Ubu probably in August 1946, not long before Picasso and Gilot were due to leave for Paris in November. During their absence from the Côte d'Azur the owl was cared for by Lionel Prejger. Eventually he decided to return the now healthy bird to Picasso in Paris.[105] In *The Owl Cage* of 21st March 1947, the composition is remarkably close to mediaeval bestiary imagery (see below), and based upon the same tendency of other birds to mob a solitary owl. Picasso shows the sour-tempered Ubu in his cage, surrounded by the cheerful turtledoves. This painting, and a later ceramic of an *Angry Owl*, seem to commemorate Picasso's standoff with the owl, as he attempted to gain its confidence:

> Every time the owl snorted at Pablo he would shout, 'Cochon, Merde,' and a few other obscenities, just to show the owl that he was even worse mannered than *he* was. He used to stick his fingers between the bars of the cage and the owl would bite him … Finally the owl would let him scratch his head and gradually he came to perch on his finger instead of biting it, but even so, he still looked very unhappy.[106]

It is interesting to note that the painting of the caged owl was produced on the same day as the much better known *Cock and Knife*, another image of a cockerel with its throat cut.[107] This perhaps mollifies the humour which one sees in the caged owl as an isolated canvas.

As usual, even though there is a 'real-life' model for the owl compositions, it is not always a safe assumption that they were painted from life or based on a particular scene. In a conversation with Brassaï in Paris on 28th December 1946, Picasso said that the owl's story was:

> … running around in my head right now… Although I don't copy anything, my surroundings appear in my canvasses in one manner or another.[108]

Perhaps one of the paintings which they looked at together was *Still-life with an Owl and Three Sea Urchins*, now in Antibes. It is

OPPOSITE, ABOVE: Picasso, *The Owl Cage*, 21/3/47, oil on panel, 80 x 100cm, Picasso Estate (Inv 13129). Courtesy of Musée Picasso, Paris. © DACS 1995.

OPPOSITE, BELOW: Picasso, *Dead Cock and Jar*, Vallauris 13/12/53, oil on canvas, 88 x 116cm, Stenersen Collection, Bergen (Z.XVI.54). © DACS 1995.

ABOVE: Abraham van Beyeren, *Still-life with Turkey*, 17th century, oil on panel, 74 x 59cm, Musée du Louvre, Paris. © Photo RMN.

BELOW: *Owl*, MS Harley 4751, Bestiary in Latin, c1230-40, f. 47. By permission of The British Library.

probable that at that date the owl had not yet been restored to Picasso by Prejger, and so this owl appears out of Picasso's memory rather than at first hand. The painting is unusual for the use which it makes of the wood grain of the panel on which it was painted. The composition contrasts the spiny urchins with the rounded owl, both on the same sort of chair as appeared in *Child with Doves*. At the same time it is central to the subject that the urchins specifically mimic the large staring eyes of the owl.

Picasso had long recognised that the eyes of a figure or an animal are of special importance to a painter, who is effectively representing the sense which he is both using and addressing. The threat and reality of blindness becomes for Picasso a constant source of fascination during and after the 'blue period', and will be explored in more detail in the case of the Minotaur in Chapter Nine. For now it is worth noting that, in recalling an old practice amongst keepers of songbirds, Picasso once paradoxically connected blindness to greater creativity:

> And they ought to put out the eyes of painters as they do
> goldfinches in order that they can sing better.[109]

Thus we can see that it was the presence of Ubu the owl with his grumpy stare that brought home to Picasso the special role which owls could play in symbolising the faculty upon which his powers rested. The owl can stand for sight, and especially a piercing painter's *in*sight that penetrates the night of ordinary experience.[110] It is clear from what has been said about the earlier range of meanings of the owl, however, that Picasso's gesture cannot be taken without irony.

OPPOSITE: Picasso, *Child with Doves*, Paris, 24/8/43, oil on canvas, 162 x 130cm, Musée Picasso, Paris (MP 192; Z.XIII.95). © Photo RMN. © DACS 1995.

CATS AND DOGS

Cats and dogs form a contrasting pair in Picasso's work, as they had for the Comte de Buffon. Both domestic pets, their character and usefulness are at odds. The cat is an unfaithful, false and perverse creature in Buffon's eyes, only to be kept if one has a more serious domestic infestation. The accompanying Picasso print (see p105, above) shows a large duplicitous cat, apparently licking its lips. Dogs for Buffon are notable not so much for their intelligence and guile but for their feelings of affection which make them entirely dedicated to their master or mistress. Unlike the cat, the dog has helped 'mankind' in his peaceful dominion over the land.[1] This contrast is entirely in keeping with the general tenor of traditional attitudes towards cats and dogs: cats are cunning opportunists and, therefore, are considered as 'women's pets'; dogs, on the other hand, are generally characterised by their faithfulness. Yet with an ambivalence characteristic of animal lore and representation, the dog could also be considered an exemplar of the basest and most foul of bestial instincts and behaviour.

In the bestiaries, the text describing the cat is very short; there is little elaboration, no detailed exegesis. The cat, simply, has acute sight and catches mice:

> She is called MOUSER because she is fatal to mice. The vulgar call her CATUS the Cat because she catches things (*a captura*) while others say that it is because she lies in wait (*captat*) ie because she 'watches'. So acutely does she glare that her eye penetrates the shades of darkness with a gleam of light.[2]

As compensation, though, the illustrations can be amongst the most charming and rich of the bestiary, succinctly elaborating on the meagre text. In MS Bodley 764, in a domestic scene appropriate to this most home-loving of animals, set against the backdrop of the night sky, one cat sits by the fire licking its genital region; one reaches inside a birdcage to snatch its terrified occupant and the third, having leapt up on its hind legs, has just caught a mouse which desperately tries to escape. The image summarises those qualities which earned for the cat such approbation: its love of luxurious warmth; its over-fastidious and impudent preening; its sharp sight and its predatory habits – no matter that these latter were also considered so useful. Although, in dynastic Egypt, the cat had been revered as a god and credited with magical powers, the

OPPOSITE: Picasso, detail of *Woman Playing with a Dog*, 8/3/53, ripolin on plywood, 81 x 100cm, Picasso Museum, Lucerne, Rosengart Donation. (Z.XV.246). Courtesy of Galerie Rosengart. © DACS 1995.

ABOVE: *Cat*, MS Bodley 764, Bestiary in Latin, *c*1250, f. 51. The Bodleian Library, Oxford.

Anon. Pompeian, *Cat Stealing a Bird*, Pompeii, AD 1,
mosaic, 51 x 51cm, Museo Archelogico Nazionale,
Naples. Photo Scala, Florence.

distinction earned it no favours for, by the Middle Ages, the cat's magic was black and of Satan.[3] Cat worship was considered an abomination, the practice of heretics such as the Cathars who, as Alain of Lille explained, '... are called after the cat, because they kiss the posterior of a cat in whose shape, it is said, Lucifer appears to them...'.[4] This identification with the Prince of Darkness, undoubtedly encouraged by the cat's nocturnal habits, is certainly responsible for the widespread belief, common in classical writings[5] and rife in the Middle Ages, that cats, especially black ones, were the familiars of witches, given by the Devil himself.[6]

From earliest times, however, the cat was represented in a more innocuous, but all the same derogatory, light: as scavenger and opportunist. *Cat Stealing a Bird* is a much reproduced mosaic from Pompeii which depicts the cat in the act of stealing from the kitchen table, a subject that became especially popular in the seventeenth and eighteenth centuries, as a vehicle for the skilful representation of foodstuffs with added interest provided by the mischievous and occasionally cruel antics of the cat.[7] In other pictures, however, a kitchen maid sleeps whilst in the background a cat stealthily grabs a chicken portion, exemplifying the proverb that 'a kitchen maid must keep one eye on the pan and the other on the cat', a warning against the consequences of inattention to one's rightful duties.[8]

Similarly, in Goltzius' print *The Holy Family with Saint John* more is intended by the small detail of a cat catching a bird than additional interest as a genre detail. As in other pictures the cat betrays its satanic associations, as a reminder of the original sin which necessitated the Incarnation of Christ, the only hope for humanity's Redemption. In Hieronymus Bosch's Paradise panel from the *Garden of Earthly Delights* triptych, a cat carries off a mouse; cats flee from the Archangel Gabriel's advance in some Annunciation scenes[9] and in others watch silently from the threshold of the Annunciate's room.[10] These presences, as in Goltzius' print, possibly signify the cat as the Devil, catching the soul or 'mouse'[11] and perpetuate the function of Christ as 'fleshly bait for the devil', occasionally represented by various symbols of the Cross which trapped Satan: the mousetrap, bait box for catching fish, or Christ as bird-decoy, caught in the nets.[12] It is no coincidence, perhaps, that mice, birds and fish are the cat's favourite food.

Given, however, the multi-layered nature of mediaeval and renaissance symbolism, it is equally likely that the cat in Annunciation and Holy Family scenes, or representations of the Fall, could represent Eve – the Devil's familiar[13] – or even the Virgin herself, in her capacity as the 'new Eve' who undid

ABOVE: Picasso, *Cat seizing a Bird*, Paris 22/4/39, oil on canvas, 81 x 100cm, Musée Picasso, Paris (MP 178; Z.IX.296). © Photo RMN. © DACS 1995.

BELOW: Hendrick Goltzius, *The Holy Family with Saint John* from the *Life of the Virgin* series, 1593, engraving, 46 x 35cm. Copyright British Museum.

the harm that the first Eve had done.[14] In Cornelis van Haarlem's *Adam and Eve*, discussed in the Ape section, the cat is firmly in the grip of an ape, as Eve was used by Satan as his instrument for the Fall. In Dürer's *Fall of Man*, reproduced in the Introduction, the prominent cat and mouse in the foreground possibly foretell the moment when, not only did animal turn on animal, but Eve was caught by the devil and, in effect, committed adultery with him. In turn, Eve trapped Adam. Her great sin was to disobey both God and her husband and since, from earliest times, it had been considered that the Fall had something to do with sexual awareness, it was a small step to equate the biting of the apple with her illicit relationship, whether sexual or otherwise, with the devil.[15] In the late fifteenth century, in his *Das Narrenschiff* (*The Ship of Fools*), Sebastian Brant used the example of a cat chasing mice to illustrate comparable ideas, perpetuating Aristotle's belief that the female cat is lascivious and sexually insatiable:

> The cats pursue the mice in haste
> When once they've had a little taste.
> Women who try out other men
> Become so bold and shameless then.[16]

The sharp-witted wife tickles her husband's nose with a feather to distract him from her adultery whilst the hapless cuckold, characteristically of those who do not wish to see what is in front of their eyes, looks through his fingers. The implication is that the 'cat's' power to trap 'mice' lay in the acuity of sight which the husband lacks. Topsell noted that 'her eies glister above measure especially when a man commeth to see a cat on the sudden, and in the night, they can hardly be endured, for their flaming aspect'.[17] In Francesco Ubertini's strange *Portrait of a Lady* both woman and cat look slyly out at the viewer to entice and bewitch. The cat was the animal representative of sight, for example in Goltzius' series of The Five Senses.[18] But it was also associated with the sin that, above all, was slave to the pleasures outward appearance affords the eyes: *Superbia*, or Pride, often represented by a woman, like Venus looking at herself in a mirror. 'A cat,' Topsell tells us, 'is much delighted to play with her image in a glasse', and is notoriously fond of grooming itself, like those women who, as in the personification of *Superbia* in Bosch's *Tabletop of the Seven Deadly Sins* in the Prado, prink and preen in front of a mirror and concern themselves only with their superficial outward appearance rather than engaging that insight which reveals the true inner person.[19] In Bosch's representation a cat, like those in Annunciation scenes, sits just beyond the threshold, and perhaps here too was intended as a reminder that the pride, root of all evil,[20] of both Satan and Eve, was responsible for the Fall. The Serpent entranced Eve, as Milton relates, by his 'tortuous train' which 'curled many a wanton wreath in sight of Eve to catch her eye'.[21] In turn, Eve used her charms to cajole her husband into eating the forbidden fruit, like the she-cat who, as Topsell wrote, 'flattereth by rubbing her skinne against ones Legges',[22] a reminder of all those women who proudly spent hours in front of the mirror, practising the seductive arts that beguiled men too blind to see beyond outward appearance.[23]

In such paintings, as in a mirror, human behaviour is held up to inspection and the painting makes us reflect on what we see reflected there. The presence of a cat neatly underscores the message and as Bosch's depictions of hellfire make clear, the consequences are fearful for those who choose to ignore its import. Some hundred and fifty years later, however, Jan Steen manipulated this association of the cat with sight in a painting intended as much to amuse as to teach.[24] In *The Drunken Couple*, a drunken woman sprawls, legs apart, and a cat peers upwards, its acuity of sight contrasted with her blind drunkenness and that of her companion, indicated by the print on the wall bearing the familiar owl, candle and spectacles.[25] The cat appears to be looking at the pipe the woman suggestively holds limply across her lap[26] but it is also in an ideal position to see, perspicaciously, up the woman's skirts, a bawdy exposition of the moral laxity which accompanies heavy drinking, and a sly acknowledgement of the 'Freudian' aspect of the cat. Inevitably, mouse and mousetrap could, in more disreputable forms of literature, be equated respectively with the male and female genitalia, for example in The *Mouse's Tail*, a bawdy Yorkshire ballad published in 1753 and *The Mousetrap*, a pornographic novel published in 1794.[27] In an old French song, the woman who bemoans 'Mon père m'a donné un mari/ Mon Dieu quel homme, qu'il est si petit' adds that 'le chat l'a pris pour une souris', underscoring the deficiencies of the marital penis[28] which will clearly impel her, like Brant's wife, to go after other 'mice'.

In the eighteenth century, the erotic possibilities afforded by representing cats and women together were exploited in otherwise elegant boudoir scenes such as Boucher's *La Toilette* of the 1730s in the Thyssen collection. Even Reynolds, an artist not generally associated with such frivolity, sketched *Woman tying her Garter* in one of his notebooks. In pictures like this, the addition of the cat embellishes the character of the woman with a frisson of dubiousness, identifying her as, at very least, promiscuous.[29] The term 'cat' came to be synonymous with 'prostitute' and it is particularly appropriate that, in Nathaniel Hone's *Kitty Fisher*, the old association of cats and women as predators of 'mice', 'birds', 'fish' and men,[30] is recast, with

OPPOSITE ABOVE: *On Adultery* from *Das Narrenschiff* by Sebastian Brant, 1494, woodcut.

OPPOSITE BELOW: Hieronymus Bosch, *Superbia* from the *Tabletop of the Seven Deadly Sins*, 1490, oil on panel whole, 120 x 150cm, Museo del Prado, Madrid. All Rights Reserved © Museo del Prado, Madrid.

ABOVE: Jan Steen, *The Drunken Couple*, n.d., oil on panel, 52.5 x 64cm, Rijksmuseum, Amsterdam. © Rijksmuseum-Stichting Amsterdam.

BELOW: Sir Joshua Reynolds, *Woman tying her Garter*, 1752, leaf from a sketchbook. British Museum, London (201a 10, f. 15). Copyright British Museum.

the image of the cat fishing in a goldfish bowl 'which reflects a window crowded with eager spectators', as a rebus-like pun on the name of this famous courtesan.[31] Doubtless it also comments on her predatory activities which will perhaps earn her the fate of Horace Walpole's 'Pensive Selima', the cat that drowned in a goldfish bowl. The incident inspired Thomas Gray to write a fine poem in which he drew the moral that:

> From hence, ye Beauties, undeceiv'd,
> Know, one false step is ne'er retriev'd,
> And be with caution bold.
> Not all that tempts your wand'ring eyes
> And heedless hearts, is lawful prize;
> Nor all that glisters, gold.[32]

Only gradually, it appears, have cats gained acceptance in art and literature as admired animals and much-loved pets, rather than scavengers, symbolic presences or merely utilitarian 'mousers'. Occasionally, it was possible to represent cats or kittens with children whose innocence precludes censorious comment, but by the nineteenth century, it was also possible to represent respectable women and cats without any apparent ulterior motive. Manet's picture of his wife and her cat in *Woman with a Cat* is a study of repose, taken from life and intended to be nothing more. This is also the case with his numerous exquisite and amusing sketches of cats from life,[33] even though he was evidently aware of the more negative associations of their relationship, for example in the infamous *Olympia* (Paris, Musée d'Orsay). It was also in Manet's circle that it became respectable to represent men together with their pet cats. Although the affection of many men for their cats, famously Dr Johnson for Hodge and Christopher Smart for Jeoffrey, 'servant of the Living God, duly and daily serving him'[34] is well documented, tradition had decreed that painters steer clear of such subjects.[35] For Manet and his friends however, cats frequently functioned as a sign of literary kinship. Manet produced the famous poster, *Cats Rendezvous*, for Champfleury's 1868 *Les Chats*,[36] and in this book, Baudelaire and Champfleury himself are represented, by Edmond Morin, with their cats. The art dealer Vollard was particularly fond of cats, and the two portraits of him by Bonnard are probably the first full-scale paintings to represent man and cat apparently enjoying each other's company. Bonnard's example probably inspired his friend Vuillard to paint Théodore Duret with a cat.[37] But beneath the calm exterior of these paintings, perhaps there is a hint of unease. Vollard claimed that he had not been able to sleep during the sittings for his portrait because of the cat and in Bonnard's print, *Portrait of Ambroise Vollard*, the cat seems no longer to appreciate the affections of its master.[38] The hand

OPPOSITE, ABOVE: Édouard Manet, *Woman with a Cat*, c1882-83, oil on canvas, 92 x 73cm, Tate Gallery, London.

OPPOSITE, BELOW: Nathaniel Hone, *Kitty Fisher*, 1765, oil on canvas, 75 x 62.2cm, National Portrait Gallery, London. By Courtesy of the National Portrait Gallery, London.

ABOVE: Picasso, *Studies of a woman with striped stockings; black cat; caricatures*, 1902, China ink on paper, 20 x 31.5cm, Picasso Estate (Inv 224). Courtesy of Musée Picasso, Paris. © DACS 1995.

OVERLEAF: *Dog*, MS Harley 3244, Bestiary in Latin, c1255, f. 45. By permission of the British Library, London.

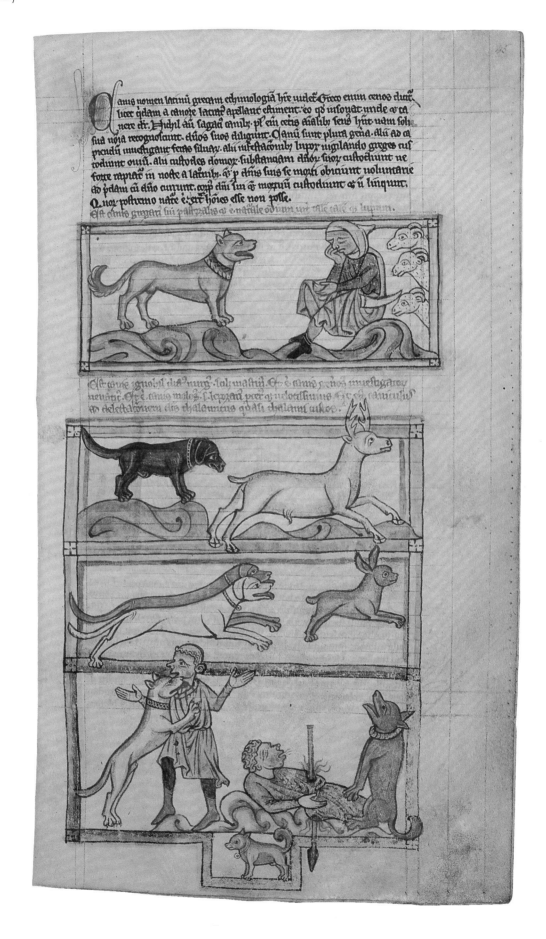

that Vollard uses to stroke his cat may be read as ever so tentative and the cat, one paw raised, stirs and looks round, with its large eyes, at the viewer.

By contrast, the faithful dog has eyes only for its owner and commensurate with the high regard this praiseworthy tendency elicits, the bestiary description and illustration depict the dog in a glowing light and in the most fulsome terms. Often the accompanying miniature, like that reproduced here, (see opposite) depicts in several 'frames' those various virtues which make the dog such a useful and fitting companion to its master – bestiary dogs are truly 'men's dogs':

> Dogs are of various kinds; some track wild beasts in the forests, others guard flocks of sheep from the attacks of wolves, others guard the houses and wealth of their master, lest they are robbed at night by thieves, and will lay down their lives for their master. They go willingly to hunt with him and will guard his dead body, never leaving it.[39]

The text that follows largely consists of the retelling of well-known historical anecdotes, occasionally with additional illustrations, amplifying these traits. Predictably, the bestiary drew several positive morals from the habits of dogs. The dog that diligently seeks to pick up a scent finds the truth. Watchdogs were like preachers:

> … who by warnings and by righteous living turn aside the ambushes of the devil, lest he seize God's treasure, namely the souls of Christians, and carry it off. As the dog's tongue heals a wound when he licks it [a habit which often merited a picture of its own], so the wounds of sin are cleansed by the instruction of the priest when they are laid bare in confession.[40]

The dogs of the bestiary are pre-eminently the servants of warriors and hunters. In commissioned royal portraits of later centuries such as Velázquez's *Il Cardinale l'Infante Fernando Cacciatore* to be represented as a hunter, accompanied by a faithful working hound, signalled the strength, valour, honesty and loyalty expected of a present or future monarch. Like the equestrian portraits of the family discussed above in Chapter Two, this painting was intended as a companion: to the same artist's *Philip IV as Hunter* and *Baltasar Carlos as Hunter* (both in Madrid, Prado) and a match for Titian's *Charles V with Hound* – proclamations of the past, present and future splendour of Europe's most powerful family.[41]

Adoption of this pose, gun in hand, dog by one's side, became commonplace in English representations of the land-owning classes but in the Middle Ages and Renaissance, representation of men and their dogs, aside from the hunting

ABOVE: Diego Velázquez, *Il Cardinale l'Infante Fernando Cacciatore*, 1635, oil on canvas, 191 x 107cm, Museo del Prado, Madrid. All Rights Reserved © Museo del Prado, Madrid.

BELOW: Picasso, *Self-portrait with a Dog*, Paris, 1902, pen on paper, 11.5 x 13cm, Museu Picasso, Barcelona (MPB 110.443). © DACS 1995.

scenes so popular in tapestries and manuscripts, had been relatively scarce when compared with the great proliferation of pictures in which elegant, courtly women are accompanied by their faithful little lapdogs. Sculpted on mediaeval effigies, 'Reclining at the feet of a man, the dog came to symbolise strength and courage; at the feet of a woman, undying love'.[42] Similar intentions perhaps inform the inclusion of the small griffin-like terrier that looks so alertly and attentively out at the viewer in Jan van Eyck's *Arnolfini Portrait*. In this exemplary picture of a pious couple plighting their troth, surrounded by symbols announcing their faithfulness to each other and to God, the small dog that, as in so many other representations of fashionable women, is never away from its mistress's skirts, exemplifies the faithfulness that exists between lovers or married couples.[43] Andrea Alciati expressed similar sentiments in his emblem 'In fides uxoriam' from the 1542 dual-language *Emblematum libellus*. In the words of the German text:

> Einer erfrawen trewe.
>
> Die zway so eins dem andern peutt
>
> vnder eimm apffelbaum die hand,
>
> Das hundle so sich bey in freudt,
>
> Thuen unnß einr frawen trew bekant:
>
> Ein hund is ein gar trewes pfand,
>
> Der apfel einn bitzige frucht,
>
> Damit Venus offt hat geband
>
> Zwen gmahel in lieb, trew und zucht.[44]

Alciati's verse draws together several strands of thought which were pivotal to the role of the dog in representations of human love and sexuality: the faithfulness of the dog and the agency of Venus in engendering lust, essential to the fruitfulness that both sustains marriage and was its *raison d'être*. Venus is frequently represented with a small dog, evidence not only of its faithfulness, but also its carnality: antique erotic reliefs of copulating couples sometimes include a small dog on or by the bed.[45] Yet typically, both attributes were susceptible as much to negative as to positive interpretation, depending on context. The faith and faithfulness of the good marriage sanctified and legitimised sexual activity, as both Jan van Eyck's portrait and Alciati's emblem signify. Pontormo's dignified *Portrait of a Woman* is no more amenable to attracting censorious comment than *The Arnolfini Portrait*: whether or not the dog was explicitly intended as a symbol of fidelity, the mood of the picture merely suggests that it was this lady's favoured and devoted little pet. But Topsell, for one, wrote most scathingly of those little lapdogs that women were wont to carry about with them, '... the delicate, neate, and pretty kind of dogges called the Spaniell gentle, or the comforter...':

OPPOSITE, ABOVE: Jean Honoré Fragonard, *Girl and Dog* ('La Gimblette'), c1770, oil on canvas, 89 x 70cm, Alte Pinakothek, Munich.

OPPOSITE, BELOW: Picasso, *Woman Playing with a Dog*, 8/3/53, ripolin on plywood, 81 x 100cm, Picasso Museum, Lucerne, Rosengart Donation. (Z.XV.246). Courtesy of Galerie Rosengart. © DACS 1995.

These dogs are little, pretty, proper and fine, and sought for to satisfy the delicatenes of dainty dames, and wanton women's wils, instruments of folly for them to playe and dally withall, to tryfle away the treasure of time, to withdraw their mindes from more commendable excercises, and to content their corrupted concupiscences with vain disport (A selly shift to shunne yrkesome idlenesse.) These puppies the smaller they be, the more pleasure they provoke, as more meete play-fellowes for minsing mistresses to beare in their bosomes, to keep company withal in their chambers, to succour with sleep in bed, and nourish with meat at bourde, to lay in their lappes and licke their lips as they ride in their Waggons...[46]

His explanation accords with the common representation of these small dogs as lover-substitutes dancing to their mistress's command[47] or sleeping on her pillow, literally dog-tired after nightly exertions.[48]

It does not take much imagination also to equate these dogs with the phallus. Traditionally, the hunter and his (two) dogs represent the male genitals, a metaphor which recurs in several English and French seventeenth-century poems: 'the dogs wait patiently by the side of the symbolic pond into which their master has plunged',[49] a meaning expressed ribaldly, if exquisitely in Fragonard's *Girl and Dog* ('*La Gimblette*'). The viewer peers through the painted curtain, like a voyeur, and there sees a young girl, naked from the waist down and balancing her small pet with its cunningly concealing long tail on her knees. The picture is so freshly painted that it is difficult to consider it in the same light as Greuze's more heavy handed and sly variations on the theme of pubescent sexuality (described in Chapter Three), but whereas Greuze's pictures, initially at least, were much admired, Fragonard's '*Gimblette*' was so 'piquant' that his shocked contemporaries forbade the work and the engraving after it to be shown.[50] This despite the common pictorial device of representing dogs in genre paintings engaged in sexual intercourse to make explicit the promise, actuality or fulfilment of the sexual act between the men and women who were the main subject of the picture. Often, the detail is included in a spirit of robust good humour, but in Veneziano de' Musi's engraving after Raphael's *Rape of Lucretia*, the explicit nature of the dogs' coupling and the obvious distress of the bitch, is clearly meant to elicit a sense of disgust at the bestiality of the rape.

This carnal side of dogs, though fully acknowledged in other medieval writings as it had been in biblical and antique texts,[51] was by and large ignored by the bestiarist who described them as moderate in their way of life:

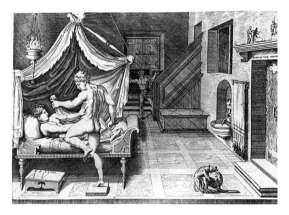

PREVIOUS PAGE, ABOVE: Jan van Eyck, *The Arnolfini Portrait*, 1434, oil on panel, 82 × 59.5cm, National Gallery, London. Reproduced by courtesy of the Trustees, The National Gallery, London.

PREVIOUS PAGE, BELOW: Picasso, *Untitled [Naked Man and Woman with a Dog]*, 22/6/68 (I), etching, 12.5 × 9cm, Galerie Louise Leiris, Paris (B 1658). Courtesy of Galerie Louise Leiris, Paris. © DACS 1995.

OPPOSITE, ABOVE: Jacopo Carucci Pontormo, *Portrait of a Woman*, Städelsches Kunstinstitut, Frankfurt am Main. Photo © Ursula Edelmann, Frankfurt am Main.

OPPOSITE, BELOW: Picasso, *Woman with a Dog*, 31/5-7/6/62, oil on canvas, 146 × 114cm, Picasso Estate (Inv 13439; Z.XX.244). Courtesy of Musée Picasso, Paris. © DACS 1995.

ABOVE: Agostino Veneziano de' Musi (after Raphael), *Rape of Lucretia*, 1534, engraving, 253 × 401cm, Albertina, Vienna. Courtesy of Albertina, Vienna.

BELOW: Adriano Cecioni, *Defecating Dog*, c1880, plaster, 3.5ins, coll. Aldo Gonelli, Florence.

ABOVE: William Hogarth, *The Painter and his Pug*, 1745, oil on canvas, 90 x 69.9cm, Tate Gallery, London.

BELOW: Sir Edwin Landseer, *The Old Shepherd's Chief Mourner*, oil on panel, Victoria & Albert Museum, London. Photo © Victoria & Albert Museum, London.

... as he who is set above others must be watchful in the study of wisdom and avoid all kinds of inebriation, for Sodom perished from an excess of good things. For gluttony is the way by which the Devil most easily corrupts men.[52]

Although one revolting doggy habit in particular was singled out for comment – 'When the dog returns to his vomit, it signifies those who fall into sin again after they have confessed'[53] – there is no mention of the untrained dog's complete lack of regard for the appropriateness of time, place and circumstance in matters faecal, exquisitely expressed in Adriano Cecioni's tiny plaster *Defecating Dog*. The delicate irony of such a mismatch between the scatological subject and its representation in this 'miniature shocker'[54] is more in the spirit of manuscript marginalia than any impulse towards 'realism' per se, and a welcome antidote to the sentimental anthropomorphism of other nineteenth-century depictions of dogs.

Sir Edwin Landseer is the undisputed master of this latter genre and *The Old Shepherd's Chief Mourner* one of his most successful, earning him (from John Ruskin) the title 'The Man of Mind'.[55] Although this picture lacks the arch humour of works such as *Alexander and Diogenes* (London, Tate Gallery) and *Laying Down the Law* (Chatsworth House), it nevertheless appeals to the recognition 'that animals had feelings different from our own only in degree rather than kind' – a sentiment which, though today unfashionably anthropomorphic, must be applauded if only for its contribution to the founding of the Royal Society for the Prevention of Cruelty to Animals in 1824.[56] Yet although Landseer's picture may be considered unquestionably 'Victorian' in the way that it teeters on a very fine line between bathos and pathos, it is a direct descendant of the bestiary image of the grieving dog unwilling to leave its master's dead body.

Dogs, it is said, resemble, or act like, their owners. This is a common notion which so often is shown to have a ring of truth about it. After all, as the examples we have been looking at demonstrate, men are expected to acquire (and are represented with) large, strong working dogs and women have little, dainty and pretty specimens. William Hogarth, however, had no such manly pretensions in his *The Painter and his Pug*, but a playful deviance from this norm and an artful manipulation of expectations of similitude between man and faithful beast, invest the painting with wit, and Hogarth the artist with more of an air of honest sincerity than can be mustered by a grand, posturing portrait. Commonly, dogs were represented exercising their incomparable faculty of smell, for example in kitchen or banquet scenes like Frans Snyders' *Still-life with a Swan* in which the dog cannot resist sniffing and drooling over the extravagant variety of foodstuffs on display. In Hogarth's painting, however, the dog is intimately associated with another sense, that of sight. In this exercise in the nature of realism and artifice, the dog becomes an integral part of Hogarth's visual exposition of the nature of beauty and of artistic practice, later expounded in his treatise *The Analysis of Beauty*. In the foreground, on a palette bearing the words 'The Line of Beauty and Grace' is the three-dimensional 'serpentine line' which encapsulated, for Hogarth, the essence of artistic practice. By adhering to, or deviating from, this curvaceous line, the artist may produce, when appropriate, beautiful images or ugly ones; sincere or caricaturistic. The set of three books by great English writers underscore the point: Milton, Shakespeare and Swift, the consummate satirist. This picture suggests that painting is an art of contrived imitation. Hogarth's portrait appears to be on an oval panel within the painting, but the drapery within it extends out into the picture, into the space where Trump sits, depicted exactly the same size as Hogarth, and rather like him: not beautiful, not particularly ugly, but faithful – the dog to his master, the master to his art.

ABOVE: Frans Snyders, *Still-life with a Swan*, c1615-20, oil on canvas, Pushkin Museum of Fine Arts, Moscow.

BELOW: Picasso, *Dog and Cock*, Paris, 1921, oil on canvas, 155 x 76.5cm, Yale University Art Gallery, Gift of Stephen C Clark, BA 1903. (Z.IV.335). © DACS 1995.

ABOVE LEFT: Picasso, *Portrait of a Bearded Man [Ambroise Vollard] with a Cat*, c1937, oil on canvas, 61 x 46cm, Picasso Estate (Inv 12902). Courtesy of Musée Picasso, Paris. © DACS 1995.

ABOVE RIGHT: Pierre Bonnard, *Portrait of Ambroise Vollard*, c1924, etching on heavy laid paper, plate 34.6 x 22.8cm, sheet 45 x 33.9cm, Brooklyn Museum, New York. Loeser Art Fund.

BELOW LEFT: Picasso, *Cat and Mice*, 1952, crayon and cut-out, Picasso Estate (Inv 6752-6758r). Courtesy of Musée Picasso, Paris. © DACS 1995.

As we noted in the Introduction, Picasso delayed making the cat print for the Buffon series in order to tease Ambroise Vollard, who was a great cat lover. *Portrait of a Bearded Man with a Cat* is a very fine and undated painting, which bears a close resemblance to Vollard and shows him clutching at a cat in the throes of testing its claws. Vollard's cats were something of a trademark in the very numerous portraits of him by various artists (for example see opposite, above right).[57] The cat is not at home with the man, and in general paintings of men with cats are – as we shall see – not the norm in Picasso's work, any more than they are in European art of earlier periods.

Buffon, like the earlier bestiarists, remarks on the peculiar eyes of the cat, and in *Head of a Cat*, one the earliest known drawings on the subject by Picasso, these eyes are so magnified as to imply that this cat wears glasses. Picasso drew the cat in La Coruña in 1892, aged eleven. It plainly shows that, unless a remarkable revolution took place in a year, the artist could not after all draw 'like Raphael' at the age of twelve,[58] but much like any other schoolboy with artistic pretensions. Whatever the level of skill on show in this funny and cramped little drawing, it can be seen that like the owl in the previous chapter, this animal subject attracts Picasso for its display of prodigious vision – that quality most valuable to a visual artist. The vision of the cat has the particular quality of acquisitiveness – these are the eyes of a stealthy 'cat-burglar', a thief.

The cat as a thief, and the cat as a killer who takes satanic pleasure in inflicting a slow death, are two of the most important subjects in Picasso's depictions of the animal. Surprisingly, there is only one instance of a game of 'cat and mouse', in *Cat and Mice*, seven paper cutouts made in 1952, probably for the artist's children. By contrast, there are two paintings of a cat relishing seafood. In the lesser known and smaller painting *Cat eating a Fish*, from 15th December 1953, Picasso shows a very scraggy cat with a small fish in its mouth. The painting is strange for its ambiguous viewpoint – it is difficult to decide which is the right way up, and this in turn leads one to imagine which way up it was painted. It is as if another kind of 'cat and mouse' game is being played. A much more famous and dramatic fish-eating cat appears in *Still-life with Cat and Lobster* of 23rd October to 1st November 1962. This grand canvas closely echoes Chardin's famous *The Ray* (discussed in detail in Chapter Six), not least in the display of brushwork. Like Chardin, whose great canvas was well-known to him, Picasso enjoys the opportunity of painting such a varied set of creatures, and capturing their precarious perching on the table top. In a characteristic spirit of parody, Picasso inverts the

OPPOSITE, BELOW RIGHT: Picasso, *Head of a Cat*, La Coruña, 1892, pencil on paper, 16.4 x 20.2cm, Museu Picasso, Barcelona (MPB 110.998). © DACS 1995.

ABOVE: Picasso, *The Cat*, Spring 1936, sugar lift aquatint, 36 x 28cm, Victoria & Albert Museum, London (B 333). Photo © Victoria & Albert Museum. © DACS 1995.

BELOW: Picasso, *Cat eating a Fish*, 15/12/53, oil on canvas, 19 x 24cm, Picasso Estate (Inv 13265). Courtesy of Musée Picasso, Paris. © DACS 1995.

ABOVE: Picasso, *Cat and Cock*, Vallauris 13/12/53, oil
on canvas, 89.5 x 116cm, Musée National d'Art Moderne,
Paris, (Z.XVI.55). Courtesy of the Centre Georges
Pompidou. © DACS 1995.

OPPOSITE, ABOVE: Picasso, *Seated Woman with a Dog*,
1914, pencil on paper, 36 x 24.5cm, Collection Marina
Picasso, Geneva (Inv 1720; Z.XXIX.109). Courtesy Galerie
Jan Krugier, Geneva. © DACS 1995.

OPPOSITE, BELOW: Picasso, *Man with a Wolf*, 1914-15,
pencil on paper, 32.5 x 23.5cm, Collection Marina
Picasso, Geneva (Inv 1719; Z.XXIX.107). Courtesy Galerie
Jan Krugier, Geneva. © DACS 1995.

dominance of the fish over the cat in *The Ray*. As has recently been pointed out,[59] this large canvas shows a confrontation of the living and the dead, but the lobster, from its colour evidently cooked, shows little sign of lying down and accepting its fate. Picasso presumably could not resist the lush reds of the traditional lobster still-life (see p140), or the dramatic clash of claws in fur and shell. The cat is almost certainly a female cat judging by its appearance (and the evidence of tradition). It clambers over the catch set out on the table, presumably in the absence of the cook or the fisherman, under the light of a lamp recalling that in the centre of *Guernica*. The intense stare of the diabolic cat in this picture contrasts with the helpless waving of the lobster with its eyes almost popping off the end of their stalks.

Almost a decade before, on the same day that Picasso painted the doom-laden *Dead Cock and Jar*, the female cat appeared in another *grisaille* painting, *Cat and Cock*, apparently just a few moments after the slaughter of the cockerel. Once again there is a strong visual contrast between the spiny, disordered forms of the cockerel and the highly directed and poised cat, whose interest is emphasised by the strong line of shadow above its back. Cats, for the Comte de Buffon, are destined to become determined thieves.[60] This one seems to intrude in a rather disturbing way on the slaughtered corpse, like a grave robber. Although female, its phallic tail and head mock the former prowess of the cockerel.

In a recent catalogue it has been noted that this painting, like the later cat and lobster composition, seems to invite allegorical reading.[61] Perhaps, given the previous connection in Picasso's work between *grisaille* and political allegory, it has a political message? Yet as the authors note, the naturalism of the scene and scale of the cat and cock suggests something more banal, or at least we could add, less literal, more allusive.

The problem of choosing between the personal and political is evident if we go back further in time, to the horrifying *Cat seizing a Bird*. This painting is often related to the tension in Picasso's personal life between Marie-Thérèse Walter and Dora Maar. Yet, as a work of 22nd April 1939, one can hardly neglect the possibility that it reflects, expresses or crystallises in some way general anxiety over the situation in Europe. The gruesome image of the bird being torn apart, which obviously has its precedents in the drawings of the carnivorous bulls discussed in Chapter One, has been painstakingly grubbed out of the paint. Picasso uses the hard end of the brush to scratch the claws of the cat into the dull surface. *Study for Cat eating a Pigeon [bird]* is one of numerous drawings in which it is clear that Picasso found it impossible to bestow any grace on this cat, and instead

Picasso, *Study for Cat eating a Pigeon [bird]*, 22/4/39,
China ink on paper, 23 x 29cm, Picasso Estate (Inv 4075;
Z.IX.295). Courtesy of Musée Picasso, Paris. © DACS 1995.

it grips the earth stiffly as the bird is ripped open. The face of the cat makes it the ancestor of that in the *Still-life with Cat and Lobster*, but somehow it is more sadistic. If we turn once again to Picasso's written texts for some clues as to the register of this work when it was made, the situation is made darker, richer but no clearer. On Valentine's Day 1939 Picasso wrote:

> … noble daughter of wild arab joy all in Louis XV crystal of its smoke helps the flight of pigeons impaled on his naked body which bleeds on the blue tambourine full of sand overflowing with his tears…

Texts written a week or so after the painting was completed are full of bleak and bloody imagery: nails tearing and wings beating, but at no point does a cat appear.[62] Instead, two embryonic characters are at work, named simply 'I' and 'II'.

Picasso allowed birds their revenge only once, in *Owl attacking a Cat* in which one night-hawk, a cat, is pitted against another, the owl. This complex, airy and decorative charcoal drawing from 1946 seems the antithesis in other ways of the sombre and congealed painting of 1939. Unlike the bull, the horse, or the birds discussed so far, it seems that Picasso never identifies with the figure of the cat, although on several occasions he confessed himself an admirer of a certain kind of cat, the street cat:

> Now, I am starting on a cat … I want to make a cat like those true cats that I see crossing the road. They don't have anything in common with house pets; they have bristling fur and run like demons. If they look at you, you would say that they want to jump on your face and scratch your eyes out. The street cat is a real wild animal.[63]
>
> And have you ever noticed that female cats – free cats – are always pregnant. Obviously they don't think of anything but making love…[64]

Similarly, the Comte de Buffon made this observation: '[The cat] is always ready for love; and, a rare thing in animals, the female seems to be more ardent than the male.'[65]

Picasso's entirely conventional association of cat, woman, and urban promiscuity, was made explicit in his remarks on the sculpture of a pregnant *Cat* of 1941.[66] It was further revealed in the evolution of a sculpture politely called a *Seated Cat* by Brassaï, but which is unmistakeably a *crapping* cat:

> [In] the sculpture studio, I notice that the tail of the plaster *Chat Assis* is broken. One day, some time ago, Picasso had confided the secret of this cat's history to me. He had modelled it first as the figure of a standing woman but had not been satisfied with it. Then he had the idea of transforming the woman into a cat. Her breast had become the cat's head, and her legs the cat's two forelegs.

ABOVE: Picasso, *Owl attacking a Cat*, Golfe-Juan, 3/8/46, pencil and charcoal on paper, 66 x 50.5cm, Musée Picasso, Paris (MP. 1376; Z.XIV.199). © Photo RMN. © DACS 1995.

BELOW: Picasso, *Cat*, Paris 1943, bronze, 36 x 17.5 x 55cm, Musée Picasso, Paris (MP 324; S.278 (II)). © Photo RMN. © DACS 1995.

ABOVE: Picasso, *Woman with a Cat*, Mougins 30/8/37, oil on canvas, 81 x 65cm, ex collection Dr Henri Laugier, Paris, present whereabouts unknown, (Z.VIII.373). Courtesy of Archives 'Cahiers d'Art'. © DACS 1995.

BELOW: Francesco Ubertini, *Portrait of a Lady*, n.d., present whereabouts unknown. Courtesy of Dr Nikolenko.

Then he had added the rest of the body and the tail. No one else knows of this metamorphosis. But the secret of its birth is always present now, between myself and the cat. I can no longer look at it without seeing a woman.[67]

Brassaï's story of the origin of the sculpture is obvious if one masks the front from the hind quarters, allowing the headless standing woman to reappear. Two bronze casts of these cats moved from house to house with Picasso, like familiars. The one a pregnant demimondaine, the other a woman become scatological cat.

There are numerous drawings and paintings made in the spirit of this equation of the lascivious woman with the cat. In 1902 Picasso made a sheet of studies showing women with striped stockings, apparently displaying their wares in a brothel, or at least in the artist's fantasy (see p95). At the top right of the drawing a bulky but well-dressed man marches with his arm irrepressibly erect. Further down the page, two clothed figures seem in listless negotiation. At the bottom centre sits a knowing black cat, worthy of that in Manet's famous *Olympia*.[68] The unmistakably old equation is being made. At the other extreme of Picasso's career, in the 1964 *Woman Playing with a Kitten*, a more complicated but no less ancient theme persists. Here the woman teasing the cat could be taken for a temptress or a mistress of dissimulation, as unwise (she might get scratched), or the whole could be a crude joke about female masturbation. There are a number of other canvases on the theme of the naked woman teasing a cat from the late period, which is often noted for its salacious content.[69] A work by one of Picasso's favourite French poets, the symbolist Paul Verlaine, emphasises the tension between sensuousness and satanic danger which lurks beneath the play of woman and cat.[70]

Yet one of the oddest pictures to link a cat and a woman was *Woman with a Cat* painted on 30th August 1937. In this painting a grinning woman with the physiognomy, if not the mood, of the famous *Weeping Woman*[71] of the same year, suckles a kitten in her lap. The witch and familiar in this perverted woman with a cat composition began, according to one source, as a portrait of Picasso's friend the poet Paul Eluard in the costume of an 'Arlesienne'.[72] This painting teeters on the cusp of folly and nightmare. Perhaps that is not inappropriate in the aftermath of *Guernica* and the physical and mental exertions, the unfamiliar high moral stand it represented for the artist.

In addition to the print of the cat for the Buffon book, Picasso had made a rare image of a lioness. Similarly, on turning to the dog, Picasso found room not only for a mongrel, but also for a gruesome wolf. The silvery coat of this snarling predator distinguishes it from an overgrown wood into which, according to Buffon, wolves had been forced by the human beings they love to eat.[73] Picasso's skilful print recalls a large and little-known canvas sketch of a dog from 1930 (see below). Once again the animal is captured as it turns aggressively to face an enemy. The print in particular gives rise to a pose favoured by Picasso elsewhere in depictions of people as well as animals, and which he sometimes achieves through distortion, where the subject wraps around on itself, allowing simultaneous views of front and back.[74] This device is as much about getting a forceful and tactile presence of the animal or person into the picture as it is about solving the old pictorial problem of representing three dimensions in two.

For Buffon the dog and the wolf were of similar appearance, but opposite temperament. The similarity seems borne out in the two works just considered, but is confirmed in an amusing way in the case of two 'cubist' drawings from 1914, entitled *Seated Woman with a Dog* and *Man with a Wolf*, which both now belong to Picasso's granddaughter Marina Picasso. Cubism is perhaps the pictorial manner for which Picasso is most famous, and although the questions of its invention, development and most of all its 'meaning' remain open, there is no doubt that nearly all of Picasso's work after 1907-1914 is continually exploring ideas he discovered during those years. Although there is not the space here to attempt an explanation of Picasso's cubism, it is clear from these two drawings that it can be enjoyed for its humour as well as its for its intriguing implications for the understanding of past and present visual art.[75] The compositions of the drawings are remarkably similar: a ridiculous smirking dog sits at the feet of a mass of boxes and squiggles which just about add up to a figure. In fact, the more cubist pictures one sees, the easier it can get to spot the elements of such figures. For now it is worth pointing out the two feet which poke out at the bottom, and the snakelike arms ending in doorknob hands on either side of the dog. In *Seated Woman with a Dog*, the left hand of the figure clasps the dog's collar. Floorboards are visible, as is something like a military drum towards the bottom left. There also seems to be a piece of newspaper or a poster on which we can read the word 'JOLIE', meaning 'pretty'! The word also relates to a code in Picasso's paintings of the time for a mysterious woman with whom he was in love, Eva Gouel.[76] Perhaps it was this detail that led Christian Zervos, the publisher who attempted to catalogue Picasso's work as it evolved, to christen the drawing *Seated Woman with a Dog*. Yet Zervos obviously had other thoughts about the second drawing, where an almost identical animal becomes a wolf! The titles now have to be retained, of course,

ABOVE: Picasso, *The Wolf*, Spring 1936, sugar lift aquatint, 36 x 28cm, Victoria & Albert Museum, London (B 337). Photo © Victoria & Albert Museum. © DACS 1995.

BELOW: Picasso, *Woman with a Cat*, 1964, oil on canvas, 97 x 195cm, Private Collection. Photo Hans Hinz. © DACS 1995.

ABOVE: Picasso, *The Dog*, 1930, oil on canvas, 114 x 154cm, Picasso Estate (Inv 12548). Courtesy of Musée Picasso, Paris. © DACS 1995.

BELOW: Picasso, *The Vauvenargues Buffet and a Blue and White Spotty Dog*, 21/6/59 (I), oil on canvas, 55 x 46cm, Picasso Estate (Inv 13377). Courtesy of Musée Picasso, Paris. © DACS 1995.

in order to avoid more confusion.

Most of Picasso's dogs present problems of identity at a more specific level, because so many of them are known to be particular pets of the artist. Just as Buffon had suggested that the behaviour of dogs reflected the habits of their master, or as English folk-wisdom claims that 'people begin to look like their dogs', so it has been argued that the particular dog or dogs which happened to live with Picasso at any one time might influence the mood and look of his works, or even the 'look' he gave to his sitters.[77] It certainly seems that Picasso relished the decorative stimulus of his Dalmatian 'Perro' ('dog' in Spanish) during the late fifties and early sixties, evident in *The Vauvenargues Buffet and a Blue and White Spotty Dog*. The coat of this energetic but lanky animal made Picasso see spots before his eyes. The physique of the dog is contrasted in a series of paintings – of which this is one – with an elaborate old sideboard in the Château de Vauvenargues. The amusement Picasso found in the spotty dog coincided with his continuing pleasure in the efforts of his two children, Claude and Paloma, to draw like their father.

It is perhaps more difficult to accept the view that Picasso always based his portrayal of his *human* subjects on the physiognomy of his current canine best friend. Although there is often some consonance between the two, it might be misguided to put the dog before the person. Nevertheless, in *Woman Playing with a Dog*, the face of the woman (purportedly Jacqueline Roque) does perhaps bear the squashed look of the dog (Yan, a blind boxer) with which she is 'wrestling'.[78] The subject of this painting, expressive of 'misery' according to one author,[79] is rather exceptional, and the closest earlier parallel to be found is perhaps in the much more sensuous Fragonard's *Girl and Dog* (*'La Gimblette'*).

In 1895 Picasso had painted his pet 'Klipper' over an earlier study of St Anthony of Padua.[80] However, it is in *Self-portrait with a Dog*, thought to be from the latter part of 1902 when Picasso was in Paris, that an indication is given of the real importance of a dog to an artist. In the early years of Picasso's visits to Paris (1900-1903), the pet dogs he kept were easy company. At this point in his artistic career Picasso was stealing pennies from friends and sharing a room with the poet Max Jacob – the two were reduced to eating rotten meat sausages.[81] For a brief period, Picasso was indeed the 'bohemian' artist struggling against penury, although he seems to have been less enthralled with the condition than the romantic stories of Henri Mürger would suggest.[82] This might help to explain the inscription under the smiling face on the drawing: 'sigo igual' or 'still the same'. The young Picasso, wearing an enormous overcoat, confronts adversity alone save, of course, for his dog. In 1904 Picasso settled in Paris, and did so with three dogs: Gat (Catalan for cat) which he brought from Spain, and Feo and Fricka acquired in Paris.[83] As Gat became sick, Frika bore pups in 1907.[84] This moment of fecundity became symbolic for Picasso, who was in the process of working out his most ambitious and original work to date, *Les Demoiselles d'Avignon*.[85] The drawing *Dog (Fricka) suckling her Puppies*, one of a series in a sketchbook, may relate to an abandoned plan to include the dog suckling her pups in the foreground of that painting of a brothel interior, rather in the manner that cat and dogs featured as minor but telling details in works of earlier centuries (for example see Venziano de' Musi's *Rape of Lucretia*).

One of the most famous dogs owned by Picasso, Kazbek, is best known not in paintings but in photographs. Kazbek was the Afghan hound who was present at all the intellectual soirees in Picasso's studio during the German Occupation of Paris. Although an earlier familiar of Picasso, a dog called Elft, is described by Brassaï as a regular attender of prewar cafe visits,[86] Kazbek is the memorable sidekick:

> At about one o'clock, the house finally empties out. We are left alone. Kazbek, that strange, always silent and apparently sad dog, stretches his cadaverous frame and poses his delicate interminable paws in front of him in an attitude resembling a sculpture.
>
> Picasso: Have you ever noticed that he can assume poses that are so extraordinary they make you think of anything in the world except a dog? Look at him over there. Doesn't he look more like a giant ray than a dog? Dora [Maar] thinks he resembles an enormous shrimp. Man Ray took some photos of him. Maybe you will too, some day.[87]

It is Brassaï's photographic record of Kazbek which renders the dog so significant, and what is clear in these casual remarks is that Picasso was instrumental in having himself thus commemorated in the guise of his animal companion. Photographs of Picasso in the company of animals become increasingly common after the war. The association between the artist and his pet dog returns us to the image of Picasso as Orpheus, charming the animals, but also recalls the idea of the magician's familiar, or Hogarth's *The Painter and his Pug*.[88]

Seeing Picasso's pet dogs as creatures magically imbued with his *persona* is suggestive in looking at some other works. In *Woman with a Dog* of 1962, for example, another Afghan is seen with paws outstretched on the lap of a woman. The complex but imposing figure of the woman pats the dog on the head. Certainly, the features of this woman conform to the style of representation associated with Picasso's last wife,

Picasso, *Woman playing with a Kitten*, 7-9/5/64, oil on canvas, Picasso Estate (Inv 13484; Z.XXIV.140) Courtesy of Musée Picasso, Paris. © DACS 1995.

Jacqueline Roque. Meanwhile, Picasso had an Afghan at this time called Kabul. It is thus not difficult to see the painting as 'Jacqueline and Pablo', with the dog standing in for the painter. Similarly, in *Untitled* [*Man, Woman, Girl and Dog*], which undoubtedly represents Piero Crommelynck, his wife Landa and daughter Carine dressed in high (early seventies) fashion, another lively Afghan bedevilled by flies occupies centre-stage. Piero Crommelynck, and his brother Aldo, assisted Picasso in his extensive printmaking activities between 1963 and 1972. In the print, Piero Crommelynck, carrying a portfolio of prints, probably for signing by the artist, presents a flower to his wife, seated on the right. If we see a little of Picasso in his dog jumping up at the printer,[89] then we have a whimsical reversal of roles, whereby the 'Master Printer' becomes the print artist's master.[90]

The last of the numerous identifiable canine personalities to be considered in this Picasso Bestiary is a dachshund called 'Lump', who plays a squat but important role in *The Piano*. This painting, one of the most inventive of the fifty-eight variations which Picasso executed during 1957 in response to Velázquez's great *Las Meninas*, is easiest to figure out by beginning with this dog.[91] The dog in *Las Meninas* is a royal hound, whose repose is disrupted by a prod from the foot of the Italian child-jester Nicolasito Pertusato, a minor figure on the far right of the composition.[92] When Picasso painted his variations, Lump had recently been given to him by the photographer David Douglas Duncan, and was thus presumably in his mind:

> The only place [Lump] was not allowed to go was the second floor, where [the variations on] Las Meninas and the dovecote were. He would undoubtedly have eaten the pigeons.[93]

Like the figures in Velázquez's painting, Lump was not 'really' present in the studio as Picasso painted, but he seemed a fitting model to replace the seventeenth-century dog and enter Picasso's parodic royal family. Roland Penrose explains how the boy ended up as a pianist:

> As he pokes the good-tempered dog with his foot the boy's hands seem to flutter nervously. This tempted Picasso to think that he might be playing an invisible piano, and to paint a study of him seated at a piano well lit with candles. He also noticed in the original a black line in the panelling that rises from the nape of the boy's neck. This in turn suggested to him a cord by which the young pianist was hanged like a helpless tinkling marionette.[94]

The dog, though squashed under foot, has its revenge…

Beyond works which feature identifiable dogs, there are some impressive pieces which seem closely related to earlier examples

OPPOSITE: Picasso, *The Piano*, Cannes, 17/10/57, oil on canvas, 130 x 96cm, Museu Picasso, Barcelona (MPB 70.472; Z.XVII,404). © DACS 1995.

ABOVE: Diego Velázquez, *Las Meninas*, 1656, oil on canvas, 318 x 276cm, Museo del Prado, Madrid. All Rights Reserved © Museo del Prado, Madrid.

BELOW: Picasso, *Untitled* [*Man, Woman, Girl and Dog*], 7/3/71 (I), etching, 15 x 21cm, Galerie Louise Leiris, Paris (B 1924). Courtesy of Galerie Louise Leiris, Paris. © DACS 1995.

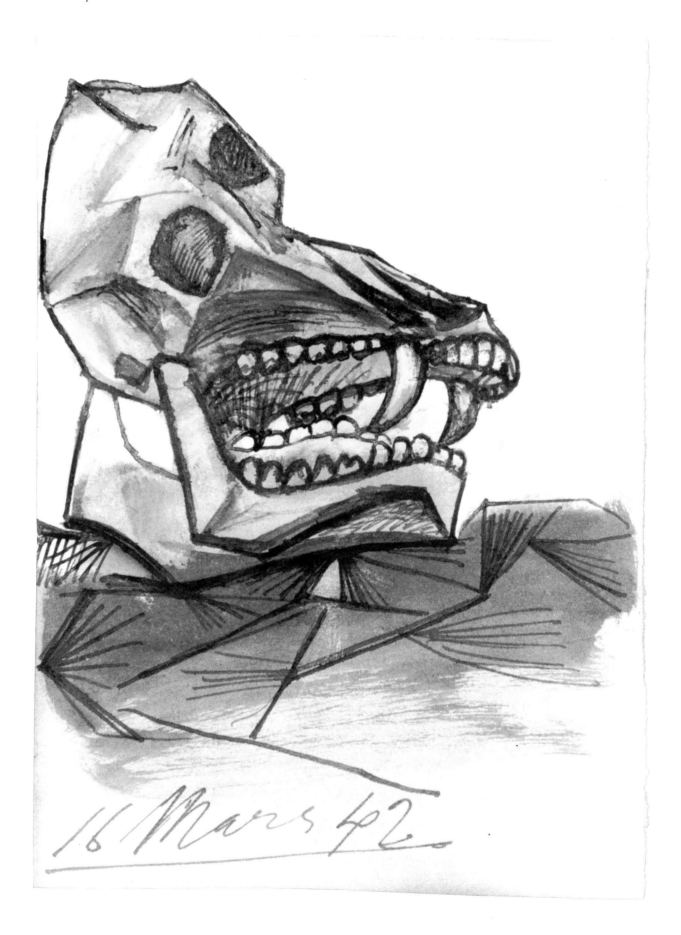

of the depiction and symbolism of the dog. An untitled print of 1968 [*Naked Man and Woman with a Dog*] is absurd in itself, but when paired with Van Eyck's *The Arnolfini Portrait*, Picasso's jolly hirsute trio act as a wonderful lampoon. Only the dog is unmoved in its steadfast role as symbol of fidelity, albeit fidelity stripped bare. A similar degree of closeness to a traditional composition is to be seen in *Dog and Cock* of 1921. As has been noted by other writers, this painting, like *Still-life with Cat and Lobster*, may be based on a large work by Chardin, in this case a corner of *Le buffet* of 1728, which Picasso must have seen in the Louvre.[95] In fact, the depiction of a dog sniffing at a table decked with game, weaker willed than the thieving cats we have encountered, was a subject treated in many paintings before Chardin, for example Frans Snyders' *Still-life with a Swan*. It has been claimed that this colourful cockerel antici-pates in tone those later more morbid dead birds of the late forties and fifties which were discussed in the previous chap-ter.[96] Certainly the tightness of the composition might be taken as evidence of such a mood. On the other hand, the playful comparison of table and dog legs, and the great balance of the colour scheme does not lead forcefully, as later canvasses would, in the direction of meditation on death.

Such a sentiment seems much less contentiously present in the almost unique *Dog's Skull* of 16th March 1942. Picasso apparently had dog's skulls amongst his large collection of bones at Boisgeloup, but in that lean period of the Occupation, it may be that Picasso acquired a dog's skull after the animal had been eaten by some hungry Parisian family.[97] Perhaps the study was not made from life, after all? It is in any case one of a procession of skulls, mostly of sheep and rams, which were studied at the beginning of the war and again and again during it.[98] Were it not for the timing of this interest, it would be possible to look at the general category of skull studies as simple exercises in artistic comprehension. But even if this dog's skull had been done after the war, the significance of the dog in a very intimate corner of Picasso's bestiary implies an elegy with a more private pathos than that conjured by any sheep.

OPPOSITE: Picasso, *Dog's Skull*, 16/3/42, China ink and gouache on paper, 23 x 17cm, Picasso Estate (Inv 4335). Courtesy of Musée Picasso, Paris. © DACS 1995.

GOATS AND SHEEP

This group of animals occupy a middle ground in Picasso's Bestiary, and in this book. They are, like birds, both animals to be farmed and companions for human beings. Sheep carry great symbolic weight in their dependence on the shepherd, which must end paradoxically at the dinner table. The paradox was not lost on the authors of the bible and other Christian thinkers. The ram features less often, although its spiralling horns prompted one of Picasso's finest late cubist still-lifes, *The Ram's Head*. Goats, with their devilish behaviour, attracted Picasso enough for him to demand one as a present, and to be commemorated in two very different but significant sculptures. Goats also bring about one of Picasso's most explicit reflections on the nature of sacrifice – outside of the bullring, that is. In general, the decaying heads of these creatures are peculiarly favoured by Picasso for still-life paintings in the memento mori tradition. In these pictures, as with those of the bull, we see Picasso's engagement with the grandeur, the weight and the pathos of centuries of ritual association. Yet we also see a playful delight in the frolicsome sexuality of these creatures, in those antics for which they have been denigrated, but which to Picasso were an enduring source of irreverent pleasure.

By nature and etymology the goat is 'capricious', so much so, that the bestiary takes great care to differentiate between two quite distinct types.[1] First to be considered is 'caper' (see above), 'the tame goats, which the Greeks called gazelles because they had such keen sight.'[2] These goats, we are told, live on high ground, their sight being so keen that they can recognise from a long way off whether approaching humans are hunters or travellers.[3] The remainder of the bestiary description elaborates on this rather meagre information, interpreting 'caper' as a type of Christ, who also loves high hills, who sees and knows all things and who, like the goat, can see 'through the wiles of those who betrayed him'.[4] A variety of biblical texts are used to corroborate these assertions, from the *Song of Songs*, to extracts from Psalm 33 and Matthew 26. Similarly, the wild goat, (*Caprea*) moves higher and higher as he grazes (like good preachers who, 'feeding on the Law of God and on good works ... rise up from one virtue to another'[5]), chooses good herbs from bad by sight, and heals its wounds with the herb dittany. This latter characteristic and its interpretation is

OPPOSITE: Picasso, detail of *Three Sheep's Heads*, Paris 17/10/39, oil on canvas, 65 x 89cm, Collection Marina Picasso, Geneva (Inv 12961; Z.IX.349). Courtesy Galerie Jan Krugier. © DACS 1995.

ABOVE: *Goat*, MS Royal 12 C xix, Bestiary in Latin, c1200-10, f. 31v. By permission of the British Library, London.

ABOVE: Annibale Carracci, *The Butcher's Shop*, c1582-83, oil on canvas, 185 x 266cm, Christ Church Picture Gallery, Oxford. The Governing Body, Christ Church, Oxford.

BELOW: Pieter van Boucle, *Butcher's Table with Cat and Dog*, 1651, 113 x 149cm, Musée du Louvre, Paris. © Photo RMN.

considered by White to be one of the more successful of bestiary puns: 'Christ heals: dittany heals. Christ is to be called '*beneditantius*' [sic]: the Latin for dittany here is '*ditannus*'.[6]

The association of the goat with Christ, perpetuates distant reminiscences of pre-Christian sacrifice: goats, like bulls, were commonly sacrificed animals, and as in the case of the bull or ox, the goat could be a prefigurative symbol of the sacrificed and resurrected Christ whose birth, as a man, was precondition for his rebirth and eternal life as God. The goat shares this distinction with other, related ruminants. *Agnus*, the lamb, '... is a symbol of our mystic Saviour, whose innocent death saved mankind, as John says: 'Behold the Lamb of God, who taketh away the sins of the world [I:36]'[7] and as *agnus dei* was commonly represented with the banner of the Resurrection (a red cross on white).

Sheep may also be considered, according to the bestiary, as the faithful flock, encapsulated in the image of Christ as the good shepherd carrying a lamb over his shoulders, the models for which were antique sculptures such as the Greek *Moskophorus* (*Man with a Sacrificial Calf*) and numerous Old Testament and Jewish texts which demonstrated how deeply this pastoral imagery was felt in Jewish thought.[8] But in this image (representing a calf not a lamb, but illustrating comparable concerns) there is an evident tension between the young animal being returned to its herd or flock, and the animal carried to slaughter. This tension was inherited by the Christian religion with its substitution (described in Chapter One) of the sacrifice of Christ for the actual, ritual sacrifice of goats and sheep recorded in the Old Testament. The bestiary duly records this earlier fate of these animals in its etymologies: The sheep, *Ovis* '... gets its name '*ab oblatione*' – from the burnt sacrifice-because in the old days among the ancients it was not bulls but sheep which were offered up';[9] *Aries* the ram, '... may get its name because it was originally immolated on altars – from which 'aries' because he was sacrificed '*aris*' (with altars) – and thus we get the ram in scripture who was offered up at the altar (*ad aram*).[10]

Naturally, a prime consideration for killing these beasts was simply that they were good to eat, but as the discussion of Aertsen's *Butcher's Shop* in the bull section demonstrates, even these practical considerations could be turned, by those so inclined, to didactic purpose. Annibale Carracci's own great *The Butcher's Shop* possibly offers a similar commentary. Meat is matter-of-factly displayed on the butcher's slab, cut into neat joints out of the haunches of venison. In the foreground, a sheep, its legs tied, awaits the same fate, recalling the hobbled lamb that so often appears in representations of *the Adoration of the Shepherds* as a prefiguration of Christ's sacrifice. The image also recalls the Sacrifice of Isaac, and it is significant perhaps that in the Old Testament description of this event, Isaac had asked his father 'where is the lamb for a burnt offering', to which Abraham replied: 'God will provide himself a lamb'.[11] When Abraham's hand was stayed by an intervening angel, saving his son:

> Abraham lifted up his eyes, and looked, and behold behind him a ram caught in a thicket by his horns; and Abraham went and took the ram, and offered him up for a burnt offering in the stead of his son.[12]

This episode, 'an echo of the historical change from human to animal sacrifice in primitive society ... was seen as a foreshadowing of the death of Christ, himself a sacrificial substitute for mankind.'[13] *The Butcher's Shop* is also an exposition of cruelty and carnality, intended to provoke sustained reflection – and self-reflection – in the viewer. The consumption of meat was considered with deep suspicion in some quarters, and butchers themselves were widely considered odious and not unlike the public executioner – throughout the seventeenth and eighteenth centuries in England, butchers were ineligible for jury service in capital cases owing to their cruel inclinations.[14] In Carracci's painting, these general considerations are given specific focus by additional details. In the background, an old woman takes a joint of meat, nonchalantly passed to her by an assistant who pretends to be concentrating elsewhere. To the left, above the frightened sheep, the butcher weighs a lump of meat for a customer, dressed in the ridiculous costume of the *lansquenets*, the Swiss mercenaries, fingering the pieces of silver in his purse, a correlate of the *bursa*, coddled in the padding of his absurd codpiece.[15]

Under the butcher's table, regarding the imminent fate of the sheep with the concern it would give a nice bone, is a dog, its keen nose having led it to the irresistible odour of the meat-shop where it lurks, eager for the few scraps it can purloin. These dogs are a common, almost indispensable, element in many seventeenth-century kitchen and butcher's shop scenes such as Pieter van Boucle's *Butcher's Table with Cat and Dog*, where they provide contrasting animation to an elaborate still-life display. Here, the carnage on the table includes a sheep's head, like that of the bull in Aertsen's *Butcher's Stall* the more startling for being detached from its body and recalling the image of the head of John the Baptist that Salome earned with her erotic dance. As Sir Matthew Hale confessed in the seventeenth century, the sight of sheep grazing always made him feel that God must have intended 'a more innocent kind of food for man'.[16] Boucle's sheep's head is the more poignant for

Picasso, *Three Sheep's Heads*, Paris 17/10/39, oil on
canvas, 65 x 89cm, Collection Marina Picasso, Geneva
(Inv 12961; Z.IX.349). Courtesy Galerie Jan Krugier. ©
DACS 1995.

being ignored by the cat and dog, neither of them food for humans except in the most extreme circumstances, snarling at each other across the table: two carnal creatures and the head of the innocent animal.

So far, we have seen that goats and sheep were largely considered in a positive sense, but like all other creatures, this was tempered by equal emphasis on their own carnal nature. The bestiary urges the reader to 'Note also the wicked sheep in the Psalter: "Like sheep they are laid in the grave, and death shall feed on them"';[17] the kid (having been likened to Christ) 'can also be Antichrist';[18] rams (having signified the Apostles or the princes of the Church) 'Elsewhere … represent wicked rulers.'[19] The he-goat, however, was carefully distinguished from all other types of goat, being considered:

> … a stubborn and lascivious animal, always eager to mate, whose eyes are so full of lust that they look sideways, from which they get their Latin name 'hircus', for Suetonius calls the corner of the eye the 'hircus'. Its nature is so hot that diamonds, against which fire and iron are powerless, dissolve in its blood.[20]

It was an opinion shared by many authors and has survived into today's English slang and idiom: to roger (to copulate) derives from the pet name for a goat and it is still customary to say of a rapacious man, especially an old one, that he is 'as randy as a goat'.[21] Unlike bulls, which were considered sexually temperate, goats engaged in intercourse when they were barely weaned:

> To show the member of a fecund man, they draw a goat, not a bull, for the bull cannot serve a cow before he is a year old, but the goat covers the female seven days after birth, discharging a sterile and empty sperm. But nevertheless, it matures before all other animals.[22]

From earliest times, goats or a goat-god were symbols of the active male principle and it was in this capacity that the goat (again, like the bull) was sacred to Dionysos and was yet another embodiment of the corn spirit.[23] One of his names was 'kid' (in his youth, his father Zeus changed him into a goat to save him from the wrath of Hera) and at Athens and Hermion he was worshipped under the title of 'the one of the Black Goatskin'.[24] Goats as well as bulls were torn to pieces by his followers and its flesh devoured raw.[25] As a goat, Dionysos can hardly be distinguished from all those other minor deities associated with him and with Bacchus: the Fauns, Pans, Silenuses and Satyrs, described as being half-man, half-goat, all lustful creatures and most avid participants in ritual orgies.[26]

With the spread of Christianity, pagan religion was consigned by the Church Fathers to the Kingdom of the Devil:[27]

Hendrick Goltzius, *Luxuria*, n.d., 13.8 x 10.7cm, Bibliothèque Royal Albert Ier, Brussels. Copyright Bibliothèque Royal Albert Ier, Brussels.

William Holman Hunt, *The Scapegoat*, 1854, oil on
canvas, 33.7 x 45.9cm, Manchester City Art Gallery,
Manchester. © Manchester City Art Galleries.

One of the most effective tactics of the Christian Church in dealing with converts or potential converts who continued to worship their pagan gods was to demonise those gods – to claim that those deities were actually demons of the Devil himself.[28]

Because there was no existing image of the Devil, medieval artists appropriated his form from the old gods, from Pan and his like, and the satyr become the model, in the Middle Ages, for representation of the Devil as 'goatee' bearded, cloven hoofed, prong-tailed and horned.[29] Witches, who were widely believed to have entered in a pact with the Devil,[30] were, therefore, commonly depicted with a goat, for example in Hans Sebald Beham's engraving *The Witches' Sabbath*, in which an old hag of a witch flies through the sky on a goat, whilst below her sisters prepare potions amidst a detritus of skulls and bones. Notably, the other animal sharing their sorcery is a cat. The choice of the lustful goat was particularly apt, considering that witches were not only considered to have made a pact with the Devil, but to have copulated with him[31] – the goat was the attribute of *Luxuria* who is also depicted, as in Hendrik Goltzius' print with a bird, or pair of copulating birds on her hand.

The goat, therefore, may be said to carry within it all the sins of the world, and Holman Hunt's *The Scapegoat* expresses wonderfully the pathos of this exiled creature, banished to the wilderness to die. As Frazer explains, animals are often employed in the transference and banishing of evil and although in different cultures other animals, even humans, were employed in this capacity, as the word suggests, goats were the commonest 'scapegoats'.[32] Leviticus 16 describes the Jewish ritual of choosing two goats for the rites of the Great Atonement (perhaps why the bestiary takes such pains to keep the two types of goat separate). The one was to be consecrated, and offered 'for a sin offering';[33] the other:

> … shall bear upon him all their [the children of Israel's] iniquities unto a land not inhabited: and he shall let go the goat in the wilderness.[34]

According to the bestiary:

> The he-goat, which in Jewish law was offered in atonement for sins, shows us the sinner, who in pouring out his blood (that is, in the tears of penitence) dissolves the hardness of his sins.[35]

This is an image which, yet again, is remarkably like to that of Christ, who atoned for human sin with his own blood, bringing full circle the paradoxes and anomalies that characterise our reception of this much maligned and 'capricious' creature.

The ambiguous position of the goat in human thought and action is well captured in Picasso's *Vase with Goats*, which was decorated in 1952. This pot, of which a copy is reproduced overleaf, shows on one side the head of a goat, nibbling cheerfully at an overhanging branch reminiscent of the bestiary *Goat* (see p119), and on the other a prancing animal, full of lustful energy. It was the latter quality, noted by bestiarists and Buffon alike and shared, of course, with the bull and the cock, which perhaps made all these animals suited to the altar of sacrifice.[36] Later, the strong flavour of goat's meat seems to have been an important factor in its role as a sacrificial beast, as is attested by an ancient Greek inscription:

If I ever burnt the rich thighs of bulls and goats in your honour, grant me this prayer.[37]

The point that links the decoration with the notion of sacrifice and slaughter is the fact of the pot itself, with its archaic resonance of libation vessels, a resonance present in many of Picasso's ceramics.

There are – surprisingly – only a few occasions when Picasso exploits the old idea of the goat as a symbol of lust. In a painting of 1906, *Young Female Nude and Nude Child with a Goat*, a naked woman – inspired by sources which might include classical sculpture, Ingres, Gauguin, and Puvis de Chavannes – dresses her hair whilst an impish boy to her left balances a pot on his head and a lively white goat looks up at her. The scene is not exactly innocent, and not long after the woman found her way into a painting of a *Harem*.[38] Despite this flirtation with the erotic goat, Picasso reserved the lascivious rule of the devil over the woman for his satyrs, as can be seen in his painting of c1905, *Naked Woman and Satyrs*.

The other element of the pot, its link to ideas of animal sacrifice and slaughter, is represented explicitly in a quite horrifying drawing of 1938, *Woman sacrificing a Goat*. Unlike painters such as Annibale Carracci who, in *The Butcher's Shop*, made such a display of the craft of the *male* butchers, and secretly recalled the sacrifice of Christ, Picasso shows very little interest here in the wild colours and textures of the incident. Rather, the focus is on the gruesome pleasure which the effort of slaughter elicits from this farmer's wife. The woman's feet are visible beneath the table, as is the dish collecting the blood. The left arm of the woman seems to spring from nowhere, in between the legs of the goat and press down on its chest. Her right arm, clutching the knife, spews out of her mouth, whilst her breasts are squeezed upward to the point of bursting.[39] It is worth recalling that this drawing dates from sometime during the same year, probably the summer, as the *Woman with a Cock* discussed in Chapter Three. In 1947, Picasso wrote a playlet

OPPOSITE: Picasso, *Young Female Nude and Nude Child with a Goat*, Gosol, 1906, oil on canvas, 146 x 114cm, Barnes Foundation, Merion Penn. (Z.I.249). Photo © 1995 by the Barnes Foundation. All Rights Reserved. © DACS 1995.

ABOVE: Picasso, *The Ram*, Spring 1936, sugar lift aquatint, 36 x 28cm, Victoria & Albert Museum, London (B 332). Photo © Victoria & Albert Museum. © DACS 1995.

BELOW: Picasso, *Woman sacrificing a Goat*, Paris, 1938, pencil on paper, 24.2 x 45.5cm, Musée Picasso, Paris (MP 1205v; Z.IX.116). © Photo RMN. © DACS 1995.

entitled 'The Four Little Girls', in which one of the participants slaughters a goat and then dances about the garden
with its corpse. Another takes its heart from its chest, but the
heart still beats and is thrust by another little girl into the
mouth of a doll.[40]

Against this background, Picasso's repeated efforts to represent the theme of the good shepherd, the man carrying a lamb,
takes on a gendered interest. On the other hand, a look at some
examples of his treatment of the theme once again corrects the
impression that the sheep, the ram and the goat have only the
farmer's wife and sadistic little girls to fear. The earliest
representation of the basic theme is an 'Academy' drawing (see
overleaf).

Picasso underwent at least some of the conventional training
which mainstream artists had followed in Europe from the
seventeenth century onwards. Broadly speaking, students of
painting were obliged to consider drawing before colour. They
began by copying from prints of major artists' work, then
progressed to drawing plaster casts of antique statues, and were
finally permitted to draw from life. Picasso's most extensive
period of following such precepts was in Barcelona at the
School of Fine Arts known as La Llota, although on completion
of a standard entrance exam in September 1895 he gained
direct admission to the class in 'Antique, Life, Model and
Painting'.[41] The drawing of the cast must have come soon after
the date of admission, since Picasso seems to have preferred
working from life. It represents an antique sculpture which is in
fact of a faun or satyr carrying a kid rather than a man carrying
a lamb. The original sculpture (see opposite, above left), about
four and a half feet in height, was in Madrid in the then Musée
Royal. It was originally found in Rome in the church of St
Maria in Vollicella.[42] Casts of the restored version proliferated:
in addition to the cast in La Llota,[43] there was one in Malaga
where Picasso's father had taught,[44] and one in the Royal
Academy in London, to name but a few. Picasso represents it in
half restored form, so presumably it was possible to remove the
sections which had been added on the original. There is no
doubt that the focus of achievement for Picasso was to model
the complex arrangement of 'man' and kid in the deep light and
shade encouraged by the medium of charcoal. There is nevertheless something uncanny in the fact that the subject was to
be spectacularly revived at two later junctures. The 'man with a
lamb' is a lesser version of the bullfight or the dove: themes with
antique resonance on the one hand, and early personal icons on
the other.

Picasso did not take the *Academy* drawing with him to Paris,
but its memory must have lived on. In early 1943, almost fifty

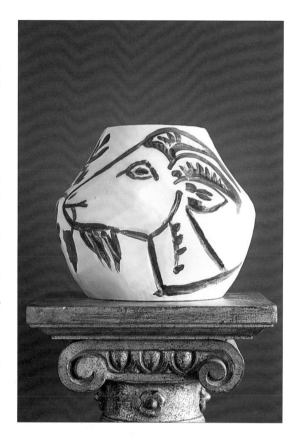

OPPOSITE, ABOVE LEFT: Anon., *Faun carrying a Kid*, Museo
del Prado. All Rights Reserved © Museo del Prado, Madrid.

OPPOSITE, ABOVE RIGHT: Picasso, *Man with a Sheep*,
1943, bronze, 222.5 x 78 x 78cm, Musée Picasso, Paris
(MP 331; S.280.II). © Photo RMN. © DACS 1995.

OPPOSITE, BELOW LEFT: Anon. Greek, *Moskophorus (Man
with a Sacrificial Calf)* 7 BC marble, Acropolis Museum,
Athens. Courtesy of the Acropolis Museum, Athens. Photo ©
Mario Bettella.

OPPOSITE, BELOW RIGHT: Picasso, *Man with a Sheep*,
Paris 27-29/3/43, China ink and scraping, 65 x 50.5cm,
Musée Picasso, Antibes (MP 1990-75; Z.XII.297).
© DACS 1995.

ABOVE: Picasso, *Vase with Goats*, 6/6/52, original print:
white earthenware clay, deep engraving filled with oxidised
paraffin, dipped in white enamel, brown, green, 19 x 23cm,
Private Collection, Roxburghshire (AR 156; R 399).
© DACS 1995.

years later, Picasso made one of his most ambitious sculptures, the *Man with a Sheep*, which was modelled in clay on an iron armature in the space of a few days, and then cast in plaster *in situ* due to the fragility of the life-size piece.[45] As has been noted before, this rapidity of execution was possible because Picasso had planned the sculpture in advance in a large number of drawings.[46] The drawings were more than simple plans, however, as is proven by their occasional degree of finish, and by the fact that Picasso continued to draw the man for some weeks afterwards. Here Picasso has worked carefully on the stern bearded face of the naked 'shepherd', adding the head of a ram in the bottom right-hand corner. This drawing, like a number of others in the series, drifts in the direction of the prelude to a sacrifice by subtle twists and turns of the figures:

> This poor beast, with its head desperately and pathetically raised towards the heavens, is it not the very image of all those victims executed in these evil times?[47]

The sculpture and drawings clearly echo both the tradition of the procession to the place of sacrifice, represented by the *Moskophorus*, and that of the Christian theme of the 'Good Shepherd', where the shepherd sacrifices himself to save the beast. An earlier writer has pointed out, however, that Picasso's composition, where the man carries the animal in front of him rather than across his shoulders adds a technical challenge, which in turn symbolises the unbalancing struggle between the sheep and its sacrificer/saviour.[48] The *Man with a Sheep* himself became something of an icon after the war, one of the three casts of it being inaugurated in the main square in Vallauris (Place de la Libération) on 6th August 1950, where it still remains, watching over the market.[49] Another cast followed Picasso from residence to residence and provided a pissing-post for his numerous dogs.[50] This seems to bear out Picasso's contention that in his eyes the sculpture had no particular symbolic meaning:

> There's nothing religious about it at all. The man might just as well be carrying a pig, instead of a lamb. There's no symbolism in it. It's merely beautiful... In the *Man with a Sheep* I have expressed a human feeling, a feeling that exists now as it has always existed.[51]

Yet as we have seen in the Introduction, Picasso was most unlikely to give his man a pig! Moreover, his gesture towards an eternal human feeling emphasises the archaic ancestry of the composition. Most telling, however, and in a manner identical to the critical fortunes of *Guernica*, the sculpture clearly had its symbolism for Picasso's left-wing admirers. On the day he gave it to the town of Vallauris in the presence of local communists, the council offered him the chapel for what would be the *War and Peace* murals,[52] and at around the same time the communist party may have asked him to paint a *Massacre in Korea*.[53]

Another burst of interest in the theme occurs in the early sixties with two sheet metal sculptures,[54] but Picasso's final shepherds are in a number of drawings executed towards the end of that decade, one of which is *Man with a Lamb, Watermelon Eater and Flautist*.[55] In this series of pastoral scenes, the shepherd has lost any menace which he may have had in 1943, and instead is accompanied in his work by a boy eating watermelon and an enthusiastic flautist. Picasso clearly found in the visual similarity of the two acts – eating a melon and playing a flute – an amusing juxtaposition. Hélène Parmelin describes Picasso miming the efforts of a flautist:

> ... Picasso sat down to the music-stand on the stool that was our only chair, and, turning the invisible pages, played the flute on our fly-tox squirt, his little finger in the air, flapping his elbows to the tune. He imitated the gestures admirably. He said he undoubtedly had a gift for it.[56]

The combination of the flute, or at least the pipes, with the shepherd is another classical one; the satyr in the cast which Picasso had drawn in 1895 has a *syrinx* or pan-pipe at his side. The reason for shepherd's music is less clear, and troubled the Comte de Buffon in his text on 'The Ram', which was illustrated with this print (see p127, above):

> It is said that sheep are sensitive to the sweetness of song, that they graze more assiduously, that they carry them-selves better, that they fatten to the sound of the pipes, that music attracts them; but then again they also say, with more basis and more often, that music does at least serve to enchant the shepherd in his boredom; and that it is to this type of solitary and idle life that one can attribute the origin of this art.[57]

Picasso produced two other works showing a goat rather than a ram being serenaded, firstly by a shepherd,[58] and secondly by some priapic fauns, *Fauns and Goat*. Amongst the three animals in this chapter, goats, rather than sheep or the ram, preoccupied Picasso for some fifteen years after the end of the Second World War. In 1946, in his first season of painting in the beautiful light and stone of the Château Grimaldi in Antibes, Picasso sketched out a fine and quite naturalistic study of *The Goat*, a shaven goat at rest. The choice of medium was unusual, reflecting a difficulty at that moment in obtaining canvas: Picasso worked on fibrocement, which gives a plaster-type surface, and in oil and ripolin. On the back of the painting he wrote: 'If this man had worked harder, you feel he would have made it.'[59]

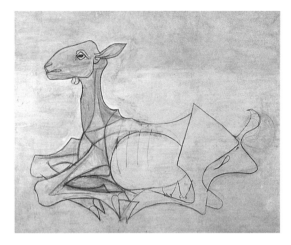

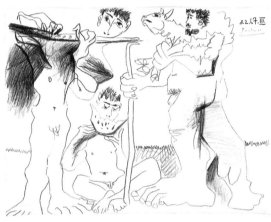

ABOVE: Picasso, *The Goat*, 1946, oil and ripolin on fibrocement, 120 x 150cm, Musée Picasso, Antibes (Z.XIV.241). © DACS 1995.

BELOW: Picasso, *Man with a Lamb, Watermelon Eater and Flautist*, 3/2/67, bistre crayon on paper, 48 x 63.5cm, Courtesy Thomas Ammann Fine Art, Zurich (Z.XXVII.436). © DACS 1995.

ABOVE: Picasso, *The Goat*, 1950, original plaster, 120.5 x 72 x 144cm, Musée Picasso, Paris (MP 339; S.409.I). © Photo RMN. © DACS 1995.

BELOW: Picasso, *Flayed Head of a Sheep*, Royan 4/10/39, oil on canvas, 50 x 61cm, Musée des Beaux-Arts, Lyon (MP 1990-20; Z.IX.351). © Photo RMN. © DACS 1995.

Looking at the care with which the intertwining forms of the goat's body are rendered, and in particular the effort with which Picasso has articulated the area of the neck and head, it would seem that considerable hard work had already gone into the piece. The intellectual scrutiny of the joints and muscula-ture of this goat lay dormant for a few years, but finally found its expression in the famous *The Goat* assemblage of 1950, where the sense of anatomy that is present in the painting comes magically to life.

The goat was improvised in Picasso's studio at Vallauris. The challenge was a more extreme version of that met in the *Head of a Bull* of 1942: to transform oddments of rubbish from local heaps into a very convincing representation of the animal, although in this case plaster was used as the binding agent on a wood frame. Picasso had some of the elements of the goat already, including a tatty wicker basket which was probably the one painted in the same year alongside a startled cock.[60] Bits of the finished work, like many of Picasso's other larger sculp-tures, were prone to falling off,[61] and this partly explains the need to cast the piece in bronze.[62] The energy of the work, and its remarkable incarnation of the obstinacy of the animal, may reflect Picasso's newly acquired familiarity with a goat which he and Françoise Gilot won in a local lottery around 1950. If that is the case, Picasso obviously preferred to change its sex, since although the prize was supposed to be a nanny-goat, it turned out to be a very smelly billy-goat. The billy-goat conducted itself so badly that, much to Picasso's chagrin, Gilot gave it away to some gypsies.[63]

Picasso did not forget his affection for the goat. In 1956 the local branch of the French Communist Party and other worthy organisations wanted to give the artist a present for his seventy-fifth birthday. Jacqueline Roque informed those at the head of the operation that Picasso wanted a goat, which, in spite of the excess of goats in the Côte d'Azur, threw the *apparatchiks* into heated debate. The concerns of the Party over potential embarrassment meant that the goat was a long time in coming. In the interim, Jacqueline found another small goat, christened Esmerelda, which she bought from a neighbour for Picasso. When the Party eventually did produce a goat, it was an ancient, shaggy and rather terrifying specimen. Not long after, Picasso discovered that it had a tumour, and it had to be put-down. Picasso took his macabre revenge by insisting that the meat he served up for lunch to the editor of *La Patriote de Nice* was none other than the goat's tumour.[64]

As the joke suggests, despite his pretensions to the role of Dr Doolittle or Orpheus, Picasso was no squeamish vegetarian.[65] After Françoise Gilot gave away his first goat, Picasso acquired a goat's head which he set on the branch of a tree to dry, although the precise date when he began the drying process is unclear.[66] Certainly, the large number [67] of fine drawings of a head, for example *Skull [Head] of a Sheep*, which seem to be contemporary with the famous sculpture known as the *Goat's Skull, Bottle and Candle*, reveal the fruits of observation, as do the slightly later paintings.[68] In the charcoal drawing, many of the features stylised in the sculpture are apparent: the ribs on the horns, the coarse hairs on the brow, the bulging eyes (effectively but sadistically imitated by large screw heads in the sculpture), and the ever-tightening skin progressively revealing the lower teeth. Once again Picasso used a variety of materials in transforming the head into sculpture, and in this case he may have been partly inspired to do so by an object in his own collection, a *Saga Ram Mask* from Mali. Yet the use of diverse materials in each shows a different interest: for Picasso in matching a material to a quality in the real object; for the artist who made the mask a process of more abstract embellishment.

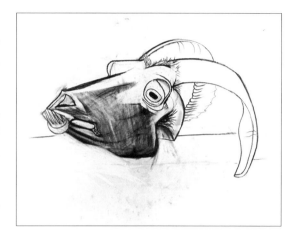

If Picasso's studies of this head had come a little later, they might have been seen as a tribute to Paul Eluard, who died on the 18th November 1952. Their appearance without any such landmark to underwrite them is a reminder that one cannot always attribute intimations of mortality to the *nature-morte* (still-life), nor simple motives to the person that paints it.

However, it is difficult to resist expressive interpretations of two earlier works on a similar theme. Two burning, putrid and barren paintings of sheep's heads date from the beginning of the Second World War. *Flayed Head of a Sheep* was painted on the 4th October 1939 and *Three Sheep's Heads* was painted in Paris on the 17th October 1939. It has been suggested both that the paintings derived from visits to a butcher's or an abattoir undertaken during October 1939, and that they also closely echo Francisco Goya's *Sheep's Head and Ribs* of around 1810 which Picasso knew from the Louvre.[69] The manner of the two paintings is different: the earlier work, although constructed in a taught geometry of red and black, has a more eerie presence than the later, whose pungent colours are ethereal – at turns thick and thin, reflecting the memory rather than the immediacy of the animal heads. In turning to a vocabulary of bloody slaughter and the incipient decay of wastage – perhaps after visiting an abattoir – Picasso followed in the steps of the poet Lorca:

Every day there are killed in New York
four million ducks,
five million pigs,
two thousand doves, to titillate the dying
one million cows

ABOVE: Picasso, *Skull [Head] of a Sheep*, Vallauris, 1951, charcoal on paper, 50.5 x 65.5cm, Collection Marina Picasso, Geneva (Inv 05727). Courtesy Galerie Jan Krugier, Geneva. © DACS 1995.

CENTRE: Anon., *Saga Ram Mask*, Mali, (MP 3641), Musée Picasso, Paris. © Photo RMN.

BELOW: Picasso, *Goat's Skull, Bottle and Candle*, 1951-53, painted bronze, 78.8 x 95.3 x 54.5cm, Museum of Modern Art, New York (S.410.IIb). Photo © 1995 The Museum of Modern Art, New York. © DACS 1995.

Picasso, *The Ram's Head*, 1925, oil on canvas, 81.6 x
99.7cm, Norton-Simon Museum, Pasadena, CA (Z.V.443).
Gift of Mr Alexandre P Rosenberg, 1978 P.1978.6.
© DACS 1995.

one million lambs
and two million cocks
that leave the sky in splinters.
[...]
The ducks and the doves
and the pigs and the lamb
slay their drops of blood
beneath the calculations... [70]

The moral paradoxes, the alienation, of industrialised mass slaughter are nowhere better brought home than in the darker aspects of the war which Picasso would live out in France – and indeed some have seen these paintings in such a light.[71] Yet once again, it is worth recalling that this kind of interpretation must be offset by the preoccupations of the painter, to emulate and surpass his forerunners. As well as Goya, Picasso may have recalled Chardin, whose *Kitchen Table and Utensils with a Rack of Mutton* he may have owned by this time.[72]

As we have seen, there were plenty of painters before Picasso who found a living in the theme of the butcher's table and whose work he must also have known from the Louvre. Picasso's desire to remake or even outdo not only the works of the great but also countless mediocre painters is a key factor behind the highly traditional nature of his compositions, and the familiarity of his bestiary. His earliest still-life paintings on the theme of *The Ram's Head* – or indeed any animal head – date from 1925. Compositional drawings indicate the care with which this wonderfully integrated work, and its *grisaille* counterpart, was conceived.[73] The surface of the painting is itself highly worked, suggesting that the drawings may have been undertaken during its creation, in order to clarify the late cubist shuffling of edges and planes. The relationship between this immensely colourful version of the composition and the *grisaille* is no less clear. Nevertheless, a persistent juxtaposition makes an appearance in this painting: of seafood and some other form of animal – alive or dead. This can be seen in *Still-life with Owl and Three Urchins*, 1946, *Still-life with Cat and Lobster*, 1962, and also *Cat and Lobster on a Beach*, 1962. To the right of the ram's head is the curve of a fruit dish on a pedestal. Below that, a scallop, and next to it a tomato. Around the grimace of the ram are a fish (whose fins are rhymed with the scallop), urchin, and lemon; whilst at the bottom right a squid mindlessly ogles us, the connoisseurs. A feast for the eyes.

WATERY CREATURES

There are not as many sea creatures in Picasso's oeuvre as birds, for instance, but these other-wordly beings in their nether region of water and salt inspired some very significant paintings and fine ceramics. The seafood still-life was one of Picasso's favourite subjects during his stays in the South of France, and especially during the years in Antibes and Vallauris. Fish and crustaceans provide a challenge to the painter in their diverse forms and glistening surfaces. Furthermore, as with the squid in *The Ram's Head* of 1925, Picasso often played games with the fixed eyes, gritted teeth, or gasping mouths of his dead aquatic subjects, enjoying the old paradoxes of the still-life – the depiction of an array of live, dead and decaying creatures in the most animated manner possible.

It is especially significant that Picasso became interested in representing sea creatures when staying in the South of France, for some of the most accomplished and decorative representations of sea-life have been produced by artists in those Mediterranean countries where fish and fishing were essential to the local diet and economy. Like them, Picasso was doubtlessly inspired by the great variety of produce daily brought to shore, and by ceramics, which seemed to him such an appropriate medium for representing fishy subjects. These factors allied him with a long Mediterranean tradition of embellishing utensils and walls with all manner of sea creatures. These affinities are most striking in a Minoan Marine-style 'pilgrim flask' in which accurate observation is combined with decorative pattern (see p144, below). The octopus motif is a study in its own right of the way in which this creature, amongst drifts of seaweed, abandons itself to the swirling currents of the sea. At the same time, the shape of the flat flask has been exploited to give substance and form to the wavy-tendrilled octopus. Equally successful is a Roman mosaic from Pompeii produced some fifteen hundred years later (see overleaf) which depicts a plethora of marine life with almost complete absence of stylisation, although there is a delicate artistry in the octopus' tendrils. The mosaicist has achieved a three-dimensionality that preserves the appearance and movement of these fish in their natural habitat, a stark contrast to their careful, inanimate arrangement on the fishmonger's slab.[1]

Measured against these achievements, the bestiary illustrations of sea creatures are fanciful and naive. As the illustration

OPPOSITE: Picasso, detail of *Eel, Big Fish, Octopuses, Sea Urchins*, 28/10/46, oil on plywood, 90 x 127.5cm, Musée Picasso, Antibes (Z.XIV.325). © DACS 1995.

ABOVE: *Fish*, MS Ashmole 1511, Bestiary in Latin, early 13th century, f. 86r. By permission of the Bodleian Library, Oxford.

Anon. Pompeian, *Fish and Crustaceans*, Pompeii, 1 BC, mosaic, Museo Archelogico Nazionale, Naples. Photo Scala, Florence.

on p137 suggests, the bestiarist compiler had a somewhat tenuous grasp of the character of certain sea creatures, relying on the expectation that certain of them, such as the sea-horse and sea-calf, mimicked their counterparts on earth.[2] This was reflected, so it was believed, in the etymology of the fish: like cattle (*pecus*) fish (*pesces*) browse in flocks (*a pascendo*) and graze (*pascere*).[3] Some types were similar in appearance to land animals such as 'frogs, calves, lions, blackbirds and peacocks with many-coloured backs and necks, and thrushes with white and other colours'; others had similar habits: 'dogfish were called after dogs because they bite; wolves got their name because they pursue other fish voraciously'.[4] In the sea, as the bestiary explains, the small are forever being devoured by those bigger than themselves:

> The smaller are subject to the larger or to the more powerful, for whoever is weaker is liable to be captured by the stronger. There are, indeed, many who feed upon vegetation, but the littler among these is food for the bigger, and again the bigger is seized in its turn by a still stronger one and becomes his food: one plunderer falling to another plunderer.[5]

For this latter reason, especially, 'fish are given to us as a parable for the instruction of men', to teach us never to attack those weaker or smaller than ourselves, for a stronger assailant may be following us.[6] This message survives in the most ancient and enduring proverb, 'Big Fish Eat Little Fish' the most famous visual exemplar of which was designed by Pieter Bruegel the Elder, in the manner of Bosch.[7] The subject and moral of the print are self-evident: the selfishness, greed and iniquity inherent in a worldly commercial society.[8]

Like all living (and inanimate) things, very occasionally, fish and crustaceans were susceptible to endowment with a sexual content. In Jan Steen's *Drunken Couple* reproduced and discussed in Chapter Four, oyster- and mussel-shells litter the floor, the former being commonly considered an aphrodisiac, the latter recurring as a symbol of the female genitalia.[9] It has also been suggested that in a *Kitchen Scene* by Joachim Bueckelaer (Louvre, Paris) a salmon steak performs the same function, on the basis that fish in general could also be likened to the phallus[10] and 'fishing' to copulation.[11] As ever, though, much depends on context: oysters could also be symbolic of the Virgin for she, like them, brought forth a glorious 'pearl'[12] and a mussel shell appears on the foreground of an *Adoration of the Magi* by Geertgen tot Sint Jans in the Rijksmuseum, together with broken pot shards, usually indicative of loss of virginity.[13] Perhaps these latter perform a comparable function to the broken pot in a sixteenth-century Nativity play by the Portuguese

Pieter Bruegel the Elder, *Big Fish eat Little Fish*. 1556-57 engraving, Bibliothèque Royal Albert Ier, Brussels. Copyright Bibliothèque Royal Albert Ier, Brussels.

Gil Vincent in which the breaking of a pot on stage 'replaces the birth of Christ that could not be represented otherwise'.[14]

The most elaborate still-lifes which include sea-creatures as an element are that group known as *pronkstilleven*, or 'luxury still-lifes', which were especially popular from the middle of the seventeenth century in Amsterdam, one of the largest and wealthiest cities in the world.[15] In Willem Kalf's *Still-life with the Drinking Horn of the Saint Sebastian Archers' Guild, Lobster and Glasses* the sumptuous food, the gleaming silverware, the precious gold, are crowned by a huge lobster. It is difficult to see how this most extravagant and costly of crustaceans could be equated with Christ, who was more generally associated with the humble fish, but according to the German poet Conrad von Würzburg, it was a symbol of the Resurrection.[16] Just as the bright red of its shell when boiled was so much more beautiful than that of the living lobster, so Christ after his death on the cross escaped the miseries of earthly life, regaining the splendour of his divinity.[17] Although the reference is rather obscure – in the bestiary where one would expect this interpretation to have been repeated, the lobster rates only a passing mention if at all – it would not be surprising had more disapproving viewers of these pieces seized on the Christian message as a rebuke to their owners and producers. The conspicuous consumption and taste for luxury they exemplified was so clearly at odds with the moderate frugality demanded by Calvinist teaching, that some artists included in their *pronkstilleven* discreet reminders (watches, the eucharistic symbols of wheat and wine) of the vanity of human desires and endeavours.[18]

Nevertheless, it is undeniable that a prime objective of these painters was to amaze the eye with a lush variety of textures and materials, arrayed with such subtle ingenuity that their creations are eminently more desirable than what they represent. In the opinion of Goethe, Kalf's paintings show:

> ... in what sense art is superior to nature and what the spirit of man imparts to objects when it views them with creative eyes. There is no question, at least there is not for me, if I had to choose between the golden vessels and the picture, that I would choose the picture.[19]

Other artists, however, were content to produce simple pictures of a few fish in modest surroundings, which are so carefully composed and executed that they are no mean artistic achievements despite the apparently reticent ambition of their producers.[20] This quiet art reached its greatest accomplishment in the nineteenth century, with Manet's fish still-lifes of which *Still-life, Red Mullet and Eel* appears especially modest. But its apparent simplicity is the source of its mastery. Humble fare requires a correspondingly unfussy treatment, and here the fish

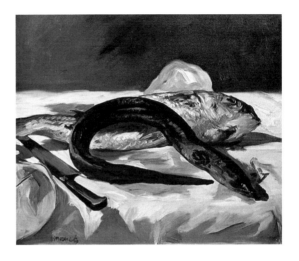

OPPOSITE, ABOVE: Willem Kalf, *Still-life with the Drinking Horn of the Saint Sebastian Archer's Guild, Lobster and Glasses*, c1653, 86.4 x 102.2cm, oil on canvas, National Gallery, London. Reproduced by courtesy of the Trustees, The National Gallery. London.

OPPOSITE, BELOW: Picasso, *Eel, Big Fish, Octopuses, Sea Urchins*, 28/10/46, oil on plywood, 90 x 127.5cm, Musée Picasso, Antibes (Z.XIV.325). © DACS 1995.

ABOVE: Edouard Manet, Still-life, *Red Mullet and Eel*, 1864, 38 x 46cm, Musée D'Orsay, Paris. © Photo RMN.

Picasso, *Cat and Lobster on a Beach*, 14/1/65, oil on
canvas, 89 × 130cm, Galerie Louise Leiris, Paris
(Z.XXV.14). © DACS 1995.

are represented as no more and no less than what they are: nourishing food on the kitchen table, their gleaming, viscous textures replicated in the medium of oil paint. The great strength of the picture lies, however, in the interplay of diagonals and horizontals, emphasised by the carefully positioned knife, literally 'on an edge', which holds the composition together. This was a method of pictorial manipulation Manet learned from looking at Chardin's equally humble still-lifes, but Chardin in turn learned much from his Dutch predecessors.[21] The careful balance of forms and textures in both his small and large pieces is greatly indebted to the producers of unassuming breakfast pieces and more elaborate banquet pieces, but he also discovered, in the half-eaten loaves of bread, the wineglasses spilled over, the crumbs on the tabletop, the eloquence with which the *absence* of men and women can invoke their *presence* and agency. The monumentality and scale of his painting *The Ray* are far grander than that generally expected and demanded of still-life. But in the tradition of the *pronkstilleven*, the intention was to push the possibilities still-life affords to their limit. The vivid reds of the gutted fish are a focus for the picture, a stunning tour-de-force of artistic execution and, a gruesome presence, its eviscerated body looking remarkably like a human face; to the left, a startled cat balances precariously on a pile of oysters. The interest of the picture, its appeal and intrigue, lies in the implied rather than visible presence of humans and suspension and anticipation of movement characteristic of Chardin's best paintings: the cat has just jumped down on the oysters, caught as it were in suspension, its arched back suggesting both its momentary balancing act and the surprise which has startled it into its frozen pose. What has frightened the cat? An unseen dog? The macabre face of the ray? Or a kitchen maid (the viewer?) beyond and in front of the surface of the picture who, having left this rich fare unattended, has just walked into the room and caught the cat in its scavenging act. However we may 'read' this picture, one thing is for certain: a split second later, the cat will move, the pile of oysters will tumble, and so will Chardin's careful and artful composition.

Jean-Baptiste-Siméon Chardin, *The Ray*, 1728, oil on canvas, 114.5 x 146cm, Musée du Louvre, Paris. © Photo RMN.

OVERLEAF, ABOVE: Picasso, *Octopus Plate*, Vallauris 29/10/47 (IV), rectangular plate in terracotta; painted in black, blue, green and red dots on enamelled white ground; engraved lines white, 32 x 38cm, Collection Marina Picasso (Inv 57217). Courtesy Galerie Jan Krugier, Geneva. © DACS 1995.

OVERLEAF, BELOW: Anon. Cretan, Marine-style flat 'pilgrim flask' from Palaikastro, 1500-1450 BC, height 28cm, Archaeological Museum, Heraklion. Photo Scala, Florence.

One of Picasso's most attractive ceramics, the *Octopus Plate*, shows how much Picasso's decorative ideas in the medium revived ancient motifs. This plate was decorated with an octopus twirling its limbs and ejecting its green-black ink on 29th October 1947. Picasso has relished creating wheels within wheels in the design, in a manner recalling early Mediterranean ceramic decoration, as well as Roman mosaics (see pp138; 144).[22] A variety of plates decorated with fishy forms similarly exploit the relationships between the fish and the roundel of the plate, so that the fish can be seen both as if swimming by a porthole or served up for supper. The fish-supper is inescapably captured in the bizarre illusionism of the *Cup: Hands with a Fish*, 1953. In the peculiar composition of this cup, one is left uncertain as to whether one pair of hands is involved or hands belonging to two different sized people – a father and son for example.

In September 1946, Picasso was offered space in the Château Grimaldi in Antibes, by the then curator of the museum, Romuald Dor de la Souchère. Picasso spent his first two month stint in the castle, a mediaeval structure piled up on the seawall, producing over twenty paintings and numerous drawings, many of which reflected his marine surroundings. The simple array of sea catches which he painted reflected his ambition to become the great people's painter in postwar France: '... this time, I know that I am working for the people.'[23]

The fish were also tokens of his delight in the food at *Chez Marcel*, a seafood restaurant he frequented with Françoise Gilot.[24] Once again, however, Picasso's surroundings and everyday environment vie with the spirit of painters long dead. In *Eel, Big Fish, Octopuses, Sea Urchins*, a still-life painted in oil on plywood, there is a clear echo of another pictorial eel curled over a fish in *Still-life, Red Mullet and Eel*, painted by Edouard Manet in 1864. Manet's painting, known to Picasso from the collection of the Louvre, is a wonderful performance, apparently casual and intimate, redolent with all the necessary clues for the discriminating observer to detect the painter's high class. Picasso's larger work, with its zesty flow of surfaces and balanced shapes, is a slightly comic update and deliberately fresh but heavy version of the Manet, a fish painting 'for the people'. Part of the comedy derives from the separation of the lively octopus, eel, fish and urchin, which allows for the fantasy that they are seen still swimming beneath the water surface.

Painting a lunch is something that Picasso had done before, and at a time when one might expect such simple gestures to be ruled out by the grave tenor of contemporary events and the artist's own works. On the 18th March 1937, between the execution of the rather disturbing *Dream and Lie of Franco*

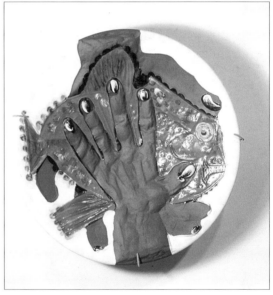

ABOVE: Picasso, *The Crayfish* [*Le Langouste*], Spring 1936, sugar lift aquatint, 36 x 28cm, Victoria & Albert Museum, London (B 352). Photo © Victoria & Albert Museum, London. © DACS 1995.

BELOW: Picasso, *Cup: Hands with Fish*, 1953, round cup; original print red earthenware clay, deep engraving painted in engobes under partial brushed glaze, russet, green, white, black, diameter 32cm, Musée de la Ville de Vallauris (AR 216; R 717). © DACS 1995.

etchings and the epic *Guernica*, Picasso painted a small *Still-life with Tuna*. The painting may not be quite as innocent as the Antibes still-life, however, since it may have given Picasso an idea. On the following day Picasso was dreaming up a 'Poisson d'avril' (April Fish), the equivalent of an April Fool, which he could send on a postcard to Dora Maar. Picasso took the name of the tradition at its word, though, and worked out a rebus around the central motif of a fish. In *April Fool [rebus]* we see a hairy fish apparently sealed like an envelope, and behind it six more similar silhouettes. Along its back run six white and six black female figures. On its head sits a bone bearing the face of a cat. The fish is supported on a sort of tripod in the form of an erupting penis. The text which forms the key to the rebus is: 'l'hache-chat d'os 7 carpes postales porte mâle heures'.[25]

When pronounced in French this means 'the purchase of this postcard brings bad luck'. The elements of the rebus, like most punning jokes, are not easy to explain. The bone-cat in the drawing is 'La chatte d'os', which sounds like 'l'achat de...'. Seven postal carp is 'sept carpes postales' which gives 'cet carte postal'. The twelve figures running along the top of the fish represent the hours of darkness and light: the 'heures'. The 'porte mâle' is the strange penis/tripod, and 'porte mâle'– 'heures' (taken together) provide for the bringing of bad luck![26] Something is inevitably lost in the translation ...

On the whole, but with one very important exception, Picasso was most obsessed by the subject of crustaceans. The fascination of the crayfish found expression in the Buffon series (see p145, above), although no text was printed to accompany the print. The bubbling and darkened environment of this weed dweller was captured with clever use of aquatint.

It is, however, much more common for crustaceans to appear out of the water in paintings. On Boxing Day 1948, Picasso painted a lush still-life of a *Lobster and Bottle*. Picasso's translation of the traditional virulent red of the cooked lobster into a deep blue is probably no more than an exercise in colour harmony in a painting so clearly modelled on a standard composition.[27] However, the date of the work does perhaps give some credence to the idea that Picasso had an inkling of the Christian symbolism of the lobster's noisy change of colour in the boiling cooking-pot. According to one writer, these exceptional creatures, with their spiny exoskeletons, eyes on stalks, and mechanically articulated limbs had the ability to cause Picasso disquiet, or even a reminiscence of cruelty.[28] A more recent book has argued that the *Boy with a Crayfish* of 21st June 1941 alludes to paintings by Picasso's friend Salvador Dali on the theme of 'castration anxiety'.[29] In Picasso's lewd work we see a gleeful seated little boy waving a crayfish in his right hand, whilst his neat little penis points down in infantile pleasure at a fish. The round form as if on a tripod on top of the fish has been read unconvincingly as a squid.[30] The claim that a specific gesture is being made in Dali's direction seems heavy handed, although there is no doubt that this boy's ecstatic wiggling is prompted by a combination of sadism, naughtiness and fear regarding his new prisoners, and especially the unfortunate crayfish. He is the alter-ego of the quiet *Child with Doves* of two years later.

However, the notion that lobsters and other crustaceans were only summoned when anxieties and sadistic impulses afflicted the artist himself, is easy to counter. After the publication of Françoise Gilot's memoir of their relationship, which distressed the artist greatly, Picasso painted *Cat and Lobster on a Beach* in 1962:

> ...both the lobster and his companion crab have claws; they defend themselves, and the cat is kept at arm's length.[31]

As the author of the above acknowledges, the apparent moods of Picasso's pictures do not neatly map onto the vagaries of his private life. Other paintings before and after this one are perfectly jolly, and one can turn that mood back on the cat and the lobster to see a comic clash of two most unlikely combatants in a most unlikely setting. Neither looks comfortable, and the stumbling twists and turns of the cat on the slimy rocks recall the ginger steps of Chardin's cat in *The Ray*. Picasso must in any case have taken pleasure in effecting yet another inversion here – tipping the odds of his earlier confrontation of cat and lobster, in *Still-life with Cat and Lobster*, in favour of the hapless crustacean.

Undoubtedly Picasso's watery masterpiece is *Night Fishing in Antibes*. This work of August 1939, conceived on a scale smaller but no less confident than *Guernica*, is one of the most evocative depictions of the luminous depths of the sea at night in the history of western art. The canvas was part of a large roll which Picasso tacked to the flock wallpaper of an otherwise emptied room in an apartment in Antibes.[32] Most paintings of fishermen are either genre works or renditions of Christ calling on Peter to be 'a fisher of men';[33] but the subject of this painting is one well known to those who walk on the piers of seaside towns at night, as Picasso did with Dora Maar at that time. In the centre of the canvas an unnaturally bright light, an acetylene lamp, hangs over a fishing boat, attracting the fish.[34] Of the two fishermen, that in the centre wears a striped jersey and leans over the bows to spear a flatfish with an four-pronged spear by the reflection of the lamp; the other cranes towards the water surface and a passing fish whilst he awaits a tug on the

ABOVE: Picasso, *Boy with a Crayfish*, Paris 21/6/41, oil on canvas, 130 x 97.3cm, Musée Picasso, Paris (MP 189; Z.XI.200). © Photo RMN. © DACS 1995.

BELOW: Picasso, *Lobster and Bottle*, 26/12/48, oil on canvas, 50 x 61, Private Collection, Courtesy Thomas Amman Fine Art, Zurich (Z.XV.114). © DACS 1995.

Picasso, *Night Fishing in Antibes*, August 1939, oil on
canvas, 205.8 x 345.4cm, The Museum of Modern Art,
New York (Z.IX.316). Mrs Simon Guggenheim Fund.
Photograph © 1995 The Museum of Modern Art, New
York. © DACS 1995.

fishing-line tied to his toe. Moths or other insects flutter wildly in the light. To the right, two female figures stand watching on the pier; one holds her bicycle and licks a double-coned ice-cream, the other in green gestures towards the men.[35] On the far left of the painting looms the Château Grimaldi, which would become Picasso's studio after the war and then a museum dedicated to his work. The impressive rocks which lie before the sea wall hide, as we might expect: 'a crab whose soulful eyes seem to focus on the viewer.'[36]

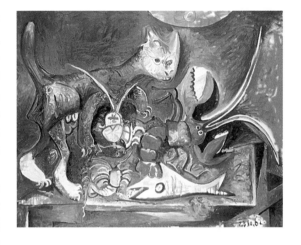

Once again, the timing of the painting has been seen as relevant to its interpretation, and it is certainly the case that the main topic of conversation at the time between Picasso and his friends in Antibes was whether, and when, to leave France.[37] The painting was subjected to a flurry of over-interpretation in the early sixties, when this and other factors were brought to bear on it, as were rather predictable Freudian interpretations of cycling, licking and ice-cream, and spearing fish.[38] More recently, it has been suggested that Picasso's choice of subject and manner of depiction are indebted to Paul Klee,[39] or to a twelfth-century Catalan fresco, showing St Peter's boat, now in Barcelona.[40] The distortion of the figures, characteristic of the period and close to that seen in *Boy with a Crayfish*, bring the human actors into alignment with the creatures. The fisherman who leans down to the water surface has repositioned eyes amusingly reflected in those of the fish he watches, and even more so in the flatfish.[41]

Watery creatures in Picasso's art, despite suggestions that they indicate something more sinister (especially when juxtaposed with a cat or an owl as in *Still-life with Owl and Three Urchins*), seem to provide the occasion for the free use of colour and playful rendering of diverse shapes. *Night Fishing in Antibes*, although a depiction of a hunt, is a hymn to recreation in an environment rich in sights, sounds, textures and smells. It is therefore an eminently rich subject for a painter, especially since:

> [Spearfishing] shares with the act of painting ... the successful and suspenseful verve of marksmanship and balance, total absorption and intense involvement.[42]

Not to mention of course, intense visual awareness. The attraction of the hunt as a subject carries over to Picasso's works involving those small creatures most difficult to spot, insects.

Picasso, *Still-life with Cat and Lobster*, Mougins 23/10-1/11/62, oil on canvas, 130 x 162cm, Hakone Open-Air Museum, (Z.XX.356) © DACS 1995.

INSECTS

For Picasso, insects were as insignificant as they were for his predecessors, but nevertheless they deserve a small chapter in a Picasso Bestiary for like sea creatures, they inspired some extraordinary works. In these, we can see several points of contact between Picasso's representation of insects and those of his predecessors: the scatological amusements afforded by the flea, the wistful evocation of childish pleasure in chasing a butterfly. But with *Composition with a Butterfly* he also produced a work in which a real butterfly joins forces with all manner of other materials to produce a witty still-life. Perhaps this work comments on the achievements of those mediaeval artists who sought to deceive the eye.

These smallest of animals were cherished by illuminators, who depicted them with loving care and minutely exact detail in the borders of manuscripts generally for no other reason than delight in their appearance and the opportunity they afforded for exercising the miniaturists' art of precise observation and skilful execution. As in the miniature reproduced here, Flemish artists of the late fifteenth century working in Ghent and Bruges[1] enlivened the borders of their pages with all manner of creepy-crawlies and different kinds of flowers, illusionistically rendered almost actual size as though casting 'real' shadows, playfully deceiving the viewer that insects had just alighted there.[2] Such displays of pictorial wit not only provided amusement for the viewer, they also recalled the jokes said to have been played by precociously talented young artists: on one of his master's paintings the pupil paints an insect, which the master then attempts to brush away.[3]

In the bestiary, however, these tiny creatures occupy the least of places. Perhaps this was because, in those days before the great classification exercises of the seventeenth century onwards, it was difficult to neatly group together insects and their kin. It was even more difficult to decide how individual species could fit into the basic bestiary categories of beasts, birds, snakes, fish and monsters. Perhaps too, because these creatures are so small, it was not easy without the as yet uninvented microscope to observe their habits and draw from them the spiritual and moral conclusions that made the bestiary so useful and attractive.[4] Only bees and ants, whose hard-working habits and efficient social structure were held up as a paradigm for human behaviour and government, rate more

OPPOSITE: Detail of Frontispiece (see p154).

ABOVE: *Coronation of the Virgin*, MS Douce 219-220, Master of Mary of Burgundy, 'The Book of Hours of Englebert of Nassau', f. 171r. The Bodleian Library, Oxford.

BELOW: Picasso, *Composition with a Butterfly*, Boisgeloup 15/9/32, cloth, wood, plants, string, drawing pin, butterfly and oil on canvas, 16 x 22 x 2.5cm, Musée Picasso, Paris (MP 1982-169; S.116). © Photo RMN. © DACS 1995.

than a passing interest. Even the spider, that most industrious and unfairly loathed of creatures is merely classed as an 'air-worm' and merits only a terse description.[5] However, this brevity is compensated for by other writers. Theobaldus in his *Physiologus* likens the spider to avaricious men who eviscerate the poor and to the Devil who traps and eviscerates sinners;[6] Topsell's lengthy account in *The History of Serpents* reveals his great admiration for the house-spider's industry and art and understandable dislike of the poisonous varieties[7] and Jacob Cats likened spiders' webs to the trap that Venus sets for the unwary.[8]

No one, however, has a good word to say about the flea. In the bestiary, it is merely an etymological curiosity: 'Fleas or "pulices" get their name because they come from dust (ex pulvere)'.[9] Yet the attentive reader of the bestiary may have been encouraged by even such a brief description to give a knowing nod at the flea's intimate association with domestic neglect. For fleas were associated with sluts and slatterns and their bite a common conceit for fornication.[10] Given this association, the quiet orderliness of George de la Tour's *Woman with the Flea* is rather startling, so much so, that Christopher Wright has even tentatively given it the alternative title *The Virgin awaiting the Light of the World*? explaining that:

> ... no authentic La Tour depicts such an obviously banal theme without a deeper meaning. The only symbol in the picture is the solitary candle burning on the chair, and it is surely not too speculative to suggest that the picture might represent the pregnant Virgin, isolated by Joseph when he discovers she is with child, the candle thus symbolising the forthcoming Christ as the Light of the World.[11]

There is no reason, however, why this painting should not represent a perfectly ordinary woman and still convey a 'deeper meaning'. The theme of the painting seems to be related to that of the Penitent Magdalene reflecting on her past iniquities, but lacks the skull and mirror which, together with the candle, positively identify her in George de La Tour's own version.[12] Yet surely this woman is, like the Magdalene, pensively dwelling on her own misdeeds, the flea and the candle indicating the direction of her thoughts away from the vain pleasures of life towards a new concern with the true light and the hereafter.[13]

In the small subsection of worms in the serpent and snake grouping of the bestiary, caterpillars are singled out for mention, for their habit of eating, and destroying, everything in their wake,[14] but there is no mention of the beautiful butterfly. The bestiary's general identification of wormlike creatures as agents of destruction is elaborated in some *Vanitas* still-lifes. In these the bloom on a peach, the fragrant petal of the rose, possess a fading beauty prey to maggots and flies, caterpillars

OPPOSITE: Picasso, *The Flea* [*La Puce*], Spring 1936, sugar lift aquatint, 36 x 28cm, Victoria & Albert Museum, London (B 359.) Photo © Victoria & Albert Museum, London. © DACS 1995.

ABOVE: Georges de La Tour, *Woman with the Flea*, n.d., canvas, 120 x 90cm, Musée Historique Lorraine, Nancy. Photo © Giraudon.

OVERLEAF, ABOVE: Matthaeus Merian the Younger, Frontispiece for *Historiae Naturalis, De Insectis* by Johann Johnston, 1657, copper engraving. Courtesy of The Library, National Museum of Wales.

OVERLEAF, BELOW: Otto Marseus van Schriek, *Serpents and Butterflies*, 1670, 70 x 55cm, oil on panel, Louvre, Paris (RF 3711). © Photo RMN.

AMSTELODAMI.
Apud IOANNEM IACOBI FIL. SCHIPPER. MDCLVII.

and beetles, which gnaw away at their tender flesh.[15] The sense of these still-lifes is retained even in illustrations to apparently dispassionate and scientific treatises, for example the frontispiece to Johann Johnston's 1657 *Historiae Naturalis, De Insectis…* Johnston's volume also deals, as the full title indicates, with serpents and dragons and although the decision to treat all these creatures – things that crawl and fly – as a group has a logical basis to it, the illustration, with the title a cartouche formed by a dragon and a snake, suggests a taxonomy that was product of the same concerns expressed by the still-life painter – or, indeed, the bestiarist. The function of the illustration is ostensibly quite different to Marseus van Schriek's *Serpents and Butterflies* but both were produced with the same knowledge that the serpent, Satan, brought sin and death to mankind. From death, however, arises resurrection and new life, represented by the metamorphosed caterpillar, the butterfly. For the butterfly had stood, since antiquity, for the soul leaving the body at death; its transformation from caterpillar and chrysalid signified immortality and to the Christian represented the resurrected human soul.[16] This is probably why, in the miniature depicting the Coronation of the Virgin reproduced on p151, both caterpillar and butterfly lurk amongst the red and white roses which elsewhere constitute the Virgin's 'rosary' crown. If caterpillar and chrysalis were also present, the eternal cycle of life, death and resurrection was invoked.[17]

This belief probably accounts for the origin of various superstitions regarding butterflies: a trio of butterflies (life, death and resurrection or, perhaps, the trinity) flying together presages death or misfortune; if the first butterfly of the year is white, good luck will prevail; it is bad luck to kill this first butterfly.[18] But the butterfly was in its turn a symbol of desire[19] and hence of transience, of fleeting pleasure. For similar reasons the *Horae*, or Hours, as in Rubens' *Allegory of Peace* in the National Gallery and the *Birth of Maria de' Medici* from the Maria de' Medici cycle in the Louvre, are sometime represented with butterfly wings;[20] the Cabbage White butterfly perched on the Tree of Knowledge of Good and Evil in Cornelis van Haarlem's *Fall of Man*, reproduced and discussed in the Ape section, may be an illusion to the heedlessness that was the undoing of Adam, and through him all mankind.[21] In Emblem LII, however, of Jacob Cats' *Sinne- en Minnebeelden* the image of a butterfly emerging from its chrysalis is the occasion for reflection on the power of love to revive a deadened spirit. In the contemporary English version:

> Like dead in grave I lay, of liffe berefte, O Venus bright,
> Until your Sonne, and Sunne revynde, & made mee stand upright.

My wings your Sonne did give, youre Sunne restord'e my liffe forlorn,

and so of a dead stock was I a lively Creature borne...'[22]

The essence of a butterfly is, however, captured most expressively in one of Gainsborough's most charming paintings, *Gainsborough's Daughter's, Margaret and Mary Chasing a Butterfly*. The unfinished state of the painting, though perhaps unintentional, gives it a fresh immediacy ideally suited to its subject, evoking the brevity of youth and beauty and the transient innocence of childhood pleasures. In the joy of the moment there is a sadness: of ambitions left unfulfilled, of dreams chased but never caught.

ABOVE: Thomas Gainsborough, *Gainsborough's Daughters, Margaret and Mary Chasing a Butterfly*, c1756, oil on canvas, 113.7 x 104.8cm, National Gallery, London. Reproduced by courtesy of the Trustees, The National Gallery, London.

BELOW: Picasso, *Child in a Sailorsuit with a Butterfly Net [The Butterfly Hunter]*, 2/4/38, oil on canvas, 122 x 86cm. Museum of Modern Art, New York. © DACS 1995.

Despite being so under-represented in the general run of the artist's work, when Picasso was invited to represent insects naturalistically for the Buffon book, he produced no less than six prints. He also produced *The Flea* which, for reasons considered below, did not appear in the book. The six insects included were, in order of appearance, the bee, the butterfly, the wasp, the spider, the dragonfly (illustrated opposite), and the grasshopper. None of the prints were accompanied by text in the finished volume, probably reflecting once again the contents of the abridged *Histoire Naturelle* which was the publisher's source. The prints made full capital of the challenge: to render the glistening wings of a dragonfly, the hairy legs of a garden spider, the myriad eyes of the grasshopper, in the same limited medium.

Beyond this series there are hardly any naturalistic studies of insects in Picasso's work, although the same sequence of drawings from June 1956 which featured *Bull on a Branch* includes *Flowers and Insects*. The fine antennae of the grasshoppers ascending the flower-stem are captured with the relish of an artist working in pen and ink.

Insects remind us of the world out of notice, of the constant, teeming and not necessarily benign activity of nature pressing-in on the hygienic environment of the house. They scuttle across the page in a caricatural drawing, *Chatter*, of around 1900. Picasso did not miss the opportunity to effect a reversal of significance familiar in children's stories about insect life, and the human figures at the top of the sheet are about the smallest to be seen. The various creatures assume the human ability to talk, a childhood fantasy which adult sobriety never quite dispels completely.

The chatter in the cartoon – a mixture of Catalan and Spanish – reads as follows. From a castle at the top left, a woman shouts 'Bina' – (probably a name) to a person running along with another, exclaiming 'No en Pescaras' (You won't catch any). A third figure with an unsheathed sword says 'mala hija el honor de mi casa lo das por un plato de lentejas' (You wicked daughter you give my family honour for a plate of lentils). To the left are two crouching rabbits: one exclaims 'Adeu: nois' (Goodbye boys), and the other 'ola' (Hello). A third, to the right says 'apa buenas' (Hey Hi), and a bird of some sort 'Quin: Bullit' (what a racket). Lower down, a rabbit in front of a snare exclaims 'No me agra esto' (I don't like this) and a group of snails 'A: ver; quien: llega: Primero' (let's see who gets there first). A mouse says 'Nevir' (either a name or a nonsense word) and next to it a toad says 'No me dejaran cantar' (They won't let me sing) while a cock replies 'Ni que fueras: Gallare' (As if you were a big cockerel). A grasshopper

OPPOSITE ABOVE: Picasso, *Flowers and Insects*, 17/6/56 (IV), China ink on paper, 66 x 50.5cm, Picasso Estate (Inv 5687; Z.XVII.126). Courtesy of Musée Picasso, Paris, © DACS 1995.

OPPOSITE BELOW: Picasso, *The Dragonfly* [*La Libellule*], sugar lift aquatint, 36 x 28cm, Spring 1936, Victoria & Albert Museum, London (B 354). Photo © Victoria & Albert Museum, London. © DACS 1995.

ABOVE: Picasso, *Chatter*, [Barcelona 1899-1900], pen on paper, 23 x 21.9cm, Museu Picasso, Barcelona (MPB 110.337r). © DACS 1995.

Picasso, *Cat and Spider*, 2/8/46, Picasso Estate (Inv
4896; Z.XIV.202). Courtesy of Musée Picasso, Paris.
© DACS 1995.

comments 'Que estau di broma: Nois' (You're joking boys) and a beetle sings 'Escarabat: Bun: Bun' (Beetle, boom, boom). Scrawled at the bottom and then obliterated is 'Por no saber firmar toda/via P Ruiz Picasso' (Unable to sign as yet P Ruiz Picasso).

The notion of an animal conversation occurs similarly in Jules Renard's collection of stories entitled *Histoires Naturelles* of 1896,[23] which was illustrated by one of Picasso's favourite artists at that time, Henri de Toulouse-Lautrec. It nevertheless seems unlikely that the young Picasso was familiar with the text, since his French was of a rather low standard.

Perhaps one reason why there are few insects in Picasso's work is contained in an anecdote concerning his fear of spiders. Toby Jellinik visited Picasso one day in his studio:

> ... I noticed that there was water all over the floor. I asked what had happened. 'I was working and I saw a huge spider, I hate spiders and this one was enormous.' He grabbed a piece of charcoal and drew the spider on the floor to show me, it was pretty lifelike. Then, as usual, we went round the studio looking at his work. I never understood why he should care what I, a young artist, thought but he would always ask. So we were walking around and suddenly he jumped about ten feet in the air ... He'd seen his own picture of the spider and thought it was the real thing. It seemed to really upset him – he got very angry and rubbed the thing out.[24]

Picasso painted a *Cat and Spider* a few years before, allowing one of his more favourite creatures to take its revenge on the arachnids in whose fear he lived. The painting shows in schematic form the attack of a playful but bemused cat on a large but leggy spider. The theme of the insect hunt also appears in *The Flea*, a print for the Buffon book which was rejected by Fabiani the publisher, although he did issue it along with the other prints as a loose suite to accompany the luxury copies of the volume. It is unclear quite why the plate was rejected: it cannot be for lack of text,[25] since this did not stop Fabiani including a large number of the other prints. The only other possibilities are prudishness in the climate of right-wing rectitude during the war, or a lack of coherence with the other illustrations, which were all simple depictions of particular animals. Whatever the reason, Picasso's work is a witty and slightly more cheeky recapitulation of the theme to be seen in de la Tour's *Woman with the Flea*.[26] Both works in turn draw upon the long-standing association between the flea and the woman, whose nakedness is shameful but not, given the sensuous treatment by the artist, an apparently unwelcome or unenjoyable sight. This seems doubly true, if the frequent identification of the voluptuous 'pucelle' as a representation of

Picasso's secret lover Marie-Thérèse Walter is taken seriously.[27] It is also worth noting that in Barcelona at the end of the summer of 1902 Picasso had made a series of drawings of a music-hall artiste known as 'La Bella Chelito', of whom he had collected several saucy postcards. The drawings were of her striptease routine 'La Pulga' – The Flea.[28]

Undoubtedly Picasso's most developed insect works are on the theme of the butterfly hunt. On 15th September 1932 he produced a mixed-media collage known as *Composition with a Butterfly*. The fragile work is related in some ways to a series of 'sand paintings', 'picture reliefs'[29] executed in August 1930.[30] These were perhaps inspired by Surrealist developments in the realm of the *tableau-objet* (picture-object), as well as by Picasso's own continued reflections on Cubism. In the sand paintings, Picasso assembled objects on a reversed canvas, using the stretcher as a frame, covered them in paint or glue, and then fixed them in place by sprinkling a layer of sand on top. The sand gave a unified colour and texture to the otherwise diverse materials. In the isolated *Composition with a Butterfly*, Picasso's only work to ever include a real dead creature, the artist enjoyed using paint rather than sand as the binding agent. Paint for painters is normally the hallowed material, to be whipped into a representation of the world. Here Picasso uses some of the qualities of oils, its viscosity and adhesiveness, for the humble task of binding some anodyne fragments together. Two different sorts of figures appear: one made of string and another from matchsticks, a drawing pin and a piece of cotton rag. Perhaps a man and woman, or a boy and a girl. Between them is a leaf – perhaps standing for a bush – and the butterfly, whose creamy hue seems to have determined the colour of the whole. The self-appointed leader of the Surrealists, André Breton, understood that the butterfly is 'immobilised forever beside a dry leaf', like a live insect straying into a honey pot, but also in exactly the way the butterfly is normally pinioned by the entomologist.[31] A true *nature-morte*.

The flurry of the two stick figures in the relief reminds us of that transient desire for which the butterfly hunt had long acted as a symbol. *Child in a Sailorsuit and with a Butterfly Net [The Butterfly Hunter]*, which Picasso kept for himself, shows a child attempting to net a butterfly, and has itself prompted a game of 'chase the lady'. The main character, standing before (or perhaps sitting on) a log, wears a sailor suit and hat.[32] Instead of a ship's name, or even a kiss-me-quick slogan on the headband, we read the word 'Picasso'. This word has much to answer for, since it has prompted many writers on the painting to see it as a self-portrait. In an exercise in interpretation worthy of a bestiarist, Jerome Seckler interviewed Picasso:

Then I described for Picasso my interpretation of his painting *The Sailor*, which I had seen at the Liberation Salon. I said I thought it to be a self-portrait – the sailor's suit, the net, the red butterfly showing Picasso as a person seeking a solution to the problem of the times, trying to find a better world – the sailor's garb being an indication of an active participation in this effort. He listened intently and finally said, 'Yes, it's me. But I did not mean it to have any political significance at all.' I asked why he painted himself as a sailor. 'Because', he answered, 'I always wear a sailor shirt. See?' He opened up his shirt and pulled at his underwear – it was white with blue stripes! 'But what of the red butterfly?' I asked. 'Didn't you deliberately make it red because of its political significance?' 'Not particularly', he replied. 'If it has any, it was in my subconscious!'[33]

The identification of the butterfly hunter as Picasso, apparently from the horse's mouth, was taken up by Alfred Barr in his major exhibition catalogue of the artist's work in 1946. More recently another scholar has seen the child as a boy with autobiographical overtones.[34] It is interesting that Barr regarded the child as: '... of the same generation as the little girl with a doll' (see p63).[35]

One could go a little further and see the child in the painting as a girl rather than a boy. The physiognomy of the figure, with jutting nose, painted lips, 'butterfly' ear, and stringy hair is closer to the woman in *Woman with a Cock*, than to contemporary paintings of male figures. There is thus every reason to believe that the painting is of a *girl* chasing a butterfly, perhaps another portrait of Picasso's daughter Maya.[36] If so, the painting becomes a camp version of Gainsborough's depiction of *Gainsborough's Daughters Margaret and Mary Chasing a Butterfly*. It would not be surprising if Picasso's delight in 'April Fools' (unfortunately, the painting is dated *2nd* April 1938) made him spin a yarn to his interviewer: the name on the headband could easily be a signature rather than a name tag.

The jokes do not end there. Picasso has relished the opportunity of placing the elusive butterfly directly before the eyes of the girl. The disjunction between the representations of these eyes is a quite typical occurrence in Picasso's work, right back to the early years of the century, but especially in the thirties and after.[37] Here, however, it is no mere stylistic device. The butterfly hunter, in concentrating on her prey, ends up literally cross-eyed – not unlike those who insist on seeing Picasso in every animal, or a political meaning in every painting!

MONKEYS

Simia quam similis, turpissima bestia, nobis.[1]

Picasso was reputedly fond of remarking to his friends, at an early lull in the conversation, 'so here we are in the monkey cage'.[2] Monkeys occupy the sort of place we might expect in a Picasso Bestiary, closely following the artist in his tracks and mimicking his behaviour. Monkeys are not as common as insects in his art, but they tend to make their appearances at special moments, especially in the later years.

Apes and monkeys are the most frequently represented creatures that inhabit the margins of medieval manuscripts, where they hunt and are hunted, ride other animals, play musical instruments, conduct religious ceremonies, eat and copulate.[3] Yet they are quite deservedly pushed to the edge of the page, where they not only entertain, but also mock the import of the most sacred texts, committing the most outrageous and scatological obscenities. The frequency with which they are represented is equal to the extent with which they were despised. Apes were evil, obscene and foolish. They literally 'ape behaviour of rational human beings':[4]

> They are called MONKEYS (Simia) in the Latin language because people notice a great *similitude* to human reason in them.[5]

Nevertheless, apes were considered not in the least 'reasonable': they represented the basest instincts, symbols of abandonment to sensuality and the senses.

The bestiary illustration generally records a most unfortunate consequence of the ape's maternal instincts:

> Their nature is such that if a mother bears twins, she will love one and hate the other. If she happens to be pursued by hunters, she will clasp the one she loves in front of her and carry the one she hates on her back. But when she is weary of running upright, she willingly drops the one she loves, and unwillingly carries the one she hates on her back.[6]

For Jacob Cats, however, the ape's love for her young was proof of the adage 'love is blind'. Emblem IV from the 1700 edition of his *Sinne- en Minnebeelden*, is illustrated with a mother ape looking dotingly at her single child, visually expressing the motto 'Amor, forma condimentum', freely translated into contemporary English in the 1627 version as:

> In true love there is no lack,

OPPOSITE: Hendrick Goltzius, detail of *Taste* from the Series of the *Five Senses* 1578, engraving by Philip Galle, 14 x 8.8cm, Print Room, Rijksprentenkabinet, Amsterdam.

ABOVE: *Ape*, MS Harley 4751, Bestiary in Latin, c1230-40, f. 11. The Bodleian Library, London.

BELOW: '*Amor formae condimentum*', Emblem IV in *Sinne- en Minnebeelden* by Jacob Cats, 1700. Photo © University of London, The Warburg Institute.

ABOVE: *Apes Mocking Writing*, MS 78 D 40, Missal 1323, by Petrus de Raimbeaucourt, f. 124r, Koninklijke Bibliotheek, The Hague.

BELOW: Cornelis van Haarlem, *The Fall of Man*, 1529, 273 x 220cm, oil on canvas, Rijksmuseum, Amsterdam.

OPPOSITE, ABOVE: Albrecht Dürer, *Virgin and Child with Monkey*, c1498-99, engraving, 19.1 x 12.4cm, The Metropolitan Museum of Art, Fletcher Fund, 1919 [19.73.49].

OPPOSITE, BELOW: Christophe Huet, detail of *singerie*, door panel, 1735, Musée Conde, Chantilly. Photo © Giraudon.

All is the bryde never so black.

Which, signifies, as the opening lines of the accompanying verse elaborates:

What blynd-folde doltinghe love is this, appearinghe in our sigt?

How that the ape takes in her younge such wonderfull delight.[7]

The ape was a particularly apt creature to prove the truth of the adage because, as Topsell noted, '... the body of an ape is ridiculous by reason of an indecent likeness and imitation of man'.[8] That is, its appearance in itself was considered a travesty of beauty, attractive only to those of its own kind. Its extreme ugliness was, above all, manifest in its extremities: 'The whole of the ape is hateful, his backside is even more horrible and disgusting.'[9] This accounts for the look of distaste on the face of a scribe in Petrus de Raimbeaucourt's *Apes Mocking Writing*. The scribe's endeavours, in the margins of this early fourteenth-century missal, are being mocked by a troupe of monkeys, one of which commits the ultimate insult by displaying to him its posterior.[10] But, as the proverb goes: 'When apes climb high they show their bare bottoms' or, rather more politely, 'pride goes before a fall'.[11] The ugliness of the ape's bottom was, to the bestiarist, more than merely unfortunate or distasteful; it was a consequence of evil, of the Devil's deceit and hypocrisy that precipitated his fall from grace and brought about the Fall. Ultimately, though, like all proud people, he will be vanquished:

A monkey has no tail (*cauda*). The Devil resembles these beasts; for he has a head, but no scripture (*caudex*)... In the same way, the Devil had a sound *foundation* when he was among the angels of heaven, but he was hypocritical and cunning inside himself, and so he lost his cauda-caudex as a sign that all of him would perish in the end. As the Apostle says: 'Whom the Lord Jesus Christ will kill with the breath of his mouth'.[12]

The most damning characteristic of the ape, therefore, was its *similitude* to the Devil, who was '*diabolus simia Domini*', the ape of God.[13] In Cornelis van Haarlem's *The Fall of Man* an ape holds a cat firmly in its grip, recalling the fable of the cat's paw in which the ape used the cat to draw hot chestnuts out of the fire, as Satan used Eve as the instrument of the Fall. The Dutch emblematist Roemer Visscher interpreted the fable more broadly as an illustration of the iniquity of those who profit by another's misfortunes,[14] and Joost van den Vondel used it as an allegory of those kings who keep themselves out of danger and use their brave countrymen to expand their kingdom, pulling as with the cat's paw all that their heart desires from war's fierce fire.[15] These provide further exemplification of the self-seeking that cares not who or what it destroys, one manifestation of which is lust, fuelled by *Superbia* or Pride. As outlined in Chapter Four, both vices were considered to have been contributory to, and a consequence of the Fall, and both were embodied in the person of the Ape-Devil as they were in Eve.[16] First, apes were considered to be particularly fond of fornication;[17] second, they were fond, like *Superbia*, of admiring themselves in the looking-glass. Aelian notes that in India, monkeys are captured with bogus mirrors into which they:

> ... gaze steadily, imitating what they have seen. And from the reflecting surface opposite their sight there is a surge of strongly gluey substance that gums up their eyelids, when they gaze intently into it. Then being unable to see, they are caught without difficulty, for they are no longer able to escape.[18]

An ape looking into a mirror could also signify the folly of being enslaved by lust, as were Adam and Eve after the Fall.[19] Fittingly, in Hendrik Goltzius' Series of the Five Senses, the monkey is animal representative of the sense of *Taste* eating a fruit – a reminder of the apple of the Tree of Knowledge of Good and Evil?[20] Considering that the animals in Dürer's *Fall of Man*, discussed in the Introduction, may be seen as representative of the humours, an alternative though not incompatible reading of the ape and cat in Cornelis' picture has recently been proposed: 'The sanguine ape is beside Adam, the hothead who yields to temptation, and the choleric cat is beside Eve to exemplify her cruel cunning'.[21] But, as the bestiary notes, the evil done by the Devil was destroyed by Christ. In Dürer's *Virgin and Child with Monkey* a chained Ape could represent the Devil, his lust and desires checked by the Incarnation and Birth of Christ: frequently, in illuminated manuscripts, the ape is represented hunting with an owl, as a lure for birds, representing the human soul[22] but here Christ has the 'bird'.[23]

A descendent of the mediaeval marginalia, though encouraged by Chinese imports, is that popular eighteenth-century art-form the *singerie*, which represented apes dressed in the fashionable attire of the day, mimicking their elegant human counterparts. There is no evidence to suggest that anything more profound is intended by these *singeries* beyond delight in their conceit and wit. In some seventeenth- and eighteenth-century paintings, however, the ape was as frequently represented in its capacity as 'the ape of nature', illustrating the tag *Ars simia naturae* – art is the ape of nature – as a metaphor for painting, that most imitative of arts.[24] Small monkeys frequently appear in representations of artist's studios, and

paintings, popular in the seventeenth century, depicting the art galleries of private collectors. In Chardin's *The Ape Artist*, produced very much in the spirit of the *singerie*, the monkey is copying, as faithfully as it can, a small statuette, itself the product of human art. But so too is the picture, a ridiculous subject which replicates not what is seen by the eyes, but that which resides in the faculty the monkey-artist lacks – the artful imagination.

ABOVE: Picasso, *The Acrobat's Family with a Monkey*, Paris, Spring 1905, gouache, watercolour, pastel and Indian ink on cardboard, 104 x 75cm, Göteborgs Konstmuseum, Göteborg (Z.I.299). Courtesy of Göteborgs Konstmuseum, Göteborg. © DACS 1995.

BELOW: Jean-Baptiste-Siméon Chardin, *The Ape Artist*, n.d., oil on canvas, 73 x 59.5cm, Musée du Louvre, Paris. © Photo RMN.

One of Picasso's two most important monkey works is *Baboon and Young*, a sculpture which he apparently liked to call 'the ancestor'. A female baboon clutches to her chest a helpless infant,[25] a subject remarkably close to bestiary and later representations of the ape (see p163), but does it have a similar meaning? The dedication of the mother to the baby is of course another kind of metaphor for the artist's care over his work, and it would not be surprising if Picasso was making the connection in 1951, when Claude Picasso was four years old and Paloma two. Yet the sculpture was not born out of family equanimity. The destructive Claude was most unhappy when Picasso hijacked two of his still unbroken toy cars in which the artist had seen a potential head of a baboon.[26] Picasso made some sketches of his *Monkey with a Car-head* which demonstrate the miraculous appropriateness of the toys for that job of representation. Following the process of scavenging and recycling which had produced the *Head of a Bull* in 1942 and *The Goat* in 1950, Picasso gave life to his ancestral figure:

> For the ears he used two handles from a pitcher he found
> in a scrap heap near his studio. He took the handles from a
> large pottery bowl called a *pignate*, the most common
> variety in use in Vallauris, and made the shoulders with
> them... The bulging front was a pot which he incised with
> a knife to make a breast and nipple.[27]

The tail was, appropriately, made from a car spring. As with *The Goat*, the remainder was modelled and carved in plaster and wood. The uncanny effect of the mischievous transformations was anticipated in the drawings, where the baboon is clearly quite alive. In fact, Picasso seems to have thought initially not of the very traditional mother-ape and young composition, but of a seated male monkey, very much like *The Monkey* he had created for the series of Buffon prints. The monkey sits and offers something – pleasant or unpleasant – to his neighbour, or perhaps to a human passer-by outside his cage. This seated monkey has an even earlier manifestation in Picasso's work, however, and one which more convincingly relates it to the sculpture. In *The Acrobat's Family with a Monkey*, the male baboon lovingly gazes on a poetic 'holy' family.[28] A number of writers have drawn attention to the origins of the composition in renaissance art.[29] Yet Picasso's use of the monkey seems unlike that found in, for example, Dürer's *Virgin and Child with Monkey*. His compassionate creature, despite its frank genital display in an otherwise chaste work, is no symbol of the fall as in Cornelis' *The Fall of Man*. The scene is not entirely fantasy either, since Picasso, along with his friends Guillaume Apollinaire and Max Jacob, had seen clowns and acrobats working with monkeys at the Cirque Medrano;[30]

ABOVE: Picasso, *Monkey [Le singe]*, 9/2/36, sugar lift aquatint, 36 x 28cm, Victoria & Albert Museum, London (B 339). Photo © Victoria & Albert Museum, London. © DACS 1995.

BELOW: Picasso, *Baboon and Young*, Vallauris, October 1951, original plaster (pottery, two model cars, metal and plaster), 56 x 34 x 71cm, Musée Picasso, Paris (MP 342; S.463 (I)). © Photo RMN. © DACS 1995.

but as Apollinaire noted in his important early text on Picasso, this 'ancestor', set slightly apart from the family group, looks on with almost human scrutiny:

> Primiparous mothers no longer expect the baby to arrive, perhaps because of certain ill-omened, chattering ravens. Miracle! They give birth to future acrobats in the midst of pet monkeys, white horses, and dogs like bears...
>
> ... placed at the frontiers of life, the animals are human, and the sexes are indistinct.[31]

Whereas Apollinaire found something moving and poetic in this idea of a lack of distinction between the monkey and the human, the Comte de Buffon had been worried by it. In the text published along with Picasso's print, we are warned not to be deceived by the monkey's apparent closeness to man. In fact, for the eighteenth-century naturalist, the monkey is far from being the most intelligent animal:

> Just as its nature is lively, its temperament hot, its nature petulant, so none of its feelings are mitigated by education. All its habits are excessive, and more closely resemble the actions of a lunatic than of a man.[32]

Picasso, of course, found something to celebrate in a hot temperament. A number of authors testify to his fascination with the activities of monkeys.[33] Aside from those he had seen in the circus, Picasso knew the resident monkey in a Montmartre cafe called the *Lapin Agile* (which means 'Agile Rabbit'), and reputedly had several pet monkeys of his own in the years before the First World War.[34] According to Penrose, Picasso also enjoyed visiting the Paris Zoo in the Jardin des Plantes, seeing in the monkeys human caricatures.

> ... one day he was present when a Swiss psychiatrist asked Picasso what he thought was the relationship between the drawings, which he had brought, of some of his patients and modern tendencies in art. The reaction of Picasso was to say nothing. Turning his back he proceeded to mime with convincing realism the gestures of a long-armed ape, and with a crayon he produced a meaningless scribble which he thrust at the professor with a chuckle.[35]

The simian artist was an image of himself that he ironically relished. In *Self-caricature and Other Sketches*, of 1903, Picasso the monkey-painter is shown scampering along with brush and chalk behind his ears, scratching his armpit. The modern artist as 'Cheetah' alongside the 'Tarzan' of classicism! In 'borrowing' his son's toys to make *Baboon and Young*, Picasso had truly acted like the thieving and cantankerous 'ancestors' he so admired. Yet the depiction of the monkey-painter had also been, as in Chardin's *The Ape Artist*, a way of attacking slavish imitation posing as originality, or of exemplifying

OPPOSITE, ABOVE: Picasso, *Picasso par lui-même: Self-caricature and Other Sketches*, 1/1/1903, pen on paper, 11.8 x 10.7cm, Museu Picasso, Barcelona (MPB 110.440). © DACS 1995.

OPPOSITE, BELOW: Picasso, *The Woman and the Monkey*, 6/7/66 (I), pencil on paper, 51 x 60cm, Picasso Estate Inv 6264). Courtesy of Musée Picasso, Paris. © DACS 1995.

ABOVE: Picasso, *Monkey with a Car-head: Study for Ape and Young*, c1951, crayon on paper, Picasso Estate (Inv 6351r). Courtesy of Musée Picasso, Paris. © DACS 1995.

Picasso, *Seated Man and Young Girl with Monkey and
Apple*, Vallauris 26/1/54, watercolour on paper, 24 x
32cm, Private Collection (Z.XVI.229). Courtesy of Archives
'Cahiers d'Art'. © DACS 1995.

the predicament of the painter – 'aping' nature – in general.

This deeper self-irony reached an almost derisive fever pitch for Picasso in the series of 180 drawings, watercolours and lithographs, known as 'The Human Comedy', which date from 18th November 1953 to 3rd February 1954, many of which feature monkey-painters or monkey-lovers. Ever since the drawings were published in an issue of *Verve* in 1954,[36] they have been seen as testimony to a gruelling encounter between the famous artist and death (in the guise of advancing old age, manifest in loss of sexual prowess), prompted by his definitive split with Françoise Gilot in late 1953.[37] In these drawings Picasso resorts to the device of the monkey painter, and also, as in *Seated Man and Young Girl with Monkey and Apple*, the monkey as ape of man, tempted in his ignorance by the voluptuous apple of Eve. Picasso was familiar with the tradition of using a monkey to play Adam to a woman's Eve. As a young man he had copied out Paul Verlaine's poem 'Cortège', in which a woman is lusted after by her pet monkey.[38] In a slightly different vain, Brassaï told Picasso a corny and very typical yarn about an amorous marmoset. An adulteress is found out because her pet monkey copulates with her 'Tahitian' lover's own pet marmoset, and as Brassaï – echoing the bestiarists – is quick to point out to Picasso, monkeys imitate the gestures and actions of humans.[39]

Despite the seriousness with which some writers have approached the Human Comedy series as a whole,[40] Hélène Parmelin nevertheless recalls Picasso amusing her with improvised comic stories about the scenes he was inventing[41] – but then, as the first and best essay on the drawings acknowledges, their humour and seriousness are not at all incompatible.[42] *Seated Man and Young Girl with Monkey and Apple* is a lewd but very fine watercolour and is as difficult to place as any good piece of irony. The old man on the left does bear more than a passing similarity to the aging Picasso, although the woman is no woman in particular. She wears a slightly outdated costume, and her monkey is dressed in absurd ruffs and laces. These *may* be another couple of circus performers. Picasso – or *perhaps* the 'Picasso' figure in the drawing – relishes the visual rhyme of the monkey's blue/brown bottom with the apple. The laughing man does not realise, however, that the joke is on him. This certainly seems to be the case twelve years later in *The Woman and the Monkey*. There the inarticulate monkey, in his dotage, faces up to a beautiful Arabian Eve.

Hendrick Goltzius, *Taste* from the Series of the *Five Senses* 1578, engraving by Philip Galle, 14 x 8.8cm, Print Room, Rijksprentenkabinet, Amsterdam.

MONSTERS

On the edge of medieval maps, where the boundaries of the known world ended, a warning is given to the intrepid traveller: 'Here be monsters', together with a myriad of illustrations depicting those creatures which were still believed to be living there.[1] Even though few actually claimed to have seen them, even in the seventeenth century intrepid travellers filled their accounts with apocryphal stories of monsters.[2] Monsters existed not in the imagination, in dreams and nightmares, even though they were the stuff that nightmares were made of, but as very real presences – creatures that battle for possession of human body or soul.

In the bestiaries, therefore, due attention was given to the description and explanation of different types of monsters, yet they are not classified as such but assimilated rather haphazardly into the general hotchpotch of beasts they resemble, however remotely. The manticora, for example, a particularly loathsome beast with the body of a lion, face of a man, a pointed tail with a sting like that of a scorpion, a hissing voice, and a triple row of teeth which delighted in eating human flesh, was placed in the company of the crocodile and the parander, a type of huge deer.[3] Even Topsell, who straightforwardly calls the manticora a 'monster' classes it as a type of hyena.[4] We may consider belief in these strange beasts to be quaint and amusing, but some ninety per cent of these creatures probably have a basis in fact, however garbled these facts may have become in centuries of telling.[5] For example, as noted in Chapter Six, life in the sea was thought to mirror that on earth; why could there not, when mammals like whales and seals and porpoises lived in the sea, be mermaids and mermen there also?[6] As White points out:

> When the dweller by the Nile saw the first Bedouin on horseback, or when Pizarro on his steed dawned dreadfully upon the Mexicans in the New World, the legend of the centaur came into being. Of cavalry we still use the word 'horsemen': and what is a horseman but a centaur?[7]

To the reality of such apparent hybrids as flying foxes, flying fish and bats (flying 'mice'), birds which cannot fly but can run (ostriches) or swim (penguins), together with other curiosities such as the duck-billed platypus and the spiny echidna, only the embellishment of the human imagination is required for monsters and fabulous beasts to emerge. It is easy to imagine

OPPOSITE: Picasso, detail of *Dancing Faun and a Faun Musician before a Naked Woman, by the Sea, an Anchor in her Hand*, 7/1/38, oil on canvas, 50 x 61cm, Picasso Estate (Inv 12823). Courtesy of Musée Picasso, Paris. © DACS 1995.

ABOVE: *Satyr*, MS Bodley 764, Bestiary in Latin c1250, f.17v. The Bodleian Library, Oxford.

Dragon, MS Sloane 278, *Dicta Chrysostomi* in Latin, mid 13th century, f. 57. By permission of The British Library.

that, when the shaman of the painted prehistoric caves donned his animal skin and mask to appropriate the strength of the bison, the stamina of the horse, the agility of the antelope, in the flickering light of a fire, he seemed to *become* that beast, conjuring up its essence and spirit which resided in the shadowy representations on the wall. When the half-memory of what had happened was passed down through the generations, and once the fiction of the half-man half-beast had become a reality in the mind, intermingled with the awful presence of the demons of the night, a monster was born. By the Middle Ages, such are those presences with which the human soul had to do battle: the entirely 'animal' such as dragons and chimeras and those hybrid creatures which share both human and bestial characteristics. In these latter, the tension between rationalism and sensuality, the conflicting demands of the body and the soul, which has characterised much of the animal lore described in the proceeding chapters, was visibly manifest in the one body, a visual exposition of the degeneration of the soul, should the senses take control over humanity's faculty of reason.

The grinning gargoyles that penetrate the deepest recess of the cathedral, the strange hybrid monsters that cavort on the margins of the medieval page, represent bestiality-in-waiting. They lurk on the edge of sacred edifices and texts, poised to divert and amuse those weary of sermons and prayer. Yet there is danger in laughter. As Michael Camille oberves:

> Like the French word *drôle*, or amusing, which has lost its original associations with the uncanny, the gargoyle's mouth becomes the clown's. Yet this process is also one of de-demonisation and lays an increasing emphasis upon human perversity and monstrosity ... No longer did the onlooker see the gargoyle as a hideous primeval beast that had been put to flight by the local bishop or as a dark succubus of the Devil, it became a reflection of the possible perversity in oneself.[8]

Yet, conversely, what causes this perversity but the temptations of the Devil himself and his succubi? We must also question whether mediaeval gargoyles had any sort of definable function. Emile Mâle argues that sometimes they were produced for no more reason than delight in fantasy, citing Saint Bernard who claimed that he did not understand them and considered them dangerous because they hindered the mind's meditation on the will of God.[9] Francis Klingender, on the other hand, argues that they are indeed highly symbolic, the error being to try and interpret them too precisely by applying to them the anachronistic classificatory procedures that properly belong to nineteenth-century science. The point is, Klingender argues, that any single image may assume a wide range of different and often contradictory subsidiary meanings depending on context.[10] This method is not dissimilar to those used by the bestiaries, and it is probably safe to assume that at very least these monsters grinning down from even the most sacred recesses of the cathedral, were calculated to instil in the congregation a sense that even where one would expect one's soul to be safe, there lurk demons. Beyond this, the mediaeval craftsman was probably free to indulge his own fancies and fantasies.

The same fancy informs bestiary representation of monsters, as we might expect amongst the most idiosyncratic of the illustrations. It could hardly be recognised, for example, that the dragon reproduced here, apparently in combat with an elephant, is that demonic creature which is

> ... like the devil, the fairest of all serpents, who often leaves his cave to rush into the air; the air glows because of him, because the devil rises from his abyss and transforms himself into an angel of light, deceiving fools with hopes of vain glory and human pleasures.[11]

Similarly, it is difficult to equate either the illustration (see p173) or the description of the satyr with its demonic goat-manifestation:

> There are also creatures called satyrs, with almost pleasing faces and strange, restless gestures, They are hairy almost all over, and are different from the others. They have beards and broad tails. They are not difficult to catch, but difficult to keep alive. They can only live under their native Ethiopian sky.[12]

These are clearly not the creatures which, as discussed in the goat section, provided the prototype for mediaeval depictions of Satan and which were 'a terrible warning of what man would become if he surrendered himself to the Devil.'[13] Neither do they appear to be the lustful creatures who, as in the detail from Rubens' *The Feast of Venus Verticordia*, perform lascivious dances with nymphs or lust after and ravish sleeping nymphs, as 'Jove once in a satyr's guise had got Antiope with twins'.[14] This latter episode, (see for example Van Dyck's *Jupiter and Antiope*) was a favourite vehicle for representing the recumbent female nude. On the contrary, satyrs are presented in the bestiary and elsewhere as rather innocent creatures and even when Dürer cast his *Satyr Family* as a sort of parodic Holy Family, the image is nevertheless idyllic rather than demonic.[15] Indeed, the satyr appears to have been the subject of some confusion. The satyr was considered a type of ape, but even this equation did not make them any more devil-like in the bestiarist's eyes. Topsell went to considerable trouble to clear the matter up, but

ABOVE: Albrecht Dürer, *Satyr Family*, 1505, engraving, 11.5 x 7cm, Clarence Buckingham Coll., Art Institute, Chicago. Photograph © 1995, The Art Insitute of Chicago. All Rights Reserved.

OVERLEAF, ABOVE: Picasso, *Dancing Faun and a Faun Musician before a Naked Woman, by the Sea, an Anchor in her Hand*, 7/1/38, oil on canvas, 50 x 61cm, Picasso Estate (Inv 12823). Courtesy of Musée Picasso, Paris. © DACS 1995.

OVERLEAF, BELOW: Sir Peter Paul Rubens, detail from *The Feast of Venus Verticordia*, mid-1630s, oil on canvas, 217 x 350cm, Kunshistorisches Museum, Vienna.

PAGE 177, ABOVE: Picasso, *Faun unveiling a Woman*, 12/6/36, aquatint, 31.7 x 41.7cm, Tate Gallery, London (B 230). © DACS 1995.

PAGE 177, BELOW: Sir Anthony van Dyck, *Jupiter and Antiope*, first half 17th century, oil on canvas, 150 x 206cm, Museum voor Schone Kunsten, Ghent. Photo Scala, Florence.

ABOVE: Jean Auguste Dominique Ingres, *Oedipus and the Sphinx*, c1826-28, oil on canvas, 17.8 x 13.7cm, National Gallery, London. Reproduced by courtesy of the Trustees, The National Gallery, London.

BELOW: *Aegopithecus*, from *The Historie of Foure-footed Beasts* by Edward Topsell, 1607, Bodleian (M.3.14 Th.). The Bodleian Library, Oxford.

although he restored to the satyr its association with the devil, and described it as being a thoroughly lustful creature, he begins his account by playing down their association with goats:

> ... the Satyres a most rare and most seldom seen Beast, hath occasioned others to thinke it was the Devill; and the Poets with their Apes, the Painters, Limners and Carvers, to increase that superstition, have therefore described him with hornes on his head, and feete like Goates, whereas Satyres have neither of both. And it may be that Devils have at some time appeared to men in this likenes, as they have done in the likenes of the *onocentaure* and wild Asse, and other shapes, it being also probable, that Devils take not any daenomination or shape from Satyres, but rather the Apes themselves from Devils whom they resemble ...[16]

As the illustration demonstrates, the satyr according to Topsell is in appearance much more like an ithyphallic ape. It is that other kind of ape, the Aegopithecus (see below) which has the appearance of a goat – according to Topsell, Pan was such a creature.[17] Equally the appearance of the Sphinx was subject to some confusion. Again, Topsell identifies it as a type of ape with female breasts (see opposite, above) which is thoroughly unlike the Sphinx of classical antiquity which had a human head and the body of a lion or griffon as depicted by Ingres in his *Oedipus and the Sphinx*.

With the hindsight of the twentieth century we may be tempted to dismiss all this conjecture as charming babble. But we have found our own monsters, conjured from the darkest recesses of the mind, and as we discover them, fresh urgency is given to the old myths.

Through the psychoanalytical writings of Freud, the name of Oedipus has become inextricably linked with the 'oedipus complex', that is, the destructive infantile fixation of a boy for his mother. In the original story Oedipus, King of Thebes, in his quest for truth, confronted the sphinx and correctly answered its riddle: 'What goes on four feet, on two feet and three, but the more feet it goes on the weaker it be?' The answer is man, who crawls as a baby and uses a stick in old age.[18] By giving the correct reply, Oedipus destroyed the Sphinx and avoided the fate of earlier travellers who, unable to answer the riddle, were devoured by this monster. It is not surprising, therefore, that the Sphinx's riddle has itself been subject to 'Freudian' interpretation:

> Róheim considered that it belonged to the group of riddles which had to do with the father and mother in bed, with the observer first seeing four legs (the man on all fours),

then the two outstretched legs of the woman, and finally the third leg which, in most variants of the riddle, mysteriously disappears.[19]

Above all, however, the Sphinx is yet another example of the predatory, destructive female, considered the most pernicious and dangerous of hybrid beasts, epitomised in the Jewish and Christian religions by Eve. Her features were sometimes, as in Hugo van der Goes' *The Fall* superimposed on the body of the serpent or snake. The Devil is therefore presented as her alter-ego and perpetuates the belief (discussed in Chapter Four) that Eve was the Devil's familiar used by him as the instrument of the Fall. Snakes have long been associated with women, and in Near-Eastern religions were thought to control wisdom, magic immortality and fertility.[20] But the snake was also, from earliest times, a phallic totem, and as Rowland points out, 'Since the church attributed pacts with the Devil to primarily sexual motives, throughout the Middle Ages he continued to be represented as a gigantic serpent or dragon with tail, penis and even arms composed of snakes.'[21] Thus 'The phallic shape of the serpent establishes his purpose turning him into an irresistible suitor for the woman calling forth from her the lust latent in her since her creation.'[22] As one of the old Jewish legends had it, '... the serpent engaged to pluck the fruit for her. Thereupon [she] opened the gate of paradise and he slipped in.'[23] Talmudic myth confused the issue still further by asserting that it was Lilith, the first woman and first wife of Adam who became a serpent and gave Eve forbidden knowledge and it was probably this myth, superimposed on the Christian one which is, above all, responsible for the representation of the serpent with a female countenance.[24]

That the quintessentially male devil could thus be given female form, is symptomatic of the extent to which the power of female seduction was considered fearsomely 'monstrous'. Various forms of monster-women expressed this belief. Mermaids, half-fish, half-women, were probably originally fertility or fish goddesses, but to the medieval imagination they were sirens, often represented with a fish's tail, as in the illustration overleaf but more commonly believed to have birdlike characteristics, on account of their irresistibly sweet voice which lured sailors to their death.[25] Typically, these 'stout whores' (as the mediaeval theologians called them) were also subject to conflicting interpretation in the bestiaries.[26] One describes them as:

> ... white serpents with wings ... which run faster than horses, and are also said to fly. Their poison is such that the victim is dead before he feels the pain of their bite.[27]

Another, states that;

ABOVE: *Sphinga* or *Sphinx*, from *The Historie of Foure-footed Beasts* by Edward Topsell, 1607, Bodleian (M.3.14 Th.). The Bodleian Library, Oxford.

BELOW: *Satyr*, from *The Historie of Foure-footed Beasts* by Edward Topsell, 1607, Bodleian (M.3.14 Th.). The Bodleian Library, Oxford.

The SIRENAE (Sirens), so Physiologus says, are deadly creatures who are made like human beings from the head to the navel, while their lower parts down to the feet are winged. They give forth musical songs in a melodious manner, which songs are very lovely, and thus they charm the ears of sailormen and allure them to themselves. They entice the hearing of these poor chaps by a wonderful sweetness of rhythm, and put them to sleep. At last, when they see that the sailors are slumbering, they pounce upon them and tear them to bits.[28]

As this bestiary points out, reiterating the *Physiologus*, the fate of these men acts as a caution to all humans who are 'tricked by pretty voices ... charmed by indelicacies, ostentation and pleasures, or when they become licentious with comedies, tragedies and various ditties.'[29] According to the *Physiologus*, the same moral may be drawn from the onocentaur, companion of the siren as the illustration reproduced here demonstrates.[30] Onocentaurs were, as their name suggests, sea-centaurs though rather than being half-horse, were half-ass, though the distinction hardly matters: just as the ass, as discussed in Chapter Two two, was considered a libidinous creature, so too was the horse.[31] Centaurs, therefore, 'always symbolised lust'.[32] Centaurs were quite unequivocally male, which makes Lear's misogynist rant so full of loathing and disgust:

> Down from the waist they are all centaurs,
> Though women all above.
> But to the girdle do the gods inherit
> beneath is all the fiend's.
> There's hell, there's darkness, there is the sulphurous pit;
> burning, scalding, stench, consumption: fie, fie, fie, pah, pah![33]

These half-human half-bestial creatures represent that duality in humans which has characterised representation of animals since earliest times: humans were made in the image of God, and the defilement of the human body with beastly characteristics was nothing short of odious. Women were not always considered in such a dim light, however. To Renaissance humanists, the centaur personified man's lower, animal nature and may be contrasted with the highest wisdom symbolised by Minerva.[34] This is possibly the meaning behind Botticelli's strange *Pallas and the Centaur* – the taming of base desire by the restraint of wisdom and reason. For once, the old gendered roles have been revised.

It remains to consider that unique monster, a dreadful beast created by a union most foul: Picasso's alter-ego, The Minotaur. It has been long believed that offspring could be engendered by sexual congress between man and beast, which as Thomas notes, shows that 'in popular estimation at least, man was

ABOVE: *Siren & Onocentaur*, MS Laud Misc. 247, Bestiary in Latin, n.d., f. 147r. The Bodleian Library, Oxford.

BELOW: Hugo van der Goes, *The Fall*, c1470, 32.3 × 21.9cm, Kunshistorisches Museum, Vienna.

not so distinct a species that he could not breed with beasts.'[35] It is on this belief that the myth of the Minotaur depends. As Ovid relates in the *Metamorphoses*, the union that produced the Minotaur was unnatural, and bestial and punished by the production of a monstrous offspring. Before considering his account, however, it is worth noting the role played by the Minotaur within the great interweaving mesh of ancient ritual that has occupied such an important place in our own bestiary. From this, we may gauge a little more of Picasso's fascination with the beast. Frazer relates the myth of the Minotaur to that of the Talos:

> … a bronze man who clutched people to his breast and leaped with them into the fire, so that they were roasted alive. He is said to have been given by Zeus to Europa, or by Hephaestus to Minos, to guard the island of Crete, which he patrolled thrice daily. According to this account he was a bull, according to another he was the sun. Probably he was identical with the Minotaur, and stripped of his mythological features was nothing but a bronze image of the sun represented as a man with a bull's head.[36]

Given the association, outlined in Chapter One, of the bull with the sun and great importance of bulls in Cretan ritual, such an origin for the myth is plausible. It is also possible that the Minotaur may illustrate a transition from the ritual sacrifice of the king to that of an animal surrogate.[37] In many cultures, the king was sacrificed at the end of a fixed term in order to ensure renewal with the godhead.[38] It is perhaps also with this connection that seven youths and maidens were sent to Minos every eight years to be sacrificed to the Minotaur – although as Graves relates, only the youths were actually killed: the maidens probably 'became attendants on the moon-priestess, and performed acrobatic feats at bullfights, such as are shown in Cretan works of art: a dangerous but not necessarily fatal sport.'[39] Ovid, however, tells a modified story.

King Minos was the offspring of Zeus, who, in the shape of a bull, had ravished Europa. In turn, the Minotaur was a result of the adulterous liaison between Minos' wife Pasiphaë and a beautiful bull. Evidently, there was one rule for gods, and another for women! This 'monstrous hybrid beast', with the head of a bull and the body of a man, 'Declared the queen's obscene adultery'[40] and even in the Renaissance stood for the flouting of natural and divine law and the overthrow of reason for the sake of passion.[41] From shame, Minos hid the beast in a labyrinth designed by the great architect Daedalus, 'and fed him twice on Attic blood, lot-chosen each nine years until the third choice mastered him.'[42] This third lot included Theseus. Minos' own daughter, Ariadne, fell in love with Theseus and

Sandro Botticelli, *Pallas and the Centaur*, early 1480s, oil on canvas, 207 x 148cm, Uffizi, Florence.

entrusted him a magic ball of thread which Daedalus had given her, thus he was able to find his way into the labyrinth, kill the sleeping Minotaur and by rolling the thread back into a ball, find his way out again. The episode was common on Greek vases[43] and found an unlikely home in mediaeval churches where the labyrinth was a symbol of Hell into which Theseus, like Christ, descended in order that humankind may be redeemed from the bestial evil that held it prisoner.[44]

Gustave Moreau chose to represent *The Athenians delivered to the Minotaur*, yet within the painting only a glimpse of this fearsome creature can be seen. Frederick Watts, however, produced a much stranger picture: the Minotaur leans on a parapet, looking out into the distance. He is represented as much more bull than man, but is no more fearsome for that. Rather, this most beastly of beasts is a pathetic creature, imprisoned by its own desires and animal nature, and condemned to a life of solitude and loneliness.

ABOVE: Anon. Greek, *Theseus and the Minotaur*, Attic black-figure amphora (Group E) from Vulci, British Museum, London (B 205, ABV 136.55). Copyright British Museum.

BELOW: Picasso, *Fauns and Goat*, 1959, colour linocut, 53 x 64cm, Galerie Louise Leiris, Paris (B 934). © DACS 1995.

It is necessary for you to see yourself die
To know that you still live
The tide is high and your heart is very low
Son of the earth flower-eater fruit of ashes
In your bosom darkness forever covers the sky.[45]

As the preceding chapters have shown, Picasso's depictions of animals generally went beyond naturalism, and drew upon the potency of animal symbolism which he knew from the pictorial tradition. In a sense, however, we have also seen that Picasso often tried to go further, to reinvigorate something more mystical. Sometimes Picasso recalled the animism of classical myth, where human and divine characters take on the forms of the beasts for some fateful purpose. At other moments he makes elaborate quasi-magical divinations, forging connections between natural phenomena and his own destiny, a practice which underpins the medieval bestiary. These habits are particularly evident when Picasso moves away from animal forms, and represents instead the imaginary creatures which exist at the boundaries of human and animal form, monsters. There were of course no monsters in the Comte de Buffon's enlightened and scientific century, and none in Picasso's prints for the *Histoire Naturelle*. It is appropriate though that a Picasso bestiary should end in the half-world of monsters, where the half-human identities which have so far been kept concealed in animal forms should be allowed their painful emergence into the artist's imagination.

Classical myths provide the main source for the particular monster so favoured by Picasso, the Minotaur. These tales represent the origins of Greek and Roman civilization in a struggle with divine will, and show how the cunning, wisdom and courage of mortals is pitted against the whims and vengeful moods of the gods. They also show that human ambition and desire has its limitations, and that when those limits are not observed things can go very badly wrong. On the one hand, then, stories of the Minotaur and other monsters can be personal allegories, diaristic confessions of a feeling of guilt or punishment for past transgressions against family, friends or lovers. On the other hand, however, Picasso's return to classical myth was a gesture, a kind of search for a story appropriate to art, at a time when – for him – art's magical power was regrettably somewhat diminished.

Picasso's forays into classical myths, much inspired by Surrealism, took place long after the rise of science had rendered these great accounts of the place of people in the world *mere* stories. Even in mediaeval Europe, when Christianity had much reason to be suspicious of pagan wisdom, the magical

Picasso, *Chimera with the Head of a Horse*, Boisgeloup 24/4/35, China ink on paper, 17 x 25.5cm, Picasso Estate (Inv 3828). Photo © ET Archive © DACS 1995.

significance of nature, and the need to tell stories about it, persisted, as the bestiary form shows. Modern science and technology, driven by ideas of utility and domination over nature, however, had little place for art. There is a long and tortuous passage from 'pagan' culture, deriving its meanings from myth and art, to mediaeval thought, combining myth and systematic religion, into modern scientific rationalism. This history gives to Picasso's bestiary its poignancy, its mood of nostalgia, which is nowhere more keenly felt than in his depictions of the monsters of classical myth. It is of course difficult to say what it would be like to live in a culture and time when animism and divination were not undermined by the rationalism of western science. Perhaps the magical appeal of such a time for artists like Picasso is more responsible for our sense of the existence of such a time than any possible historical knowledge.

For the philosopher Friedrich Nietzsche, much admired, though probably not much read,[46] by Picasso, scientific 'reason' claimed far too much 'truth' for itself.[47] Scientific belief in cause and effect could not tolerate the apparent irrationalism of art and pagan religion. Science therefore forced art to *make sense*, and thereby deprived it of its chief power: the power to make a truce with the unknowable forces of nature. Art for the young Nietzsche was a rite closely related to an acknowledgement of human suffering in the face of nature – but it was always a *joyous*, drunken, and priapic rite, as it sometimes seemed to be for Picasso:

> In song and dance man expresses himself as a member of a community; he has forgotten how to walk and speak and is on the way to flying into the air, dancing. His very gestures express enchantment. Just as the animals now talk, and the earth yields milk and honey, supernatural sounds emanate from him, too: he feels like a god, he himself now walks about enchanted, in ecstasy, like the gods he saw walking in his dreams. He is no longer an artist, he has become a work of art: in these paroxysms of intoxication the artistic power of all nature reveals itself to the highest gratification of the primordial unity.[48]

The excitable satyr in *Fauns and Goat*, who, as the colourful linocut shows, is closely related, at least in form, to the randy goat, appears additionally in *Dancing Faun and a Faun Musician before a Naked Woman, by the Sea, an Anchor in her Hand*, from 1934.[49] In this strange example, he dons a stripy bathing suit and writhes in a comical dance before a sort of sea nymph. He is accompanied by another faun on the panpipes. Yet, as if in a reminder of the tragic nature of the dance of Dionysos,[50] this merry scene came at the end of a week during which Picasso had painted three works showing the rescue of a wounded and far from priapic faun by a more ethereal nymph.[51] The painting and the lithograph are in this way atypical: Picasso's monsters are much more often shrouded in tragedy than revelling in simple bacchic merriment. In *Faun unveiling a Woman*, the faun who has the opportunity to gaze upon the object of his desire is far from overcome with mere sexual excitement, rather he is transfixed. This touching scene appeared in *The Vollard Suite*, a series of a hundred prints on diverse themes compiled by Ambroise Vollard, who also initiated the Buffon project. The use of aquatint, together with scraper and burin, allowed Picasso to obtain the dramatic effect of flooding morning sunlight or perhaps moonlight,[52] and the delicate traceries of line and wash. The result is undoubtedly one of Picasso's finest works in the print medium. *The Vollard Suite*, unlike the Buffon series, was not commissioned by Vollard, but selected from existing plates made by Picasso between 16th September 1930 and 12th June 1936, the latter being the date of the *Faun unveiling a Woman*.[53] For this reason, the make up of this imposing set of prints is very diverse. The prints come in different sizes, and the subjects vary considerably, although the prevailing style and mood is Hellenistic.

The composition of *Faun unveiling a Woman* is traditional, and has recently been compared to Ingres' *Jupiter and Antiope* of 1851.[54] Brigitte Baer has argued convincingly that Picasso's source is most likely to be a print by Rembrandt of 1659.[55] An equally close comparison, although the composition is reversed, is to be found in Van Dyck's version of *Jupiter and Antiope*. Here the leering faun draws back the sumptuous materials in which Antiope is swathed. In the myth of Jupiter and Antiope, the god visits the beautiful woman in the form of a faun, after which, in shame and disgrace, she bears twins. The focus of the subject for Picasso and his predecessors was the first sight which the god obtains of the sleeping Antiope. The attraction of the subject for Picasso, who well understood the link between sight, aesthetic pleasure and lust, is obvious.[56] Furthermore, the guise of the god in the form of a beast-man captures the ambiguities of the look which he casts over the woman: a combination of sexual desire and a chaste and elevated pleasure. The picture thus recapitulates a theme which had fascinated Picasso for many years, and which would continue to do so, particularly in his last prints.[57]

The faun seems in this way to bear comparison with the Minotaur.[58] It might be thought that the symbolic potential of the Minotaur would be similarly exhausted in his part-human part-animal desire for women. However, the immense number of Minotaurs, and diversity of situations in which they appear

in Picasso's work, indicates that there is much more to be said. Picasso's Minotaur is not merely confined to the exact details of the myth. In *The Vollard Suite* for example, Picasso imagined Minotaurs as the improbable:

> ... rich *seigneurs* of the island. They know they're monsters and they live, like dandies and dilettantes everywhere, the kind of existence that reeks of decadence in houses filled up by works of art by the most fashionable painters and sculptors. They love being surrounded by pretty women. They get the local fishermen to go out and round up girls from the neighbouring islands. After the heat of the day passed, they bring in the sculptors and their models for parties, with music and dancing, and everybody gorges himself on mussels and champagne until melancholy fades away and euphoria takes over.[59]

In *Minotaur with a Glass*, a painting of seigneur Minotaur drowning his sorrows, Picasso gives a clue to one dimension of the deeper fascination of this beast. Whereas the satyr or faun is sometimes a carefree sinner, the Minotaur is an unfortunate creature: hideously ugly, condemned to lust, cursed with self-reflection.

The idea that the personality is comprised of opposing elements or forces is of course a very old one, but one of the greatest expressions of the theme (outside of religion) is in Sigmund Freud's division of the mind into the conscious and the unconscious. The unconscious is the banished part of human life: desire for sexual gratification at any cost and by any means, even including death. The prohibitions placed upon unconscious desires by society (and in the individual by consciousness) mean that it must find all manner of avenues for expression. During sleep, the unconscious forces the mind into an apparently inexplicable realm, that of dreams, where symbols and metaphors are underwritten by desires that dare not speak their name. These aspects of Freud's theory were taken up in André Breton's Surrealism (meaning 'above' or 'beyond' realism), and one can see how poets, writers and artists might find succour in them. The unconscious represents the dark force behind true creativity, the imagination, working to find ever new means of expression for its illegal desires. Its jailor, consciousness, is the agent of social and moral order, which must limit and channel desire into fixed patterns. Consciousness is like Nietzsche's enemy rational science: it puts human desire and creativity into a straitjacket of cause and effect. For Breton and his fellow surrealists, art and poetry needed to lead the way in breaking out of this prison imposed by a social order and a scientific spirit which they viewed as completely bankrupt, both morally and politically.[60] Needless

OPPOSITE, ABOVE: George Frederic Watts, *Minotaur*, 1878, oil on canvas, 118.1 x 94.5cm, Tate Gallery, London.

OPPOSITE, BELOW: Picasso, *Minotaur with a Glass*, 29/4/58-31/5/58, oil on canvas, 146 x 114cm, Picasso Estate (Inv 13345; Z.XVIII.98). Courtesy of Musée Picasso, Paris, © DACS 1995.

ABOVE: Picasso, *Head of a Bull (Minotaur)*, Cannes 1958, wood, sawn and painted, 126.5 x 97cm, Private Collection, Courtesy Thomas Ammann Fine Art, Zurich (S.546a). © DACS 1995.

BELOW: Picasso, *Maquette for the cover of* Minotaure, Paris, May 1933, collage: pencil on paper, corrugated cardboard, silver foil, ribbon, wallpaper painted with gold paint and gouache, paper doily, burnt linen, leaves, tacks, and charcoal on wood, 48.5 x 41cm, Museum of Modern Art, New York. Gift of Mr and Mrs Alexandre P Rosenberg. Photograph © 1995 The Museum of Modern Art, New York. © DACS 1995.

to say, Surrealism saw little merit in the aesthetics of the existing social order and looked to overturn them in the artistic equivalent of a *coup d'état*.[61] Beauty would be replaced by the extraordinary workings of the unconscious laid bare, by what Breton called 'the Marvellous'. Above all else, Surrealism was a highly poetic but also intellectual movement, whose origins and aspirations went far beyond the realm of visual art.

Breton's first Surrealist Manifesto was published in 1924. In 1928 Picasso depicted his first Minotaur.[62] The destinies of the three – Surrealism, Picasso and his Minotaur[63] – were to become intimately linked in 1933 when Albert Skira published the first issue of a periodical bearing the name of the mythological beast.[64] The Minotaur was the perfect symbol for the Surrealists: for them, the struggle between Theseus and the Minotaur could represent the struggle between the conscious and the unconscious, or perhaps the Minotaur's own hybrid nature in itself enshrined the conflict?[65] Furthermore, his mythic origin echoed Freud's use of Greek myths as symbols of certain psychic complexes (eg the famous Oedipus Complex), and similarly added credence to the Surrealism's claim to reinterpret the history of human cultures. Picasso made the cover of that first issue (see below), a collage on wood, like an improvised altarpiece from a roadside shrine, showing a heroic beast holding out a dagger of defiance. The paradoxical nature of this work has been noted before[66] – the Minotaur appears to hold the short dagger employed by the matador at the very end of the bullfight, to give the *coup de grâce* to the bull.

Aside from the poetic and intellectual context of Surrealism, and the general preoccupation which Picasso had cherished for many years with the humanised animal, the mythic Minotaur has a facility which further drew the artist to him: insight. The Minotaur, like the owl, sees in the dark. In *Head of a Bull (Minotaur)*, a wood sculpture of 1958, formally related to the *Drinking Minotaur*, Picasso paid tribute to the penetrating eyes of this creature of darkness.[67] Yet the Minotaur must remain imprisoned in his labyrinth, since the bright light by which ordinary men see will blind him. Fifteen of the plates in *The Vollard Suite* are devoted to the theme of the Minotaur.[68] Two of these show the Minotaur dying in a bullring, and four others a *blind* minotaur, clutching a stick, led along a shore by a little girl.[69] Coming as they do after orgiastic and tender scenes of the Minotaur in love and in the sculptor's studio, it seems right to say that Picasso's interest in the Minotaur went further than the Surrealist adoption of the beast as an icon suggests, and that instead Picasso wanted to tell a story about him. The blind Minotaur combines a number of myths.[70] Theseus, the Minotaur's killer, blinded by the darkness of the Labyrinth, is guided to his prey by Ariadne's thread. Oedipus, blinded in punishment for unwitting incest, is led to Colonus, where he will die, by Antigone. Picasso prepared for the prints in two marvellous drawings. In the first, *Blind Minotaur led by a Little Girl*, which was made on the same day as the first of the four *Vollard Suite* prints, he took a large sheet of paper and worked in charcoal, placing the Minotaur and his guide in a sombre and barren night.[71] The Minotaur stares up into the blackness and seems to moan, struggling to speak. This grim open-mouthed posture is repeated in all versions of the composition. The little girl clutches a bunch of flowers or herbs, a detail for which there is no clear significance.[72] In *Blind Minotaur led by a Young Girl*, a study which is closer to the remaining three prints, the Minotaur is hurried by the girl, and his ghastly fate attracts the attention of two fishermen hauling in their nets from a boat near the shore.[73] This work was made using a variety of media, anticipating the coloured versions of the final print, showing the Minotaur once again led along at night. In this second study, the arms of the Minotaur distend in a visually expressive evocation of his dependency on the girl, on his need to keep her head and hand in his grasp.

In piling up story upon story, and myth upon myth, Picasso enjoyed the freedom and creative potential of what Freud called 'the dreamwork'. Symbols are 'condensed' and identities 'displaced'.[74] At the same time Picasso's use of the unforgiving print medium, under the tutelage of Roger Lacourière, reached a peak of intensity with the *Minotauromachia*.[75] The title of the work is an extension of *tauromachia*, meaning bullfight, which has been the title of Goya's famous series of prints (see p42). Sitting in Lacourière's studio on a Saturday early in 1935, Picasso began work on the comparatively vast copper plate. Etching was combined with scraper and burin, to conjure in elaborate detail from the metal seven actors on another distant shore. On the left a man in a loin cloth climbs a ladder and looks down at the scene. To his right two women look out of a window in a dark tower, either down at their two doves or towards the glimmer of a candle. The candle is held aloft by a little girl, probably the same girl who led the Minotaur in his blindness, since she also clutches a bouquet. Between her and the Minotaur is a *femme-torero*, apparently wounded, born along on the back of a gutted mare. The horse gags in the direction of the huge Minotaur, whose hand seems to touch that of the *femme-torero*, which still clasps the executioner's sword, the *estoc*. The Minotaur thus appears an aggressor at first glance, since he can be mistakenly viewed as carrying the sword. His left hand gesture, on the other hand, can seem to cover a wound, whereas in fact he is carrying a heavy sack over

ABOVE: Picasso, *Minotauromachia*, VIIth state, Paris 23/3/35, etching and scraper, 49.5 x 69.3cm, Fitzwilliam Museum, Cambridge (G 573). © DACS 1995.

BELOW: Picasso, *Blind Minotaur led by a Young Girl*, 1934, mixed media, 35 x 51cm, Klaus Hegewisch Collection, Hamburg. Courtesy of Klaus Hegewisch. © DACS 1995.

ABOVE: Picasso, *Blind Minotaur led by a Little Girl*, Boisgeloup, 22/9/34, charcoal on paper, 51 x 35cm, Klaus Hegewisch Collection, Hamburg. Courtesy of Klaus Hegewisch. © DACS 1995.

BELOW: Picasso, *The Winged Horse*, 1948, watercolour and ink on paper, 46 x 38cm, Picasso Estate (Inv 5056). Courtesy of Musée Picasso, Paris. © DACS 1995.

his right shoulder. With his right arm, however, he unmistakeably shields his eyes from the candle. This Minotaur is not blind, but is afraid of the light. On the horizon a distant fishing boat is blown along by the wind. The elements of the print recall paintings of the descent from the cross (the man on the ladder); the bullfight (the horse and *femme-torero*, the spectators); rites of passage (the girl and bouquet); and, of course, the oneiric world of the myth itself. The *Minotauromachia* has often been seen as an allegory of the clash of light (truth) and dark (evil).[76] To this one must add that once again, Picasso's identification with his beast, and especially the *blind* Minotaur, is unquestionable. In 1937 Dora Maar photographed Picasso on the beach near Mougins, eyes closed, a stick in one hand, and the bleached skull of an ox in the other.[77] Picasso's Minotaur charades, combined with the religious, mythic and sporting allusions in the *Minotauromachia*, make the print like a dream: a paradise for interpretation. The fact that the print coincides with Picasso's first intense foray into stream of consciousness prose, and a crisis in his relations with Olga Koklova, has led many to see the print as an allegory of love and separation, and to seek behind the appearances the real characters Marie-Thérèse Walter, Picasso, Olga, and Dora Maar.[78] Allegory is also an invitation to tell further stories, however, to fantasise, to invent. Like all of Picasso's work influenced by Surrealism, the *Minotauromachia* calls for a less 'scientific', more creative, response. To put it another way, what Freud called the 'manifest content' of a dream, even when its 'latent content' is puzzled out, retains its ability to haunt the waking mind.

In the second chapter of this book, it was noted that a pure white Pegasus, a classical horse which so defined one aspect of human culture for Georges Bataille, is largely absent from Picasso's work. On the other hand, as we have seen before, the horse is perfectly capable of becoming a monstrosity, especially when it has been opened up by the horns of the bull – or perhaps a Minotaur? In *The Winged Horse*, of 1948, Picasso depicted a winged horse, with its innards shooting out of a wound, surrounded by black birds of prey. The subject is close to a stage instruction in one of Picasso's own plays, *The Four Little Girls*, written during the same period:

> Enter an enormous winged white horse dragging its entrails, surrounded by wings, an owl perched on its head, it stands for a brief moment in front of the little girl then disappears at the other end of the stage.[79]

Surprisingly, the most revolting monster in Picasso's work, the most grotesque and aberrant creature, is in large part a horse. Dating from 24th April 1935, a few weeks after the *Minotauromachia*, Picasso drew a chimera (see p183) with the face of a canker-ridden horse, gave it a formless body, and the talons of a vicious bird. For Roland Penrose, this creature might have begun as a caricature of a person sitting in a cafe.[80] The result however, is a vivid embodiment of the imagery in Yeats' apocalyptic poem, 'The Second Coming':

> ... somewhere in the sands of the desert
> A shape with a lion body and the head of a man,
> A gaze blank and pitiless as the sun
> Is moving its slow thighs, while all about it
> Reel shadows of the indignant desert birds.
> The darkness drops again; but now I know
> That twenty centuries of stony sleep
> Were vexed to nightmare by a rocking cradle,
> And what rough beast, its hour come round at last,
> Slouches towards Jerusalem to be born?[81]

Yeats wrote his poem towards the end of the First World War, and his vision of a satanic new messiah is inevitably loaded with anxiety over the destiny of Europe. Similarly, it was the brutal ascendancy of the posturing fascist general Franco in Spain, and the resulting slaughter of the Spanish Civil War, which brought forth Picasso's most daemonic, freakish and hilarious invention: two prints entitled the *Dream and Lie of Franco*. They laid out some of the iconography used so effectively during the same period in *Guernica*, and like *Guernica* were produced not in poetic recollection of any myth, but in a spirit of unrelenting satire with a quite explicit propagandist function. *Dream and Lie of Franco* consists of eighteen small scenes together with a text, given in full below, written by Picasso on his first day of working on the plates.[82] Although there is still some debate on the matter, it would seem that Picasso produced the scenes with view to having them printed, cut up, and sold as individual 'postcards' in aid of the Republican cause.[83] This plan was later abandoned, and instead the two prints, together with a print of the text in Picasso's handwriting, a typescript, an English translation, and Picasso's own cover design, were sold in an edition of one thousand.

Picasso seems to have ignored the fact that everything he had drawn would appear in reverse after printing. He wrote the date 8th January 1937 on the plates, and added the date of completion (7th June 1937) on the second, without any effort at mirror writing. Similarly, the scenes were drawn on the plate from top left to bottom right, which means top right to bottom left in the print. There are nine scenes on each plate. Twelve of the scenes represent the exploits of the dreaming and lying Franco, the moustachioed 'polyp' mentioned in Picasso's text. In the eleventh panel a female soldier lies in a field, and in the twelfth a horse has collapsed on its male rider. The four last

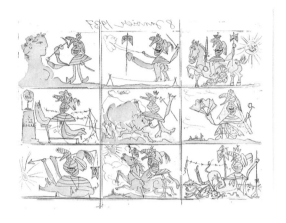

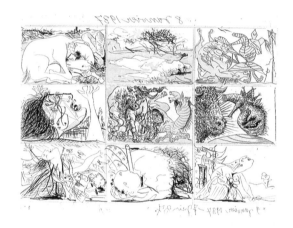

ABOVE: Picasso, *Dream and Lie of Franco I*, 8/1/37 with aquatint added 25/5/37, etching and aquatint on paper, 31.7 x 42.2cm, British Museum, London (B 297). Copyright British Museum. © DACS 1995.

BELOW: Picasso, *Dream and Lie of Franco II*, 8/1/37 with aquatint added 25/5/37 and final four panels added 7/6/37, etching and aquatint on paper, 31.8 x 42.2cm, British Museum, London (B 298). Copyright British Museum. © DACS 1995.

sections of the second plate show women and children fleeing in panic, crying at the heavens, from whence have fallen the terrorising bombs which decimated Madrid in late 1936.

There is not the space here to attend to all the complexities of political, cultural and historical reference in the prints.[84] It is worth noting, however, that the monster, like many of the creatures in Picasso's Bestiary, is prone to transformation, and is a lover of masquerades. In the first scene he poses as a Spanish King who has settled for an equestrian portrait on a disembowelled mare. He also plays at being a Spanish Lady (scene four), and is a bad Matador (scene five). Sometimes, instead of a mare, he rides a pig (scene nine), that most elusive of animals in Picasso's bestiary. Although allied with the horse (the grotesque horse, that is) in the first and fourteenth scenes, he will happily strangle (scene eight) or disembowel Pegasus (scene ten), the beautiful 'academic' horse. Certain elements of the vignettes are close to earlier works. The horse in the twelfth panel resembles the *Horse Lying Down* in Chapter Two. The confrontation of the polyp with the bull in the thirteenth panel repeats a clash of bull and horse seen in *Minotaur and Horse*, 1935. Yet in these prints, with their heavy reliance on animal symbolism, Picasso leaves behind any specific interest in the natural order for itself, and is drawn fully into his contemporary human world.

Perhaps the text for *Dream and Lie of Franco*, which Picasso read aloud to a fellow Spaniard[85] in 1936 with 'such extraordinary enthusiasm and force and violence', is thus the most appropriate way to conclude *A Picasso Bestiary*. In this book the animals scattered through the artist's work have been gathered into one small menagerie of meanings. *Dream and Lie of Franco* can return them, thus enriched, to the undiscriminating web of sensation and memory, which was for Picasso, as it remains for us, a constant resource:

> ... fandango of shivering *owls* souse swords of evil-omened polyps scouring brush of hairs from priests' tonsures standing naked in the middle of the frying-pan – placed upon the ice-cream cone of *codfish* fried in the scabs of his lead-*ox* heart – his mouth full of the *chinch-bug* jelly of his words – sleigh-bells of the plate of *snails* braiding guts – little finger in erection neither grape nor fig – commedia dell'arte of poor weaving and dyeing of clouds –beauty creams from the garbage wagon – rape of maids in tears and in snivels – on his shoulder the shroud stuffed with sausages and mouths – rage distorting the outline of the shadow which flogs his teeth driven in the sand and the *horse* open wide to the sun which reads it to the flies that stitch to the knots of the net full of *anchovies* the sky

rocket lilies – torch of *lice* where the *dog* is knot of *rats* and hiding-place of the palace of old rags – the banners which fry in the pan writhe in the black of the ink-sauce shed in the drops of blood which shoot him – the street rises to the clouds tied by its feet to the sea of wax which rots its entrails and the veil which covers it sings and dances wild with pain – the flight of fishing rods and the alhigui alhigui of the first class burial of the moving van – the broken wings rolling upon the *spider*'s web of dry bread and clear water of the paella of sugar and velvet which the lash paints upon his cheeks – the light covers its eyes before the mirror which *apes* it and the nougat bar of the flames bites its lips at the wound – cries of children cries of women cries of *birds* cries of flowers cries of timbers and of stones cries of bricks cries of furniture of beds of chairs of curtains of pots of *cats* and of papers of odours which claw at one another cries of smoke pricking the shoulder of the cries which stew in the cauldron and of the rain of *birds* which inundates the sea which gnaws the bone and breaks its teeth biting the cotton wool which the sun mops up from the place which the purse and the pocket hide in the print which the foot leaves in the rock.[86]

Picasso, *Naked Woman and Satyrs*, 1905-1906, sepia wash, 21.2 x 13.5cm, Picasso Estate (Inv 577; Z.VI.803). Courtesy of Musée Picasso, Paris. © DACS 1995.

Notes

Bibliographical Abbreviations

AR Alain Ramié, *Picasso, Catalogue of the edited ceramic works 1947-1971*, Vallauris, 1988. Detailed catalogue of the 'edited ceramics' numbered copies of originals by Picasso using various techniques.

B Georges Bloch, *Pablo Picasso, Catalogue of the printed graphic work*, 4 vols, Berne, 1968-79. Extensive print catalogue, less detailed than G below, though it includes work after 1968.

G Bernhard Geiser, *Picasso: Peintre-graveur*, 3 vols, revised and corrected by Brigitte Baer, Berne, 1990-92.

Inv Inventory number of works in the artist's possession at his death, with additions after the death of the artist's widow, as catalogued for the purposes of the legal succession. Files held in the Musée Picasso, Paris.

MP Musée Picasso, Paris.

MPB Museu Picasso, Barcelona.

r recto.

R Georges Ramié, *Picasso's Ceramics*, New York, 1976. Catalogues original and edited ceramics.

S Werner Spies, *Picasso, Das plastische Werk, Werkverzeichnis der Skulpturen in Zusammenarbeit mit Christine Piot*, Stuttgart, 1983. Definitive sculpture catalogue with few omissions.

v verso.

Z Christian Zervos, *Pablo Picasso*, 33 volumes, Paris, 1932-78. Enormously important catalogue, although disorganised and far from complete.

Bestiary Translations

Two English translations of Bestiary texts, together with reproductions of all the illustrations, are currently widely available. Our own bestiary owes a great debt to these works. They are abbreviated in the notes as follows:

Barber Richard Barber (ed. & transl.) *Bestiary*, being an English version of the Bodleian Library, Oxford, MS Bodley 764 with all the original miniatures reproduced in facsimile (Woodbridge, Suffolk, 1993).

White TH White, *The Book of Beasts*, London, 1954; Stroud, 1984, 1992.

Introduction

1 Norbert Aujoulat, *La naissance de l'art en Europe/ El nacimento del arte en Europa*, exh. cat., Union Latine, Paris, 1992, p286.

2 Michele Cremades, 'Les problèmes du sens/Los problemas del sentido', *op. cit.*, pp75-78.

3 Jean & Genevieve Guichard, *op. cit.*, p25.

4 Francis Klingender, *Animals in Art and Thought to the End of the Middle Ages*, London, 1971, p19.

5 See Arnold Hauser, 'Prehistoric Times' in *The Social History of Art 1: from Prehistoric times to the Middle Ages*, London, 1951; repr. 1962.

6 W Boers, 'Lithos van Picasso', 1947-48, transl. M McCully, *A Picasso Anthology: Documents, Criticism, Reminiscences*, London, 1981, p238; B Léal in M-L Bernadac et al, *Picasso: Toros y Toreros*, Paris, 1993, p222; G Cumont, *Picasso animalier*, Alfort, 1956, p19, and p23.

7 P O'Brien, *Pablo Ruiz Picasso: A Biography*, London, 1976, p154. Françoise Gilot and Carlton Lake give a more fluent – and therefore less vivid – version of a similar conversation in *Life with Picasso*, London, 1965, p249. Picasso's admiration of 'primitive' sculpture is also recorded by Sabartés, transl. in D Ashton, *Picasso on Art: A Selection of Views*, London, 1972, p115.

8 Picasso in 1947, quoted by Daniel Henry Kahnweiler in a letter to Alfred H Barr Jnr, received on 29th May 1947 and read by Barr at the Guernica symposium at MOMA, 25th November 1947. Typescript, Museum of Modern Art, p13.

9 In the most extended interview with the artist on the subject of symbolism, especially political symbolism, in his work, Picasso insisted that his decision to paint *Bull's Head* and *Artist's Palette* reflected only an interest in these things as things in their own right. He also recognised, however, the force of his unconscious in shaping that interest. 'Picasso Explains', interview with Jerome Seckler, 1945, in Ashton, *op. cit.*, pp133-42.

10 cf White Appendix p231.

11 JG Frazer, *The Golden Bough. A Study in Magic and Religion*, abridged ed., London & Basingstoke, 1922.

12 James Hall, *Hall's Dictionary of Subjects and Symbols in Art*, rev. ed., London,

1989, p230.

13 *ibid.*

14 Erwin Panofsky, *The Life and Art of Albrecht Dürer*, Princeton, 1943; rev. ed. 1971, p85.

15 Michael Camille, *Image on the Edge. The Margins of Medieval Art*, London, 1992, p48.

16 This was a commonplace of the Christian millennium ideal – see Keith Thomas, *Man and the Natural World. Changing Attitudes in England 1500-1800*, Harmondsworth, 1984, p288.

17 MRO James, *The Bestiary*, Oxford, 1928, p1.

18 Some were also written in French, English, Italian and Catalan. For a concise list, see the Appendix to Willene B Clark & Meradith T McMunn (ed.), *Beasts and Birds of the Middle Ages. The Bestiary and its Legacy*, Philadelphia, 1989.

19 Florence McCulloch, Medieval Latin and French Bestiaries, rev. ed., Chapel Hill, 1962, p72.

20 James, *op. cit.*, pp5; 22.

21 *ibid.* and Beryl Rowland, 'The Art of Memory and the Bestiary' in Clark & McMunn, p16.

22 eg BM Additional MS 11283 – see Anne Payne, *Medieval Beasts*, London, 1990, p13.

23 McCulloch, p72.

24 For an example, see Willene B Clark, 'The Aviary-Bestiary at the Houghton Library, Harvard', in Clark & McMunn, *op. cit.*, pp26ff.

25 Klingender, *op. cit.*, pp382ff.

26 For an account, E Mâle, *The Gothic Image. Religious Art in France of the Thirteenth Century*, Dora Nussey (transl.), New York, 1958; 1972, esp. Books I & II.

27 In general, Jean Seznec, *The Survival of the Pagan Gods. The Mythological Tradition and its Place in Renaissance Humanism and Art*, Bollingen Series XXXVIII, New York, 1953; Princeton, 1972.

28 Mâle. *op. cit.*, Book IV Chapter One pp131ff; L Réau, *Iconographie de l'art chrétien*, 5 vols, 1956-59, I Chapter IV 'Le Symbolisme Typologique ou la Concordance des Deux Testaments' pp192ff.

29 For an extensive discussion of these, see Camille, *op.cit.*, pp65ff.

30 For a brief description of Saint-Denis' exterior, 'Le trésor de Saint-Denis', *Les dossiers d'archéologie* CLVIII, March 1991; and for a more extensive account of the Abbey, its treasures and its meaning E Panofsky (ed. & transl.), *Abbot Suger on the Abbey Church of St-Denis and its Art Treasures*, 2nd ed. by Gerda Panofsky-Soergel, Princeton, 1979. For Chartres: Adolf Katzenellenbogen, *The Sculptural Programmes of Chartres Cathedral*, New York, 1959; 1964.

31 McCulloch, *op. cit.*, p46.

32 For a transl. of this, together with the cogently argued reply of an anonymous female respondent, see Jeanette Beer, *Master Richard's Bestiary of Love and Response*, Berkeley, 1986, and for a discussion, Beer's Introduction.

33 Thomas, *op. cit.*, p51.

34 S Peter Dance, *The Art of Natural History*, New York, 1978, p29.

35 *op. cit.*, p31.

36 *op. cit.*, p42.

37 For an account and transl., see Geoge Boas (ed.), *The Hieroglyphics of Horapollo*, Bolingen Series XXIII, New York, 1950.

38 For an introduction in English, see Maria A Shenkeveld, *Dutch Literature in the Age of Rembrandt. Themes and Ideas*, Utrecht Publications in General and Comparative Literature 28, Amsterdam, Philadelphia, 1991, esp. pp130ff. See also Rosemary Freeman, *English Emblem Books*, London, 1948; New York, 1966.

39 Dance, *op. cit.*, p84.

40 For a survey of the ambiguous achievements of scientific enquiry, Thomas *op. cit.*, esp. Chapter II 'Natural History and Vulgar Errors' pp51ff.

41 *op. cit.*, p69.

42 *op. cit.*, pp57ff.

43 P Caizergues and H Seckel, *Picasso/Apollinaire Correspondance*, Paris, 1992, pp78-80. According to Cumont, Kahnweiler intended to publish the poems with woodcuts by Picasso, and some of these were executed. Cumont, p21.

44 *Histoire Naturelle, générale et particulière*, the complete set of this classic of French Enlightenment literary style, when originally published, (Imprimerie Royale, Paris, puis Plassan, 1749-1804), ran to forty-four volumes.

45 According to Brigitte Baer, Fabiani was in part able to publish since he was a

collaborator. She also suggests that he may have had little or no involvement in matching plates to text, since 'there are those who say that he did not even know who Buffon was'. B Baer, *Picasso as Printmaker*, Dallas, 1983, pp102-103. The rather peculiar sounding practice of producing the plates and then searching for the text to match does in fact have a history as long as the printed book itself, as A Horodisch has suggested in *Picasso as a Book Artist*, London, 1962, p55. See also the entry on the book and suite of prints in S Goeppert et al Pablo Picasso, *The Illustrated Books: Catalogue Raisonné*, Geneva, 1983, pp104-107, (No.37).

46 G Cumont, *op. cit.* We are most grateful to Monsieur Lionel Prejger, Paris and to Monsieur Luc Deflandre of the Musée Picasso, Antibes, for drawing this book to our attention.

47 R Penrose, *Picasso: His Life and Work*, London, 1958, p270.

48 Transl. Kenneth Lyons in J Palau i Fabre, *Picasso: Life and Work of the Early Years 1881-1907*, Oxford 1981, p41.

49 See, for example, C Gottlieb, 'The Meaning of Bull and Horse in Guernica', *Art Journal*, Vol 24, No 2, 1965, pp106-12.

50 J Richardson, p29.

51 Picasso to Malraux, Quoted in *Picasso: Toros y Toreros*, *op. cit.*, p30, [author's transl.].

52 See P O'Brien, *op. cit.*, p220, characters not in the original libretto.

53 Perhaps Picasso's most significant effort at a pig is the Franco/Monster's mount in the ninth panel of *Dream and Lie of Franco I*, where connotations of stupidity, ignorance and filth are all being utilised, see Chapter Nine.

54 In a recent wave of discussion on the subject of the sociology of carnivals and their relevance to art and literature, Karen Kleinfelder amongst others has related Picasso's interest in and representation of the circus and other forms of festival and masquerade to the theory of carnival as presented in Mikhail Bakhtin's study of Rabelais (M Bakhtin, *Rabelais and His World*, transl. H Iswolsky, Cambridge, Mass, 1968). See K Kleinfelder, *The Artist, His Model, Her Image, His Gaze: Picasso's Pursuit of the Model*, London, 1993, pp163-64.

55 eg 'He took up from moment to moment with the most diverse animals, from the most simple to the most wild; as an artist, his love was always inconstant, but if it passed from owl to goat, from goat to monkey, from monkey to pigeon, he always considered them as beings which he must protect, love, and as worthy to stand in the place of his human friends.' Cumont, *op. cit.*, p17. 'Picasso's love of animals was legendary and they invariably responded to him instantly.' J Golding, 'Introduction', *Picasso: Sculptor/Painter*, London, 1994, p32.

56 M-L Bernadac & C Piot, *Picasso: Collected Writings*, New York, 1989, p1 [author's transl.].

Chapter One: The Bull

1 Rafael Alberti in LM Dominguin, *Pablo Picasso, Toros y Toreros*, Paris, 1974, p12 [author's transl.].

2 For an exception, see *The Blind Flower Seller, Young Girl and Oxen*, 1906, Barnes Collection, Merion, Penn. (Z.I.384).

3 Beryl Rowland, *Animals with Human Faces. A Guide to Animal Symbolism*, Knoxville, 1973; London, 1974, p44.

4 Géza Róheim, *Animism, Magic and the Divine King*, London, 1930, p224.

5 JG Frazer, *The Golden Bough: a Study in Magic and Religion*, abridged ed., London & Basingstoke, 1922; repr. 1987, p468. Again, this concept of the bull was widespread amongst religions. Often oxen and other animals were slaughtered for the same reason. For example, the Athenian 'murder of the ox' took place in Attica when threshing was nearly over. (*op. cit.* p466).

6 Rowland, *op. cit.*, p45.

7 *ibid*.

8 Leonard Boyle, *A Short Guide to St. Clement's Rome*, Rome, 1988, p66.

9 *ibid*.

10 Frazer, *loc. cit.* Belief in animals as embodiments of the corn spirit has been widespread, particularly in northern Europe. See *op. cit.* Chapter XLVIII, 'The Corn-Spirit as an Animal', pp447ff; also Rowland *op. cit.* p46.

11 Frazer, *op. cit.*, Chapter XXIV 'The killing of the divine King' pp264ff.

12 Further discussion will be found in Chapter Five.

13 Isaiah I:11.

14 Hebrews IX 12-14.

15 Florence McCulloch, *Medieval Latin and French Bestiaries*, rev. ed. Chapel Hill, 1962, p99.

16 Barber, p88.

17 *op. cit.*, pp88-89.

18 For accounts of the painting, much of which is echoed here, see Kenneth M Craig, 'Pieter Aertsen and the Meat Stall', *Oud Holland* LXXXXVI, 1982, pp1-15 and Paul Verbraeken in *Joachim Beuckelaer. Het markt – en keukenstuk in de Nederlanden 1550-1650* exh. cat., Museum voor Schone Kunsten, Ghent, 1986-87, cat. 1, pp114-15.

19 Verbraeken, *op. cit.*, p114.

20 For this tradition, see E de Jongh, *Tot lering en vermaak. Betekenissen van Hollandse genrevoorstellingen uit de zeventiende eeuw* exh. cat., Rijksmuseum,

Amsterdam, 1976, cat. 24, p117.

21 Kenneth M Craig, 'Rembrandt and *The Slaughtered Ox*', *Journal of the Warburg and Courtauld Institutes*, XLVI, 1983, p236.

22 Keith Thomas, *Man and the Natural World. Changing Attitudes in England 1500-1800*, Harmondsworth, 1984, p289.

23 Craig, *loc. cit.*

24 Barber, pp93-94.

25 Quoted in James Eyres, *English Naive Painting 1750-1900*, London, 1980, p111.

26 Rowland, *op. cit.*, p43.

27 *op. cit.*, pp45-46; Frazer, *op. cit.*, p390.

28 Aelian, *On the Characteristics of Animals*, transl. AF Scholfield, 3 vols, London, Cambridge, Mass., 1972, VII:4.

29 Francis Klingender, *Animals in Art and Thought to the End of the Middle Ages*, London, 1971, p62.

30 Juliet Wilson-Bareau, *Manet by Himself*, London, 1991, p37.

31 Musée Picasso, cat. no. MP 3628.

32 16th February 1935, transl. in D Ashton, *Picasso on Art, A Selection of Views*, London, 1972, p167.

33 The state numbers have been shown to be incorrect by B Baer, *Picasso the Printmaker*, Dallas, 1983, pp130-32.

34 For further discussion of this and other issues related to the prints, see I Laving, 'Picasso's Bull(s): Art History in Reverse', *Art in America*, Vol 81, No 3, March 1993, pp76-93, 121, 123.

35 H Parmelin, in Ashton, *op. cit.*, p157.

36 See M-L Bernadac, *Picasso vu par Brassaï*, Paris, 1987, p65. The bird is S 125.

37 In another example of a photographic assemblage, Picasso combined the original sculpture with a wooden arm from Easter Island. The arm covers the 'eyes' of the bull, in a gesture evoking both the desire of the bull not to see, and the Matador performing the adorno, where the head of the exhausted and defeated bull is patted between the horns, *op. cit*, p145.

38 See A Saura, 'Picasso et le taureau', in M-L Bernadac et al, *Picasso, Toros y Toreros*, Paris, 1993, pp11-27.

39 There is an excellent example in the collection of Marina Picasso, Inv 56944.

40 J Bergamin, *La Claridad de torero*, Madrid, 1987, p77, quoted in B Marcadé, 'La quadrature du cercle' in *Picasso: Toros y Toreros*, *op. cit.*, p33 [author's transl.].

41 *ibid*. Marcadé points out the similarity of this highly complex, disintegrating dialectic with that represented by the art impulses of nature, Apollo and Dionysos, in F Nietzsche's *The Birth of Tragedy*, 1871, passim. (See also Chapter Nine).

42 Years later, Picasso defended the cruelty of the bullfight to Geneviève Laporte 'by saying that it gave him a certain thrill to witness the survival of a Mithraic cult.' G Laporte, *Sunshine at Midnight*, London, 1975, transl. D Cooper, p2.

43 G Bataille, 'Rotten Sun', *Documents No.3* (Hommage à Picasso), 1930, pp173-74. This transl. A Stoekl (ed.), in G Bataille, *Visions of Excess*, Minneapolis, 1985, pp57-58.

44 The exception are *rejoneadores*, who fight on horseback.

45 See A Saura, 'Picasso et le taureau', in *Picasso, Toros y Toreros*, *op. cit.*, pp11-27.

46 *Tauromaquia* no 33.

47 eg MP 77. The two deaths were also important in works by Hemingway and Bataille.

48 From Federico García Lorca, *Selected Poems*, (transl. and introduced by M Williams), Newcastle upon Tyne, 1992, p187.

49 FG Lorca, 'Lament for Ignacío Sánchez Mejías', (part 1, 'The Tossing and the Death'), transl. in *ibid.*, pp189-91.

50 *ibid*.

51 Examples include a drawing and painting from 1934: Boisgeloup 16/7/34, Private Collection, Paris, and Jacques and Natasha Gellman Collection, reproduced in *Picasso: Toros y Toreros*, cat. no 67 & p169, Fig. 9.

52 P Picasso, *Les quatre petites filles*, [*The Four Little Girls*], transl. in R Penrose, *Picasso: His Life and Work*, London, 1958, p335.

53 See E Cowling, 'Catalogue', in *Picasso Sculptor/Painter*, London, 1994, p274.

54 In the Kunstsammlung Nordrhein-Westfalen, Dusseldorf; Jesi Collection, Milan, respectively.

55 FG Lorca, 'Lament for Ignacío Sánchez Mejías', (part 4, 'Absent Soul'), transl. in Williams, *op. cit.*, p199.

56 Penrose, *op. cit.*, p287.

57 M-L Bernardac et al, *Picasso et les choses*, Paris, 1993, pp254-57.

58 *Picasso vu par Brassaï*, *op. cit.*, p92.

59 J Richardson, *A Life of Picasso, Vol.1 1881-1906*, London, 1991, p51.

60 In conversation with Jerome Seckler, Picasso objected to the idea that the bull represented fascism, but suggested that it stood for 'brutality and darkness'. He did not comment on Seckler's claim that the palette might stand for 'culture and freedom'. J Seckler, 'Picasso Explains', 1945, in Ashton, *op. cit.*, pp133-42, this reference pp136-37.

61 See Chapter Seven, on Georges de la Tour's *The Woman with a Flea*.

62 FG Lorca, 'Lament for Ignacío Sánchez Mejías', (part 3, 'The Body Laid

Out'), transl. in Williams, ibid., p197.

63 'In Malaga, his native town, I found an explanation … of what Picasso is and I understood to what degree he is a toreador – gypsies are the best toreadors – and whatever he may do, it is in reality bullfighting.' Ramón Gomez de la Serna, 'Le toréador de la peinture', *Cahiers d'Art*, Paris 1932, pp3-5.

64 *Picasso, Toros y Toreros*, *op. cit.*, p31, n.8.

65 See note 1 and J Richardson, *A Life of Picasso*, *op. cit.*, p8.

66 Picasso concludes in this reported speech 'And there's no need even for a bull.' The metaphorical sense of mortality he describes, however, clearly invokes a metaphorical bull: failure before public opinion. H Parmelin, *Picasso Plain*, London, 1963, p163.

67 Picasso used these words of one of the 1938 series according to Ashton, *op. cit.*, p156.

68 *Picasso et les choses*, *op. cit.*, p330.

69 P Eluard, 'A Pablo Picasso', IV, 1938, in *A Pablo Picasso*, London/Geneva/Paris, 1947, p78 [author's transl.]. Although this poem may well have been written in response to the 1938 series, it seems to work even more literally with the 1958 work. See also 'l'oreille du taureau', *ibid.*, pp83-84.

Chapter Two: The Horse and the Donkey

1 eg Barber, p104.

2 *op. cit.*, p101.

3 Dom Pierre Miquel, *Dictionnaire symbolique des animaux. Zoologie mystique*, Paris, 1991, p88.

4 Barber, p102.

5 Edward Topsell, *The Historie of Foure-footed Beastes*, facs., The English Experience, no. 561, Amsterdam, New York, 1973, pp281-434.

6 Miquel, *op. cit.*, p89 citing Aristotle's *Historia animalum* VIII, XXIV.

7 *op. cit.*, citing Alain of Lille's *Anticlaudianus* 11-111, *PL* 210, pp521-22.

8 Beryl Rowland, *Animals with Human Faces. A Guide to Animal Symbolism*, Knoxville, 1973; London, 1974, p105.

9 White, p86 who notes drily (n. 1) that 'It was because he [the horse Opus] came from a Greek town of that name, not because he worked so hard.'

10 Rowland, *op. cit.*, pp104-105.

11 *op. cit.*, p104.

12 *ibid.*

13 For an accessible account, amongst many others, Walter S Gibson, *Bruegel*, London, 1977; repr. 1988, pp85-88.

14 JP Filedt Kok et al, *Livelier than Life. The Master of the Amsterdam Cabinet or The Housebook Master, c1470-1500*, exh. cat. Rijksprentenkabinet, Amsterdam, 1985, cat. 61i, p158.

15 Alexander S Murray, *Who's Who in Classical Mythology. Classic Guide to the Ancient World*. 2nd ed., New York, 1989.

16 Rowland, *op. cit.*, pp103-104.

17 Ovid, *Metamorphoses* V: 268-9.

18 Rowland, *loc. cit.*

19 Ernest Jones, 'The Madonna's Miraculous Conception through her Ear' in *Essays in Applied Psycho-Analysis*, London, Vienna, 1923, p301.

20 Edgar Wind, *Pagan Mysteries in the Renaissance*, London, 1958; rev. ed. Oxford, 1980, p252. The biblical reference is from Genesis I:2: 'And the spirit of God moved on the face of the waters'.

21 Rowland, *op. cit.*, p107.

22 For an account, Jonathan Brown, *Velázquez. Painter and Courtier*, New Haven, London, 1986, Chapter IV 'Images of Power and Prestige' pp107-28.

23 *op. cit.*, p115.

24 *Ingres* exh. cat., Musée du Petit Palais, Paris, 1967-8 cat. 161, p226.

25 Basil Taylor, *Stubbs*, London, 1971, pp32-33. See especially his fig 14, a Roman copy of a late Pergamene original in Rome, Museo del Palazzo dei Conservatori.

26 For reproductions, see Constance-Ann Parker, *Mr Stubbs the Horse Painter*, London, 1971, pp75-81.

27 Taylor, *op. cit.*, p32.

28 Lorenz EA Eitner, *Géricault, His Life and Work*, London, 1983, p131 & ff. for Géricault's influences.

29 *op. cit.*, p117.

30 *op. cit.*, pp234-35.

31 *op. cit.*, p235.

32 I Corinthians III:18-19; IV:10.

33 Comte de Buffon in the Fabiani edition, *Histoire naturelle du Comte de Buffon*, Paris, 1942, p7, p14 [author's transl.].

34 M-L Bernadac et al, *Picasso: Toros y Toreros*, Paris, 1992, p117.

35 See p155 on *The Butterfly Hunter*.

36 J Sabartés, *A los toros avec Picasso*, Monte-Carlo, 1961, p64.

37 R Otero, *Forever Picasso*, New York, 1974, pp43-44.

38 M-L Bernadac and C Piot, *Picasso: Collected Writings*, New York, 1989, p129 [author's transl.].

39 *ibid.*, texts dated 14/1/36; 13/8/36; 20/1/36; 18/2/37.

40 In the mediaeval tradition, horses are usually equated with woman, Rowland, *op. cit.*, p105.

41 See *Picasso: Toros y Toreros*, *op. cit.*, p158.

42 See Chapter One.

43 Picasso uses the sky as an interchangeable term for the horse in a number of writings (eg Picasso, *Selected Writings*, *op. cit.*, texts dated 15/2/37; 18/9/40).

44 According to G Cumont, *Picasso animalier*, Alfort, 1956, p14, gods personifying the sun or the moon were worshipped into the beginning of the nineteenth century in Spain under the name of *Astarté*. During *Astartia*, this star was represented by a head with two horns representing that of a bull or cow… In 1956, Picasso made twelve prints of prancing horses to illustrate an epic poem by Roch Grey (Baroness Hélène d'Oettingen) entitled *Chevaux de minuit* (Midnight Horses), the poem was dedicated on 1/1/36.

45 I am grateful to Hélène Lasalle of the Musée Picasso, Paris, for this suggestion.

46 Topsell, *op. cit.*, pp334-39, Rowland, *op. cit.*, p110.

47 The main example would be that of the Pegasus pulling the plough in the *Peace* panel of 1952, Musée National Picasso de la Guerre et la Paix, Vallauris.

48 R Penrose, *Picasso: His Life and Work*, London, 1958, p198.

49 G Bataille, 'Le cheval académique', *Documents*, No 1, April 1929, pp27-31.

50 Bataille's point is borne out by the fact that the investigation of the proportions of the horse through anatomy was initially the work of artists Cumont, *op. cit.*, p9.

51 Other possible influences recently suggested by John Richardson include a cast of a Javanese sculpture then in the café *Le lapin agile*; El Greco's *St. Martin and the Beggar*; a Kouros figure from the Louvre; and Cézanne's bather compositions. See J Richardson, *A Life of Picasso, Vol 1: 1881-1906*, London, 1991, pp427-28.

52 For differing opinions on this see *ibid.* and W Rubin, *Picasso in the Collection of the Museum of Modern Art*, New York, 1972, p34. It is interesting to note that around 1906 Max Jacob wrote a poem entitled 'Le cheval', which, because it was dedicated to the artist, became known amongst his friends as 'Le cheval de Picasso'. See J Richardson, *op. cit.*, p464.

53 Bataille, *op. cit.*, p29.

54 Penrose, *op. cit.*, pp334-35.

55 For remarks on the symbolism see KH Keen, 'Picasso's communist interlude: the murals of "War" and "Peace"', *Burlington Magazine*, Vol 72, No.928, pp464-70.

56 G Schiff, 'The Sabines Sketchbook No.163, 1962', *Je Suis le Cahier: The Sketchbooks of Picasso*, London, 1986, pp179-189 (the sketchbook discussed is in fact number 162); R Rosenblum, 'War and Peace: Antiquity and Late Picasso', in G Tinterow (ed.), *Picasso Classico*, Malaga, 1992, pp365-72.

57 *Rape of the Sabines*, 9/1-7/2/63, oil on canvas, Boston Museum of Fine Arts.

58 See Schiff, *op. cit.*, p179.

59 J Sabartés, *Picasso, Portraits et Souvenirs*, Paris, 1946, p199 [author's transl.].

60 *Histoire naturelle du Comte de Buffon*, *op. cit.*, pp17-22.

61 Picasso in 1935, quoted in D Ashton, *Picasso on Art: A Selection of Views*, London, 1972, p49.

62 *Carajo!* – Ass's Prick! – is a Spanish expletive. For the pagan origin, see esp. Apuleius' *The Golden Ass*.

63 Alanus de Insulis, in Rowland, *op. cit.*, p24.

64 Another version of this same composition, painted on the same day and reflecting a subtle change of mood, exists in a private collection in Basel, Switzerland. Picasso also painted his first son Paulo on a donkey in 1923 and then on a rocking horse in 7/2/26 (Z.VII.16). Photographs exist of his grandson Bernard on a metal horse constructed in 1960 according to Picasso's design by Monsieur Tiola, of Lionel Prejger's factory in Vallauris (See E Cowling and J Golding, *Picasso: Sculptor/Painter*, London, 1994, p242).

65 For more thoughts on Picasso imitating childish vision and drawing, see W Spies, *Picasso's World of Children*, New York, 1994, eg p96.

Chapter Three: Birds

1 Picasso to C Zervos, 'Conversations avec Picasso', *Cahiers d'Art X*, 1935, pp173-78, transl. in (ed.) D Ashton, *Picasso on Art*, London, 1972, p11.

2 White, p161.

3 Florence McCulloch, *Medieval Latin and French Bestiaries*, University of North Carolina Press, rev. ed. 1962, p111.

4 John Oliver Hand, '*Saint Jerome in his Study* by Joos van Cleve', *Record of the Art Museum, Princeton University*. XLIX, 1990, p7.

5 Barber, pp161-63.

6 ed. Xenia Muratova and Daniel Poirion, *Le Bestiaire*, Paris, 1988, plate 19.

7 Respectively, White, p145 and Barber, p163.

8 Barber, p164.

9 Muratova *op. cit.*, table of the colored plates.

10 In the Vulgate, 'columba' is used throughout.

11 Alan Wood Rendell (ed. & transl.), *Physiologus: A Metrical Bestiary of Twelve Chapters by Bishop Theobald*, London, 1928, pp42-43.

12 Ernest Jones, 'The Madonna's Miraculous Conception through her Ear' in

Essays in Applied Psycho-Analysis, London, Vienna, 1923, pp261ff.

13 In MS Bodley 764 f. 85v for example, the cock's beak is closed, indicating its present silence. It looks upwards, into the night suggested by a dark, starry border, as if waiting for the first sign of daybreak, which it will signal by its crow. Illustrated in Barber, p172.

14 cf Chaucer, *The Parlement of Foules* 350: 'The cok, that orloge is of thorpes lyte' Walter W Skeat (ed.), *The Complete Works of Geoffrey Chaucer*, Oxford, 1912; repr. 1949, p106. The hours of night were divided into first, second, third cock, eg Chaucer, *The Reve's Tale* 4233: 'Til that the thridde cok bigan to singe', *op. cit.*, p472.

15 White, p151.

16 Opening line of a hymn from BM MS Add. 34193 f. 119v of the late fifteenth century, quoted in Douglas Gray (ed.), *English Medieval Religious Lyrics*, Oxford, 1975; rev. ed. Exeter, 1992, no 75 p79.

17 White, *loc. cit.*

18 George Ferguson, *Signs and Symbols in Christian Art*, Oxford, 1954; repr. 1961, p14.

19 Gray, *loc. cit.*

20 cf the opening stanza of Chaucer's *Compleynte of Mars*
'Gladeth, ye fowles, of the morrow gray,
lo! Venus risen among yon rowes rede!
And floures fresshe, honoureth ye this day;
for when the sonne uprise, then wol ye sprede.
But lovers, that lye in any drede,
Fleëth, lest wikked tonges yow espye;
Lo! yond the sonne, the candel of jelosye!'
op. cit., p97.

21 Jeanette Beer (ed. & transl.), *Master Richard's Bestiary of Love and Response*, Berkeley, 1986, p3.

22 *ibid.*

23 *op. cit.*, ppxvi-xvii. Beer cites Isidore of Seville, *Etymologiae* XII, vii, 50 for this association. cf also White, p150, 'The COCK (*gallus*) is called the cock because it gets castrated. It is the only member of the bird family whose testicles are removed. Indeed, the ancients ued to call the Galli [the priests of Cybele] the "cut-offs"'.

24 Beer, *op. cit.*, pix.

25 Aelian, *On the Characteristics of Animals*, transl. AF Scholfield, 3 vols, London, Cambridge, Mass., 1972, IV 29.
'If the Hen dies the cock himself sits on the eggs and hatches his own eggs in silence, for then for some strange inexplicable reasoñ, I must say, he does not crow. I fancy that he is conscious that he is then doing the work of a female and not of a male.'

26 Beer, *op. cit.*, p43.

27 This is probably the original meaning behind the nursery rhyme:
'Cock-a-doodle-doo
My maid has lost her shoe
My master's lost his fiddling-stick
And doesn't know what to do.'
As the Opies point out, rather archly, in their commentary to 'There was an old woman who lived in a shoe' 'The shoe has long been symbolic of what is personal to a woman until marriage', *The Oxford Book of Nursery Rhymes*, Oxford, 1951, p435.

28 Early fifteenth-century verse, BM MS Sloane 2593 f. 10v in ed. RT Davies, *Medieval English Lyrics. A Critical Anthology*, London, 1963; repr. 1991, no 64, pp153-54.

29 For this latter see Hugh Honour, *Neo-classicism Style and Civilisation*, Harmondsworth, 1968; repr. 1983, p47. Eduard Fuchs, *Geschichte der Erotischen Kunst*, Munich, n.d., reproduces several examples, including Ginelli's, from different periods and cultures, of these 'cock-birds'.

30 Dou's picture entered the Louvre in 1742; van Beyeren's in 1900 – *Catalogue sommaire illustré des peintures du Musée du Louvre I: Ecoles flamande et hollandaise*, Paris, 1979, pp26 & 48.

31 Jochen Becker, 'Are These Girls Really so Neat. On Kitchen Scenes and Method' in David Freedberg and Jan de Vries (eds.), *Art in History, History in Art. Studies in Seventeenth-century Dutch Culture*, Getty Center Issues and Debates, Santa Monica, 1991, pp139-73.

32 E de Jongh, 'Erotica in vogelperspectif. De dubbelzinnigheid van een reeks 17de eeuwse genrevoorstellingen', *Simiolus* III, 1968-69, pp45-46. A similar suggestiveness is provided by the juxtaposition of chamberpot and candle (the candle broken, the chamberpot upturned) in Pieter Coecke van Aelst's *Joseph and Potiphar's Wife* second quarter of the sixteenth century, Rijksmuseum het Catharijneconvent, Utrecht, see *De Bijbel in Huis. Bijbelse Verhalen op Huisraad in de Zeventiende en Achttiende Eeuw* exh. cat. Rijksmuseum Het Catharijneconvent, Utrecht, no 8 pp84 reproduced as fig 40, p45. This, and other examples, also given by de Jongh, *op. cit.* p45.

33 For example in Gabriel Metsu's *Hunter's Gift*, Rijksmuseum, Amsterdam – see Peter C Sutton et al, *Masters of Seventeenth-Century Dutch Genre Painting*

34 exh. cat., Philadelphia Museum of Art, 1984, cat. 71, pp250-51.

35 E de Jongh *op. cit.*, pp22-74 esp. p27 and repeated by many authors.

36 See Chapter Five.

37 Becker, *op. cit.*, p142.

38 *op. cit.*, pp142-44: '... outer and inner purity can be contrasted: he or she who only cleans the outside of a vessel is a hypocrite or a pharisee.' On the tensions in Dutch portraiture and genre between appearance and reality, the façade of social *decorum* 'beneath which lurk sinful realties' see David R Smith, 'Irony and civility: Notes on the Convergence of Genre and Portraiture in Seventeenth-Century Dutch Painting', *Art Bulletin* LXIX, 1987, pp407-430.

39 Scott A Sullivan, 'Rembrandt's *Still-life with a Dead Bittern*', *Art Bulletin*, 1980, pp236-43 and *The Dutch Gamepiece*, Montclair, Totowa, NJ, 1984, esp. Chapter Four: 'Hunting and Dutch Society', pp33-45.

40 Sullivan, *The Dutch Gamepice op. cit.*, p77. See also his Chapter Eight 'The *Vanitas* Still-life with Game' pp73-77 for general observations on the genre.

41 cf 'het vogeltje was lang ontvlangen' (the bird had long flown), the concluding line of Constantijn Huygen's 'Wie zoeckt, die vindt niet' of 1671 from his *De Gedichten*, quoted in Hans van Straten (ed.), *Razernij der Liefde. Ontuchtige poësie in de Nederlanden van Middeleeuwen tot Franse tijd*, Amsterdam, 1992, p92. On the symbolism of the birdcage in Dutch genre painting, see E de Jongh, *op. cit.*, pp48-52.

42 See, for example, Annunciations by Crivelli in the National Gallery, London, and the Städelsches Kunstinstitut, Frankfurt.

43 Paul Vernière (ed.), *Diderot. Oeuvres Esthétiques*, Paris, 1968, pp533-37.

44 *op. cit.*, p536.

45 Edmond and Jules de Goncourt, *French Eighteenth-Century Painters* transl. by Robin Ironside, Oxford, 1948; repr. 1981, pp248-49. Significantly, the three subjects the Goncourts single out for mention here (*The Broken Pitcher*, *The Dead Bird*, *The Broken Mirror*) are all concerned with loss of virginity.

46 E de Jongh, *Tot lering en vermaak. Betekenissen van hollandse genrevoorstellingen uit de zeventiende eeuw*, exh. cat., Rijksmuseum, Amsterdam, cat. 33, p248.

47 Carl Kerény, *The Gods of the Greeks*, Harmondsworth, 1958, p111; Robert Graves', *The Greek Myths*, 1955, 2 vols, rev. ed., repr. Harmondsworth, 1984, 97.4, I p336. According to Graves, (25.2, I p99), when Athene was in her Crone (oracle-presiding) aspect, she was accompanied by an owl and a crow.

48 Kerény, *op. cit.*, p104. The poetical epithet for Athena, *glaukopis* means 'owl-eyed', and also refers to the sea- or olive-green of her eyes (p113).

49 See Isaiah XXXIV 13-15; Psalms CII 6; Job XXX 29; Jeremiah L 39; Micah I 8. In Isaiah XXXIV 14, the owl is specifically identified, in the King James transl. as a 'screech-owl', presumably after the Hebrew *lilith*, night owl (Robert Young, *An Analytical Concordance to the Bible*, Edinburgh, New York, 1881, p728 'Owl', 4).

50 *Metamorphoses* V 549-50.

51 See Iona Opie & Moira Tatum (ed.), *A Dictionary of Superstitions*, 1989; Oxford, 1992, pp295-96.

52 Barn Owl; although the bestiaries are usually concerned with *noctua* or *bubo* there is some confusion in the bestiaries concerning the different types of owl – see Brunsdon Yapp, *Birds in Medieval Manuscripts*, London, 1981, pp39-42.

53 Barber, p170.

54 *op. cit.*, p146.

55 Yapp, *op. cit.*, p37. On the bas-de-page of f. 14r of the Arundel Psalter (BL MS Arundel 83) he reproduces as Plate 27, a man in a pink gown crouches under a bush, holding an owl to attract the other birds. As Yapp points out (p132), the use of an owl as decoy is mentioned in the early thirteenth-century poem 'The Owl and the Nightingale'.

55 Barber, *op. cit.*, p149.

56 HT Riley, *Dictionary of Latin Quotations, Proverbs, Maxims, and Mottos*, London, 1860, p126 where it is identified as proverbial. According to Tapié, who transcribes the inscription (*Les Vanités dans la peinture an XVIIc siècle*, exh. cat., Musée des Beaux-Arts, Caen; Musée du Petit Palais, Paris, 1990-91, cat. O.10 p234) the saying is scriptural but I have been unable to locate it there, although a similar sense is meant in Proverbs XII 1; XII 18; XV 10 and Sirach XIX 5 & XXI 7. Nevertheless, the saying is common enough (see, for example, Shakespeare, *Troilus and Cressida* IV v 223: 'The end crowns all,/ and that old common arbitrator, Time,/ Will one day end it.')

57 Tapié, *loc. cit.*

58 Ecclesiastes II 14.

59 For examples of these proverbs in use see ed. FP Wilsom, *The Oxford Dictionary of English Proverbs*, 3rd rev. ed., Oxford 1970; repr. 1979, p67.

60 For a modern critical edition of the oldest surviving printed edition, (ed.) Dr Loek Geeraerdts, *Het Volksboek van Ulenspieghel. Naar de oudste, bewaard gebleven druk van Michiel Hillen van Hoochstraten te Antwerpen uit de eerste helft van de 16de eeuw* Klassieke Galerij Nr 42, Amsterdam, 1986. On this aspect of the fool, Kaiser, Walter Kaiser, *Praisers of Folly*, London, 1964, p8.

61 Geeraerdts, *op. cit.*, reproduces several examples; an account is given on pp37-40.

62 On the properties of mirrrors, see Hubert Grabes, *The Mutable Glass: Mirror-Imagery in the Titles and Texts of the Middle Ages and the English Renaissance*, New York, 1982.

63 Stanislas Klossowski de Rola, *The Golden Game. Alchemical Engravings of the Seventeenth Century*, London, 1980, p24.

64 E de Jongh, *tot lering en vermaak*, no 65 [Steen's *After the Drinking Party*] p247.

65 *ibid.*, 'Wat baeter kaers of bril, als den uijl niet sien en wil' – what need of spectacles or candle if the owl cannot and will not see.

66 *ibid.*, de Jongh also reproduces (fig 65c p248) an engraving by Hendrick Barry, after Frans van Mieris, of a drunken woman, slumped by a candle with an owl in the shadowy background, being mocked by a fool, entitled 'De Wijn is een Spotter' – wine is a mocker.

67 For a brief account see Christopher Brown, *Scenes of Everyday Life. Dutch Genre Painting of the Seventeenth Century*, London, 1984, p100.

68 Mentioned, but not reproduced in *op. cit.*, p88 where Brown states that the picture is in a New York Private Collection. It does not appear to be included in Karel Braun, *Alle tot nu bekende schilderijen van Jan Steen*, Rotterdam, 1980).

69 Eleanor A Sayre, *The Changing Image: Prints by Francesco Goya*, exh. cat., Museum of Fine Arts, Boston, 1975, no 89 p118, also the source for the translation of the caption.

70 See Picasso's *The Piano*, reproduced p114.

71 E Quinn, *Picasso at Work*, London, 1965, np, Section Three, plate one.

72 M-L Bernadac and C Piot, *Picasso: Collected Writings*, London, 1989, p186 (text dated 1/3/38), [author's transl.].

73 Picasso thought of this, perhaps unhelpfully, as influenced by childrens' drawings. See Ashton, *op. cit.*, p164.

74 F Gilot and C Lake, *Life with Picasso*, London, 1965, pp255-56.

75 P Cramer *et al*, *Pablo Picasso: The Illustrated Books*, Geneva, 1983, p168. *Picasso: Collected Writings*, *op. cit.*, text dated 2-7/2/38, contains a reference to a pigeon with a rainbow.

76 Cramer, *op. cit.*, No.62. The lithograph is B 687.

77 P Daix, *Picasso: Life and Art*, London, 1985, p301.

78 *Histoire naturelle du Comte de Buffon avec des eaux fortes de Picasso*, Paris, 1942, p128.

79 Text dated 23/5/36 [II], *Picasso: Collected Writings*, *op. cit.*, p136.

80 See, for example, *Couple with Bird*, 17/1/69, Z.XXXII.31.

81 Gilot and Lake, *op. cit.*, p140. In Brassaï's version the birds in question are lovebirds. See Brassaï, *Picasso & Co*, London, 1966, p195.

82 J Sabartés, *Picasso: portraits et souvenirs*, Paris, 1946, p15.

83 Daix, *op. cit.*, p29.

84 Sassier is depicted helping her son (according to A Barr, *Picasso: Fifty Years of his Art*, New York, 1946, p232, or daughter (according to W Rubin, *Pablo Picasso: A Retrospective*, New York, 1980, p352, on his/her *First Steps* in a painting of the same year, now in Yale University Art Gallery. This is not the first case of gender problems in the identification of a child in a painting – see Chapter Seven on *The Butterfly Hunter*.

85 W Spies, *Picasso's World of Children*, New York, 1994, p107.

86 H Parmelin, *Picasso Plain*, London, 1963, pp181-82. For more on the film, *Picasso*, (dir. L Emmer) see M-L Bernadac *et al*, *Picasso à l'écran*, Paris, 1992, pp51-59.

87 R Penrose, *Picasso: His Life and Work*, London, 1958, p325.

88 Parmelin, *op. cit.*, p181.

89 See E Cowling and C Piot, 'An Interview with Lionel Prejger', *Picasso: Sculptor/Painter*, London, 1994, p252.

90 Picasso in a text dated 18th April 1935, *Picasso Collected Writings*, *op. cit.*, p9.

91 W Misfeldt, 'The Theme of the Cock in Picasso's Oeuvre', *Art Journal*, Vol.XXVIII, No 2, Winter 1969, pp146-54 & 165.

92 MP 1332-1336.

93 *Histoire Naturelle...*, *op. cit.*, p114.

94 X Gonzalez, 1944 in Ashton, *op. cit.*, pp34-35. Examples of these cockerels are Z.IX.113 and 114.

95 As Elizabeth Cowling has suggested in *Picasso: Sculptor/Painter*, *op. cit.*, p271.

96 J Golding, 'Introduction', *ibid.*, p28.

97 The first text is *Picasso Collected Writings*, *op. cit.* p79; the second an author's transl. of 'chant des coqs midi des agitations désordonnées du ciel pétrifié...' *ibid.*, p215. Picasso combines the slaughtered cock with a mood of mourning for France in another set of texts from another Christmas Eve, this time in 1939. See *ibid.*, p208.

98 A former owner of the work, Mary Callery, recalled that either Picasso or Christian Zervos 'explained that this painting symbolised the destruction of helpless humanity by the forces of evil'. Misfeldt, *op. cit.*, p150.

99 See Chapter One, n.43.

100 In the Buffon prints, *La puce* [*The Flea*] represents a woman trying to catch a flea. See p152.

101 Author's transl. of '... l'amer prix de sa vertu et faisant du vin de sa vie la puce pique le coeur du coq à gorge déployée et presse du citron l'indifference que son noir destin illumine la table dressée à l'heure du déjeuner...', *Picasso Collected Writings*, *op. cit.*, p14. Another reference to the fate of the cock occurs on p88.

102 I am grateful to my colleague John Nash for bringing these to my attention!

103 J Seigel, *Bohemian Paris*, Harmondsworth, 1986, p318. I am grateful to Carole Lyons for this reference.

104 Gilot and Lake, *op. cit.*, p139.

105 *Picasso: Sculptor/Painter*, *op. cit.*, p241.

106 Gilot and Lake, *op. cit.*, p140.

107 Z.XV.41. This grim painting was swapped by Picasso for a white Oldsmobile convertible provided by the American dealer Samuel M Kootz, underlining once again that famous gap between 'art and life'... See M-L Bernadac *et al*, *Picasso et les choses*, Paris, 1993, p312.

108 Brassaï, *op. cit.*, pp225-26.

109 Picasso to Tériade [1932], in Ashton, *op. cit.*, p78.

110 In an apparently trivial collage, now in a private collection, Picasso attached his own famous deep black eyes, photographed by David Douglas Duncan, to a drawing of an owl. Writers have been quick to see the potential of this gesture: 'One day, Picasso drew an owl and cut its eyes out to replace them with the photographs of his own. It made a curious owl, with a curious owl's look, a man to the power of an owl.' Parmelin, *op. cit.*, p56. Penrose puts it less subtly: 'Nothing unnatural seemed to have taken place except that the bird now possessed the vision of a man whose eyes could not only see but understand.' Penrose, *op. cit.*, p322.

Chapter Four: Cats and Dogs

1 *Histoire naturelle du Comte de Buffon avec des eaux-fortes de Picasso*, Paris, 1942, 'Le chat' pp39-44'; 'Le chien' pp47-54.

2 White, pp90-91.This account of the historical fortunes and misfortunes of the cat echoes and occasionally elaborates, many of the ideas contained in the study by John Nash, *Cats*, Scala Themes in Art, London, 1992, and is very much a product of our mutual interest in the subject and the small, black, fat, delightfully exasperating creature who shares our home.

3 For a brief account of this change in fortunes see Beryl Rowland, *Animals with Human Faces. A Guide to Animal Symbolism*, London, 1975, pp51-52.

4 Quoted and transl. in Sarah Lipton, 'Jews, heretics and the sign of the cat in the *bible moralisée*', *Word and Image* VIII, 1992, pp368-69.

5 Rowland *op. cit.*, p51 who notes that: 'Hecate, goddess of the underworld, transformed herself into a cat according to Ovid; the witches in Apuleius' *Golden Ass* became cats.'

6 Keith Thomas, *Religion and the Decline of Magic. Studies in Popular Belief in Sixteenth- and Seventeenth-Century England*, London, 1971; Harmondsworth, 1978; repr. 1988, p530.

7 See Pieter van Boucle's *Still-life with Cat and Dog* in Chapter Five and Chardin's *The Ray* in Chapter Six.

8 See, for example Nicholas Maes' *Idle Servant* in the National Gallery, London and E de Jongh, *Tot lering en vermaak. Betekenissen van Hollandse genrevoorstellingen uit de zeventiende eeuw*, exh. cat., Rijksmuseum, Amsterdam, 1976, cat. 33 p146.

9 For example Lorenzo Lotto's in Recanati, Pinacoteca Communale and Aertgen van Leyden's in Antwerp, Museum voor Schone Kunsten.

10 For example Jan de Beer's in Madrid, Thyssen Collection and an Anon. Flemish Annunciation, sixteenth-century, Fitzwilliam Cambridge, for the latter see Jean-Michel Massing in *Splendours of Flanders. Late Medieval Art in Cambridge Collections* exh. cat. Fitzwilliam Museum, Cambridge, 1993, cat. 8 p50.

11 Rowland, *op. cit.*, p52.

12 See Meyer Schapiro, '"Muscipula Diaboli", the symbolism of the Mérode Altarpiece', *Art Bulletin*, XXVIII, 1928, pp182-87, repr. ed. Crichton Gilbert, *Renaissance Art*, New York, Evanston, London, 1970, pp21-42.

13 For elaboration see Chapter Nine.

14 This latter is more likely in those pictures where the cat is pure white, such as the Fitzwilliam Annnuciation and Jan de Beer's.

15 JA Phillips, *Eve. The History of an Idea*, New York, 1984, p62, who on p64 cites Agrippa's belief that sexual intercourse was the occasion of the Fall.

16 Edwin H Zeydel (ed. & transl.) *The Ship of Fools*, 1944; repr. New York, 1962, p138.

17 Edward Topsell, *The Historie of Foure-footed Beastes*, facs., The English Experience, no. 561, Amsterdam, New York, 1973, p104.

18 'Taste' from this same series is reproduced and discussed in Chapter Eight.

19 Topsell *op. cit.*, p105.

20 By contrast *Humilitas*, the special province of the Virgin, was the root of all virtue – see Adolf Katznellenbogen, *Allegories of the Virtues and Vices in Medieval Art. From Early Christian Times to the Thirteenth Century*, transl. Alan JP Crick, New York, 1964, pp66-67.

21 *Paradise Lost* IX lines 516-17.

22 Topsell, *op. cit.*, p105.

23 Also visible beyond the threshold in Bosch's picture is a young man likewise preening himself in a mirror. It is significant that all the sins in Bosch's *Tabletop of the Seven Deadly Sins* surround the iris of an eye, in its pupil a despairing resurrected Christ who asks, as the inscription tells us, 'Beware, Beware, the Lord sees'. For a reasoned account of the *Tabletop of the Seven Deadly Sins* see RH Marijnissen & P Ruyffelaere, *Hieronymus Bosch. The Complete Works*, Antwerp, New York, 1987, pp329-45; Christ himself was 'a mirror without blemish in which each man may see his own face' (*Dat boeck vanden pelgherym* 1486, *op. cit.*, p335).

24 For an account of the painting which is, in many respects, similar to this one, see de Jongh *op. cit.*, cat. 65, pp247-49.

25 See Chapter Three.

26 See de Jongh *loc. cit.* In contexts such as this, in which the juxtaposition of pipe and woman's lap is precise, the pipe is clearly a phallic symbol. In a *Brothel Scene* of 1630 by Hendrik Pot in the National Gallery, an elderly procuress makes obscene gesture with a pipe (Christopher Brown, *Scenes of Everyday Life. Dutch Genre Painting of the seventeenth Century*, London, 1984, p180); in Jan Steen's *Paar in slaapvertrek* (Couple in a Sleeping-Chamber) in The Hague, Museum Bredius, an old man entreats a young woman not to leave him; by the bed a pipe has been put out in a chamberpot (see Albert Blankert, *Museum Bredius. Catalogus van de Schilderijen en Tekeningen*, Zwolle, 's-Gravenhage, 1991, cat. 158, p214). 'Schoot' or 'lap, womb, sail (of ship)' was a common euphemism for the female genitalia, being used in this context in, for example, 'Rozemond overrompeld' from the 1659 *De Nieuwe Haagsche Nachtegaal* and H van Bulderen's 1673 'Op een juffrouw die een gaatje in mijn kous stopte', Hans van Straten (ed.), *Razernij der Liefde. Ontuchtige poësie in de Nederlanden van Middeleeuwen tot Franse tijd*, Amsterdam, 1992 respectively pp103 & 118.

27 Peter Wagner, *Eros Revived. Erotica of the Enlightenment in England and America*, London, 1988; 1990, pp174-76. A reproduction of the illustrated sheet is on p174, fig. 39. See also p246.

28 Robert Delort, *Les animaux ont une histoire*, Paris, 1984, p429 with other examples of the 'female sexuality' of the cat.

29 Rowland, *op. cit.*, p53 notes the street argot 'la fille a laissé aller le chat au fromage si souvent que l'on est aperçu qu'il fallait relargir sa robe'.

30 For the vulgar innuendos of fish and birds see the respective chapters in this book.

31 Nicholas Penny in *Reynolds* exh. cat., London, RA, 1986, p195. Reynolds had portrayed Kitty Fisher as Cleopatra (no 34, pp195-96 in this cat.) the 'libidinous Queen of Egypt' who drank a pearl dissolved in a glass of wine. As Penny notes, Kitty Fisher was renowned for her voracity and extravagance.

32 From Thomas Gray, 'On the Death of a Favourite Cat, Drowned in a Tub of Gold Fishes', in George MacBeth and Martin Booth (eds.), *The Book of Cats*, Newcastle upon Tyne, 1992, p309.

33 For these, see *Manet 1823-83* exh. cat. Grand Palais, Paris, Metropolitan Museum of Art, New York, 1983 cats. 111-13, 150.

34 quoted in MacBeth and Booth, *op. cit.*, p102.

35 Keith Thomas, *Man and the Natural World. Changing Attitudes in England 1500-1800*, Harmondsworth, 1984, pp109-110.

36 Françoise Cachin in *Manet op. cit.*, cat. 113 p298; for the *Cats' Rendezvous op. cit.*, cat. 114 pp299-301.

37 John Nash, *op. cit.*, pp54-58. Bonnard's Zurich painting of Vollard and Vuillard's of Duret are reproduced as his figs. 32 & 33.

38 *op. cit.*, p58.

39 Barber, p72.

40 *op. cit.*, p76.

41 Jonathan Brown, *Velázquez, Painter and Courtier*, New Haven, London, 1986, pp132-28.

42 Rowland, *op. cit.*, p63.

43 For this interpretation, see Erwin Panofsky, 'Jan van Eyck's Arnolfini Portrait', *Burlington Magazine* XLIV, 1934, pp117-27. Debate still rages on the precise meaning of this painting – see, for example, Jan Baptist Bedaux, 'The Reality of Symbols: the Question of disguised Symbolism in Jan van Eyck's *Arnolfini Portrait*, *Simiolus* XVI, 1986, pp5-28.

44 A delightful faith. The couple who hold each others' hand under the apple tree, and the little dog sharing their joy, show us a woman's faith. A dog is a very faithful pledge, the apple a lusty fruit, with which Venus has often joined two spouses in love, faith, and decency.
Andrea Alciati, *Emblematum libellus*, Paris; 1542; facs Darmstadt, 1980, p139. With thanks to John Roberts for the transl. The Latin verses express more or less the same sentiments and are transl. in M Koortboijan, *Self-Portraits*, Scala, Themes in Art, London, 1992, p45.

45 Catherine Johns, *Sex or Symbol? Erotic Images of Greece and Rome*, London, 1982; repr. 1992, fig. 100 and Plate 35. Even in the essentially pious *Arnolfini Portrait*, the dog and shoes may be considered sexual correlates – see Chapter Three, n27.

46 Topsell, *op. cit.*, pp171-72.

47 For example in Frans van Mieris' *Woman Rising at Noon* in Leningrad, Hermitage.

48 As in Jan Steen's two versions of *The Morning Toilet* in the Rijksmuseum, Amsterdam, and Col. HM the Queen, London, and Hogarth's engravings of indoor 'Before and After' (indoor version).

49 Rowland, *op. cit.*, p65.

50 *Alte Pinakothek Munich. Explanatory Notes on the Works Exhibited*, 1986, cat. HuW 35, p210.

51 For an overview, see Rowland, *op. cit.*, pp58-66 and Thomas, *op. cit.*, pp105-106.

52 Barber, *op. cit.*, pp76-77. De Fournival also uses the image to brutally conclude his *Bestiaire d'Amour*.

53 *op. cit.*, p77 which also mentions 'The dog who lets go of the meat in the river because he is chasing his shadow signifies foolish men who abandon what is rightfully theirs because ambition makes them pursue the unknown.

54 Robert Rosenblum, *The Dog in Art from Rococo to Post-Modernism*, London, New York, 1988, p51.

55 In *Modern Painters* quoted in Richard Ormond et al., *Sir Edwin Landseer* exh. cat., Philadelphia Museum of Art, London, Tate Gallery, 1981-82, cat. 66 p111.

56 *op. cit.*, p35.

57 According to Gilot, Picasso considered his own cubist portrait of Vollard the best, F Gilot and C Lake, *Life with Picasso*, London, 1965, p41.

58 A Vallentin, *Picasso*, New York, 1963, p5.

59 See M-L Bernadac et al, *Picasso et les choses*, Paris, 1993, p338.

60 *Histoire Naturelle...*, *op. cit.*, p39.

61 *Picasso et les choses*, *op. cit.*, p327.

62 29/4/39 & 30/4/39. The subject makes a reprise in *Les quatres petites filles* of November 1947, M-L Bernadac and C Piot, *Picasso, Collected Writings*, London, 1989, pp200-205, & p297.

63 J Sabartés, *Picasso, portraits et souvenirs*, Paris, 1946, p23 [author's transl.].

64 Brassaï, *Picasso & Co*, London, 1966, p52, gives such a similar account up to this point that he and Sabartés may be reporting the same conversation.

65 *Histoire Naturelle*, *op., cit.*, p40.

66 S 195.

67 Brassaï, *op. cit.*, p120. Brassaï noticed at an earlier date that the tail of the plaster version of the cat seemed to form a white exclamation mark. *ibid.*, p52.

68 Musée d'Orsay, Paris.

69 See eg J Richardson, 'L'Époque Jacqueline', *Late Picasso*, London, 1988, p30.

70 P Verlaine, 'Cat and Lady', transl. A Symons in G MacBeth and M Booth (eds.), *The Book of Cats*, Newcastle upon Tyne, 1992, p112.

71 Z.IX.73, London, Tate Gallery.

72 R Penrose, *Picasso, His Life and Work*, London, 1958, p279; *Picasso*, [Ex.Cat. Arts Council of Great Britain], London, 1960, p47.

73 *Histoire Naturelle...*, *op. cit.*, p69-74.

74 See L Steinberg, 'The Algerian Women and Picasso at Large', *Other Criteria*, New York, 1972, pp125-234.

75 The best introductory work remains J Golding, *Cubism, A History and an Analysis 1907-14*, London, 1988 [3rd rev. ed.]. For recent work on the more complex questions raised by cubism for the theory of art, see W Rubin et al, *Picasso and Braque, Pioneering Cubism*, London, 1989.

76 Picasso painted a cubist work known as 'Ma Jolie' ('My pretty one'). For more thoughts on the words in Picasso's cubism see R Rosenblum, 'Picasso and the Typography of Cubism', in J Golding and R Penrose (eds.), *Pablo Picasso 1881-1973*, London; D Cottington, 'What the Papers Say'; C Poggi, *In Defiance of Painting*, London, 1993; Leighten, 'Picasso's Collages and the Threat of War 1912-13', *Art Bulletin*, Vol.LXVII, No 4, December 1985, pp653-72. For Eva see chronology in Rubin *op. cit.*

77 J Richardson, 'Your Show of Shows', *New York Review of Books*, Vol XXVII, No 12 17/7/80, pp16-24.

78 According to Brassaï, *op. cit.*, p245.

79 P Daix, *Picasso, Life and Art*, London, 1994.

80 Museu Picasso, Barcelona, MPB 110.083.

81 Richardson, *A Life of Picasso, op. cit.*, ch 16, passim.

82 H Murger, *Scènes de la vie bohème*, Paris, 1851. These stories provided Puccini with the basis for his sentimental opera *La Bohème*.

83 Richardson, *A Life of Picasso, op. cit.*, p295.

84 *ibid.*, p405.

85 Z.II.18, The Museum of Modern Art, New York.

86 Brassaï, *op. cit.*, p42.

87 *ibid.*, p92.

88 Quinn writes 'Dogs often have the free run of his studio. If they seem likely to threaten the safety of some object he says: "Don't worry, they seem to sense where they have no right to go."', E Quinn, *Picasso at Work*, London, 1965, np section four. Duncan recalls that the Dalmatian Perro 'developed a crush on Picasso... He was simply head-in-the-clouds in love.' DD Duncan, *Picasso's Picassos*, London, 1961, p192. Parmelin, *op. cit.*, is littered with allusions to Picasso's special relationship with his pets.

89 According to Geneviève Laporte, Picasso 'was delighted by the way dogs jump about to express happiness and thought it sad that men do not do the same', G Laporte, *Sunshine at Midnight*, 1973, London, 1975, transl. D Cooper, p2.

90 For a much more extensive discussion of the problems involved in this kind of interpretation, as well as more on this and other related prints, and the precise relationship between Picasso and the brothers, see N Cox, 'One Man and His Dog, A Narrative Episode in Picasso's Late Prints', [Paper presented at a Symposium, University of East Anglia, December 1993], publication forthcoming.

91 The variations (which comprise forty-four paintings of the *Meninas* proper, *The Piano*, nine canvasses of *Pigeons*, three landscapes and a portrait of Jacqueline) were presented to the Museu Picasso in Barcelona by Picasso in 1968; nos. MPB 70.433-90.

92 The figure is wrongly identified as the Infanta in W Spies, *Picasso's World of Children*, New York, 1994, p92.

93 Parmelin, *op. cit.*, p228.

94 Penrose, *op. cit.*, p374.

95 *Picasso et les choses*, *op. cit.*, Paris, 1993, p194.

96 W Misfeldt, 'The Theme of the Cock in Picasso's Oeuvre', *Art Journal*, Vol.XXVIII, No 2, Winter 1969, pp146-54 & 165.

97 Brassaï, *op. cit.*, p74.

98 The theme of death during the war is considered in L Steinberg 'The Skulls of Picasso', *Other Criteria*, Oxford, 1972, pp115-23. See also E Cowling, 'Objects into Sculpture', *Picasso Sculptor/Painter*, London, 1994, p238.

Chapter Five: Goats and Sheep

1 Dom Pierre Miquel, *Dictionnaire symbolique des animaux, Zoologie mystique*, Paris, 1988, p62.

2 Barber, p54. White p41 n. 2 suggests that a pun is intended here, between 'gazelle' and 'gaze'.

3 Barber, *loc. cit.*

4 *op. cit.*, p55.

5 White, p43.

6 *ibid.*

7 Barber, p81.

8 Francis Klingender, *Animals in Art and Thought to the End of the Middle Ages*, London, 1971, pp215-16.

9 White, p72.

10 *op. cit.*, pp73-74.

11 Genesis XXII 7-8.

12 Genesis XXII: 13.

13 James Hall, *Hall's Dictionary of Subjects and Symbols in Art*, rev. ed., London, 1989, p185.

14 Keith Thomas, *Man and the Natural World. Changing Attitudes in England 1500-1800*, Harmondsworth, 1984, pp294-95.

15 *Bursa*, ie money bag, since antiquity common slang for the scrotum – see JN Adams, *the Latin Sexual Vocabulary*, London, 1982; repr. 1990, pp75-76.

16 Thomas, *op. cit.*, p293.

17 Barber, p78.

18 *op. cit.*, p82 citing Luke 15,9: 'Yet thou never gavest me a kid, that I might make merry with my friends'.

19 *op. cit.*, p80, referring to Ezekiel 27:11: 'Arabia, and all the princes of Kedar, they occupied with thee in lambs, and rams, and goats.'

20 *op. cit.*, p83.

21 Oxford English Dictionary.

22 Geoge Boas (ed.), *The Hieroglyphics of Horapollo*, Bolingen Series XXIII, New York, 1950. I 48 p65.

23 Beryl Rowland, *Animals with Human Faces. A Guide to Animal Symbolism*, Knoxville, 1973; London, 1974, p81; JG Frazer, *The Golden Bough. A Study in Magic and Religion*, abridged ed., London & Basingstoke, 1922, pp464ff.

24 Frazer, *op. cit.*, pp390-91.

25 *op. cit.*, p391.

26 *op. cit.*, p464.

27 Brian P Levack, *The Witch-Hunt in Early Modern Europe*, London, New York, 1987, p28.

28 *ibid.*

29 *ibid.*; Rowland, *op. cit.*, pp83-84.

30 Keith Thomas, *Religion and the Decline of Magic. Studies in Popular Belief in Sixteenth- and Seventeenth-Century England*, London, 1971; Harmondsworth, repr. 1988, pp521ff; Levack *op. cit.*, p32ff.

31 ed. & transl. Rev Montague Summers, *The Malleus Maleficarum of Heinrich Kramer and James Sprenger*, London, 1928; repr. New York, 1971, Question VI: 'Concerning Witches who copulate with Devils...' p41.

32 Frazer, *op. cit.*, pp540-62ff.

33 Leviticus XVI: 9.

34 Leviticus XVI: 22.

35 Barber, p83.

36 *Histoire naturelle du Comte de Buffon avec des eaux-fortes de Picasso*, Paris, 1942, 'La chèvre', p57.

37 Quoted in J Boardman *et al*, *The Oxford History of the Classical World*, Oxford, 1986, p264.

38 Z. I.321, The Cleveland Museum of Art.

39 Picasso's related treatment of the woman as an assassin of men is discussed in N Cox, 'Marat/Sade/Picasso', *Art History*, Vol 17 No.3, September 1994, pp383-417.

40 *Les Quatre Petites Filles* in M-L Bernadac and C Piot, *Picasso, Collected Writings*, London, 1989, pp308-309.

41 J Richardson with M McCully, *A Life of Picasso, volume 1, 1881-1906*, London, 1991, p64.

42 G Redford, *A Manual of Ancient Sculpture*, 2nd ed., London, 1886, p270. A line drawing of the original appears in S Reinach, *Répertoire de la statuaire grècque et romaine*, Vol I, Angers, n.d., p415.

43 A drawing of the cast by a student of a few years later is just visible in a photograph reproduced in Richardson, *op. cit.*, p63.

44 In this case a cast can be seen in a photograph of plaster casts in the Malaga art school, reproduced in *op. cit.*, p35.

45 E Cowling, 'Catalogue', *Picasso Sculptor/Painter*, London, 1994, p275.

46 *ibid.*

47 B Léal in M-L Bernadac *et al*, *Picasso, une nouvelle dation*, Paris, 1990, p160 [author's transl.].

48 P Laporte, 'The Man with a Lamb', *Art Journal*, Vol 21, No.2, pp144-50. Laporte suggests that the composition is only found in 'pre-Greek relief or painting', *ibid.*, p144.

49 F Gilot and C Lake, *Life with Picasso*, London, 1965, p289.

50 H Parmelin, *Picasso Plain*, London, 1963, p59.

51 Picasso in 1964, quoted in M-L Bernadac *et al*, *The Musée Picasso, Paris*, [cat. of the collection, vol I] London, 1986, p145.

52 P Daix, *Picasso, Life and Art*, London, 1994, p304.

53 J-P Crespelle, *Picasso, les femmes, les amis, l'oeuvre*, Paris, 1967, p264.

54 S 602, 603.

55 Other examples of the set of at least eight variations include: Z.XXV.272, now in The Art Institute of Chicago; Z.XXVII.428, Collection Peter Ludwig, Aachen.

56 Parmelin, *op. cit.*, pp18-19.

57 *Histoire naturelle...*, *op. cit.*, p36 [author's transl.].

58 Z.XIV.289, Collection Marina Picasso, Geneva.

59 R Dor de la Souchère, *Picasso in Antibes*, London, 1960, n.p, entry for cat. no20 [author's transl.].

60 Cowling, *op. cit.*, p282. 'The animal's backbone and forehead were made with a palm branch Picasso had had by him for a couple of years, the rib cage and pregnant belly with a wicker basket, the haunches with metal strapping, the udder with terracotta milk jars found at the Madoura factory, the legs with branches, the sternum with a tin, the horns and beard with a section of vine, the ears with cardboard, the tail and whiskers with copper wire, the anus with a piece of metal pipe, and the vagina with a bent tin lid.' *ibid.* p279.

61 Especially the nose, according to Parmelin, *op. cit.*, p15-16.

62 Once cast in bronze, Parmelin felt the piece became more goat-like than the original; *ibid.*

63 F Gilot & C Lake, *Life with Picasso*, London, 1965, pp216-17.

64 Parmelin, *op. cit.*, pp196-200.

65 The name of Orpheus was taken up in Orphism, which, like Pythagorism, was a later sixth-century religious cult that abominated meat eating, whose crede is contained in Empedocles' poem *Purifications*. See *The Oxford History of the Classical World*, *op. cit.*, p269.

66 Parmelin, *op. cit.*, p23. According to P O'Brian, *Pablo Ruiz Picasso, A Biography*, London, 1976, p406, Hélène Parmelin and Edouard Pignon joined Picasso in Vallauris for the first time in early 1952. Although she does not give a date for Picasso tending the skull, it seems to be an early memory for her.

67 See M-L Bernadac *et al*, *Picasso et les choses*, Paris, 1992., pp314-19 for more on this group of works.

68 Cowling, *op. cit.*, p280.

69 *Picasso et les choses*, *op. cit.*, pp261-64.

70 'New York (Office and Denunciation)', in FG Lorca, *Selected Poems*, (transl. and introduced by M Williams), Newcastle upon Tyne, 1992, p147. Georges Bataille's text 'Abattoir' makes a different point, insisting on a decay of civilization which is symbolszed in the secularisation – and seclusion – of the modern abattoir. G Bataille 'Abattoir', *Documents*, No 6, November 1929, p329.

71 'For today's public, [Three Sheep's Skulls] is a truly horrifying vision which prefigures the carnage of the ovens of Auschwitz and Belsen' *Picasso et les choses*, *op. cit.*, p319 [author's transl.].

72 Musée Picasso, RF 1973-62.

73 See *Picasso, une nouvelle dation*, *op. cit.*, p34.

Chapter Six: Watery Creatures

1 For similar observations see S Peter Dance, *The Art of Natural History*, New York, 1978; 1990, p12.
2 Ann Payne, *Medieval Beasts*, London, 1990, p92; see the Preface to the fish section in Barber pp201-202.
3 White, p195; Barber p201.
4 Barber, p202.
5 White, pp206-207.
6 *op. cit.*, pp207-208.
7 Bosch was credited as 'inventor' on the print, produced 40 years after his death, presumably to capitalise on the reputation of the older artist. Walter S Gibson, *Bruegel*, London, 1977; repr. 1988, pp44-45.
8 *op. cit.*, p54.
9 E de Jongh, *Tot lering en vermaak. Betekenissen van hollandse genrevoorstellingen uit de zeventiende eeuw* exh. cat., Rijksmuseum, Amsterdam, 1976, cat. 65 p248.
10 Pieter van Thiel in *Dawn of the Golden Age. Northern Netherlandish Art 1580-1620*, exh. cat., Rijksmuseum , Amsterdam, 1993-94, cat. 274 p602.
11 cf the verse 'Van een visser die uit vissen ging' from the 1703 *De vermakelijke Buysman* quoted in Hans van Straten (ed.), *Razerny der Liefde. Ontuchtige poësie in de Nederlanden van Middeleeuwen tot franse Tijd*, Amsterdam, 1992, pp139-41.
12 Dom Pierre Miquel, *Dictionnaire symbolique des animaux. Zoologie mystique*, Paris, 1991, p177; the difficulty of opening oysters was doubtless responsible for their association with virginity – and the opposite, once they were broached.
13 PJ Vinken, 'Some Observations on the Broken Pot in Art and Literature', *American Imago* XV, 1958, pp149-74.
14 *op. cit.*, pp162-63.
15 For an overview, Ingvar Bergström, *Dutch Still-life Painting in the Seventeenth Century*, Christina Hedström and Gerald Taylor (transl.), New York, 1983, *op. cit.*, Chapter VIII: 'Willem Kalf and his Followers', pp260ff.
16 From the Greek *ikhthus*, also the acrostic of Jesus Christ, with which the early Christians, fearful of reprisal, identified him – Louis Réau, *Iconographie de l'art chrétien* vol. I, Paris, 1955, p81. The fish was also a symbol of faith, of Baptism and baptised, those Christians who, like small fish who cannot live out of water, cannot live outside the Church – Dom Pierre Miquel, *op. cit.*, pp219-20, quoting Tertullian's *Treatise of Baptism* amongst others.
17 Réau *op. cit.*, pp88-89. Norbert Schneider gives this interpretation to the lobster in Jan Davidsz de Heem's *Still-life with Fruit and Lobster* in Berlin, identifying the bunch of grapes as 'eucharistic' in *Les Natures Mortes. Réalité et symbolique des choses*, Cologne, 1990, p116.
18 Madlyn Millner Kahr, *Dutch Painting in the Seventeenth Century*, New York, 1978, pp202-203.
19 Quoted in *Art in Seventeenth-Century Holland* exh. cat., London, National Gallery, 1976, cat. 64 p56.
20 On these see Bergström, *op. cit.*, pp229-40.
21 See Charles C Moffat's discussion of Manet's *Fruit on a Table*, Musée d'Orsay, and *Still Life with Fish*, The Art Institute of Chicago in *Manet 1832-83* exh. cat., Grand Palais, Paris; Metropolitan Museum of Art, New York, 1983, respectively cats 80 & 81 pp212-16.
22 One writer has suggested Late Minoan I pottery as a possible direct source, G Schiff, *Picasso at Work at Home; Selections from the Marina Picasso Collection*, Miami, 1985, p107.
23 P Daix, *Picasso, Life and Art*, London, 1993, p293.
24 F Gilot & C Lake, *Life with Picasso*, London, 1965, p129.
25 19/3/37 [I], in M-L Bernadac and C Piot, *Picasso, Collected Writings*, London, 1989, p162.
26 This interpretation follows that given in *ibid.*, pp406-407.
27 A few weeks later Picasso made one lithograph of the same composition (B 584) and another including fish alongside the lobster (B 582).
28 Daix, *op. cit.*, pp301; 259.
29 W Spies, *Picasso's World of Children*, New York, 1994, p66.
30 *ibid*.
31 P O'Brian, *Pablo Ruiz Picasso, A Biography*, London, 1976, p466.
32 eg Raphael, *The Miraculous Draft of Fishes*, [Tapestry Cartoon], c1514, Victoria & Albert Museum, London.
33 Recently vacated by the photographer Man Ray.
34 This form has been the subject of considerable discussion, and has been plausibly alternatively identified as the moon. In describing it as a lamp, I am following the argument of William Rubin and Roland Penrose. See W Rubin, *Picasso in the Collection of the Museum of Modern Art*, New York, 1972, p232, n.5.
35 These two woman were identified as Dora Maar (with the bicycle) and Jacqueline Lamba by Maar herself in H & S Janis, *Picasso, The Recent Years*, New York, 1946, text facing plate 5. The figure with the bicycle reappears again in 1962-63 in the *Rape of the Sabines* series. G Schiff, 'The Sabines Sketchbook No.163, 1962', *Je Suis le Cahier, The Sketchbooks of Picasso*, London, 1986, pp179-89.
36 W Rubin, *op. cit.*, p156.
37 R Penrose, *Picasso, Life and Art*, London, 1958, *op. cit.*, pp289-90.
38 Rubin, *op. cit.*, pp232-33 for references and comment.
39 M Rosenthal, 'Picasso's *Night Fishing in Antibes*: A Meditation on Death', *Art Bulletin*, Vol 65, No.4, December 1983, pp649-58.
40 N Corazzo, 'Picasso's 'Night fishing in Antibes': a new source', *Burlington Magazine*, Vol 132, No 1043, February 1990, pp99-101. In another much longer and more speculative article, the painting is related to Picasso's private life, manuscript illuminations of the apocalypse, and to the artist's continuing reflection on the events of the Spanish Civil War. See TA Burgard, 'Picasso's *Night Fishing in Antibes*: Autobiography, Apocalypse, and the Spanish Civil War', *Art Bulletin*, Vol 68, No 4, December 1986, pp657-72
41 By contrast, Rubin, *op. cit.*, p156, sees him as 'equine'.
42 L Steefel Jnr., 'Body Imagery in Picasso's *Night Fishing in Antibes*', *Art Journal*, XXV, No 4, Summer 1966, p358.

Chapter Seven: Insects

1 For discussion, see JJG Alexander, unpaginated Introduction to *The Master of Mary of Burgundy. A Book of Hours for Englebert of Nassau. The Bodleian Library, Oxford*, New York, 1970, partial facs actual size of Bodley MS Douce 219-220). It is worth noting that in this MS particular pleasure has been taken in painting many different types of butterfly.
2 As Alexander, *loc. cit.*, observes, this was particularly useful in sustaining the *trompe-l'oeil* of illuminated borders, providing a series of levels of illusion each related to the other, which unified the pictorial composition of the page. 'Nearest to us are the flowers in front of the page, then comes the page itself, and finally behind it is the scene portrayed in the miniature'. This provided an effective solution to the jarring effect of juxtaposing two-dimensional script and the three-dimensional space of the main picture.
3 Ernst Kris and Otto Kurz, *Legend, Myth and Magic in the Image of the Artist. An Historical Experiment*, transl. Alastair Lang; rev. Lottie M Newman, New Haven, London, 1979. Chapter Three: 'The Artist as Magician. The Work of Art as a Copy of Reality', pp61-71, esp. p64.
4 On the impact of the microscope on the study of insects see S Peter Dance, *The Art of Natural History*, New York, 1978; 1990. Chapter IX 'Through the Microscope' pp181ff.
5 Barber, p199; White, p191. In the former, 'Spiders are worms of the air, so called because they live on air, which produce from their slender bodies long threads, and, always busy with weaving, they never cease from their labours, perpetually occupied with their craft.'
6 Alan Wood Rendell (ed. & transl.), *Physiologus. A Metrical Bestiary of Twelve Chapters by Bishop Theobald*, London, 1928, p31.
7 Edward Topsell, *The Historie of Serpents*, London, 1608, The English Experience, Amsterdam, 1973, pp246-76.
8 For example in Jacob Cats' emblem XL 'Non intrandum, aut penetrandum' from his *Sinne- en Minne-beelden*, 1618, illustrated with a spider's web, which he terms 'Venus warre-net'. This is perhaps the reason Willem Buytewech included a spider's web in his painting of two elegant couples in Rijksmuseum, Amsterdam – see E de Jongh, *Tot lering en vermaak. Betekenissen van hollandse genrevoorstellingen uit de zeventiende eeuw*, exh. cat., Rijksmuseum, Amsterdam, 1976, cat. 10, p65.
9 Barber, p200; cf White, p193.
10 Frankie Rubinstein, *A Dictionary of Shakespeare's Sexual Puns and their Significance*, London, Basingstoke, 1984, p102. cf John Donne, 'The Flea'; *Merry Wives of Windsor* IV.ii. 158; *Henry VI Part One* III.ii.56.
11 Christopher Wright, *The French Painters of the Seventeenth Century*, London, 1985, p46. Given the northern predilection for representing sacred personages as ordinary people in humble domestic surroundings, it is not entirely unreasonable to assume that something similar was intended here. Nevertheless, the propriety of representing a pregnant, half-naked Virgin indulging in such a dubious activity, has to be seriously questioned.
12 In Los Angeles County Museum of Art. For examples of the theme by other seventeenth-century painters see *Les Vanités dans la peinture au XVIIe siècle* exh. cat., Musée des Beaux-Arts, Caen; Musée du Petit Palais, Paris, 1990-91, cat. nos F24-37. In a painting by Jacob van Campen, in Museum Bredius, The Hague, given the title *Vrouw bij haar toilet* [*Woman at her Toilet*] a young woman searches for a flea. On the table is a mirror, by her feet a candle, chamberpot, comb and candle, also an attentive small dog [for the meaning of which see Chapter Four]. These objects ostensibly announce her iniquity, but aross her knee lies a rosary, prompting the speculation that the painting could represent the Penitent Magdalene – see Albert Blankert, *Museum Bredius. Catalogus van de schilderijn en tekeningen*, Zwolle, 's-Gravenhage, 1991, cat. 29 pp59-60.
13 For candles and skulls (and flies) as Vanitas symbols see Chapter Three.
14 Barber, pp199-200; White, p192.

15 Abraham Mignon was a master of this genre, and there is a fine example of his work in Aix-en-Provence, Musée Granet, reproduced in *les Vanités op. cit.*, cat. O.41, which contains a mouse, a snail, a fly, a wasp, a dragonfly, a moth and two types of butterfly, one of which appears to be a copulating pair. See Norbert Schneider, *Les Natures Mortes. Réalité et symbolique des choses. La peinture de natures mortes à la naissance des temps modernes*, Cologne, 1990, esp. Chapter Nine, pp120ff.

16 Dom Pierre Miquel, *Dictionnaire symbolique des animaux. Zoologie mystique*, Paris, 1991, p207.

17 James Hall, *Hall's Dictionary of Subjects and Symbols in Art*, rev. ed., London, 1989, p54.

18 Iona Opie & Moira Tatum (eds.), *A Dictionary of Superstitions*, Oxford, 1992, p51.

19 RH Marijnissen & P Ruffelaere in *Hieronymus Bosch. The Complete Works*, Antwerp, 1987, p466 quote the French shepherds' calendar: 'The little owl admits that it represents the soul in a state of sin, and the fluttering butterfly is an image of desire: 'The wind leads me to pleasure ... a true desire is born in me.' Unfortunately the chapter on the sayings of the birds which includes this passage has been omitted from GC Heseltine's English edition, *The Kalendar and Compost of Shepherds*, London, 1931, as noted in his introduction pix.

20 cf letter from Rubens to Jacques Dupuy dated October 29, 1626 complaining that the latter picture had been misunderstood: '... the figures that he calls Cupids and Zephyrs are the happy Hours attending the birth of the Queen; they can be recognised by their butterfly wings and because they are feminine.' In Ruth Saunders Magurn (ed. & transl.), *The Letters of Peter Paul Rubens*, Cambridge, Mass., 1955, p150.

21 Pieter van Thiel in *Dawn of the Golden Age. Northern Netherlandish Art 1580-1620* exh. cat., Riksmuseum, Amsterdam, 1993-94, càt. 7, p338. This interpretation is based on Ripa's *Iconologia*, 1644, p361.

22 From the 1627 edition, the English version being numbered as Emblem LIII.

23 J Renard, 'Au Jardin', *Histoires Naturelles*, 1896, Paris, 1984, pp107-108.

24 Interview with T Jellinik in J Auerbach, 'Brushes with Genius', *The Independent on Sunday* (magazine), 6/2/94, p22.

25 As suggested by B Baer, *Picasso the Printmaker*, Dallas, 1983, p103.

26 See also Leo Steinberg's discussion of the classical model for the pose, the Venus Callipyge (Venus of the shapely buttocks), 'The Algerian Women and Picasso At Large', *Other Criteria*, Oxford, 1972, p186.

27 P Cramer *et al*, *Pablo Picasso, The Illustrated Books, Catalogue Raisonné*, Geneva, 1983, p106. Interestingly, Picasso used a tiny carving of a lice-comb [S 187] as an excuse for teasing Françoise Gilot on one of her early visits to his studio. She also claims that Picasso thought of Dora Maar as a Kafkaesque beetle, and drew a beetle on the walls of Dora's appartment. F Gilot & C Lake, *Life with Picasso*, London, 1965, p23 & p85.

28 J Richardson, *A Life of Picasso. Volume 1: 1881-1906*, London, 1991, p243.

29 A category invented by the Musée Picasso for the purposes of classifying an unusual group of works, three-dimensional but retaining the two-dimensional surface as a 'background and foundation', M-L Bernadac *et al*, *The Musée Picasso, Paris*, cat. of the collections, vol I, London, 1986, p129.

30 MP 123-30.

31 A Breton, 'Picasso dans son élément', *Minotaure* No.1, Paris, 1933, p10. The article was illustrated with a photograph of the work by Brassaï.

32 The sailor suit appears in the writings (19/3/38), as Spies has recently noted. W Spies, *Picasso's World of Children*, New York, 1994, p90.

33 J Seckler, 'Picasso Explains', *New Masses*, New York, 13/3/45, pp4-7 in D Ashton, *Picasso on Art; A Selection of Views*, London, 1972, pp135-36.

34 Spies, *op. cit.*, p66.

35 AH Barr Jnr., *Picasso, Fifty Years of His Art*, New York, 1946, p217.

36 Maia Widmaier believes the painting to be a depiction of herself. Letter to Croydon Museum Service, May 1994.

37 cf. Gilot, *op. cit.*, p52.

Chapter Eight: Monkeys

1 The ape, that most vile beast, how like it is to ourselves! HT Riley (ed.), *Dictionary of Latin Quotations*, London, 1860, p431.

2 R Penrose, *Picasso, His Life and Work*, London, 1958, p281.

3 For an index and some illustrations see Lilian MC Randall, *Images in the Margins of Gothic Manuscripts*, Berkeley, Los Angeles, 1966, pp48-65.

4 Barber, p48.

5 White, p34. An additional etymology for *simia* is also noted here and in Bodley 764: that it comes from the Greek meaning with squashed, or pressed-together nostrils. White, p35; Barber, p49.

6 Barber, p49.

7 The English version is Emblem V in the 1627 edition.

8 Edward Topsell, *The Historie of Foure-footed Beastes*, facs., The English Experience, no. 561, Amsterdam, New York, 1973, p4.

9 Barber, p49.

10 According to Michael Camille, *Image on the Edge. The Margins of Medieval Art*, London, 1992, pp24-26, this image '... was presumably inspired by an unfortunate word division seven lines above. This line ends by breaking the word *culpa* (sin) in a crucial place, thus it reads *Liber est a cul* – the book is to the bum!'

11 'Als apen hooger klimmen willen,
Dan ziet men juist hun naakte billen'
K ter Laan, *Nederlandse spreekwoorden/spreuken en zegswijzen*, Amsterdam, 1988, 'aap' no 8 p13.

12 White, p35. The quotation paraphrases II Thessalonians 2:8 (see Barber p49). The bestiarist often made little distinction between monkeys (which have tails) and apes (which do not). Many of the variations of apes listed in the bestiary we would class as monsters (for which see Chapter Nine). Topsell does give monkeys their own chapter and illustration together with other weird ape-hybrids.

13 Louis Réau, *Iconographie de l'art Chrétien* Vol. I, Paris, 1955, p112.

14 Roemer Visscher, *Sinnepoppen*, 1614, ed. L Brummel, facs The Hague, 1949, II xxx p91.

15 Paraphrase of 'Den Aap en de Kat' from *Vorstelijke Warande der Dieren* [Stately Pleasure-Ground of Animals] of 1617 in A Verwey (ed.), *Volledige Dichtwerken en Oorspronkelijk Proza*, Amsterdam, 1937, p60.

16 Réau, *op. cit.*, p130.

17 For examples, Beryl Rowland, *Animals with Human Faces. A Guide to Animal Symbolism*, Knoxville, 1973; London, 1974, pp8-10.

18 Aelian, *On the Characteristics of Animals*, transl. AF Scholfield, 3 vols, London, Cambridge, Mass., 1972, XVII.25.

19 Rowland, *op. cit.*, p10.

20 cf. Florence McCulloch, *Medieval Latin and French Bestiaries*, Chapel Hill, rev. ed. 1962, p88: 'The probable explanation for this choice is that the monkey was associated with the Fall of Man, and it is often pictured eating an apple'. See also Rowland, *op. cit.*, p12.

21 *Dawn of the Golden Age. Northern Netherlandish Art 1580-1620* exh. cat., Amsterdam, 1993-94, cat. 7, p338. It was also believed that pride appears especially in both choleric and sanguine men – Carl Gustave Stridbeck, *Bruegelstudien*, Stockholm, 1956, p76 & p300 n. 22.

22 Rowland, *op. cit.*, p12. For the symbolism of owls, see Chapter Three.

23 cf Rowland, *op. cit.*, p13.

24 Réau, *op. cit.*, Vol. I, p112.

25 E Cowling, 'Catalogue', *Picasso Sculptor/Painter*, London, 1994, p280.

26 F Gilot & C Lake, *Life with Picasso*, London, 1965, p295.

27 *ibid*.

28 Picasso had every cause to remember this work fondly, since it was the first he sold to an important early patron, Leo Stein. M Hoog, 'Les variations de Picasso après le cubisme', G Tinterow (ed.), *Picasso Clasico*, Malaga, 1993, p333, argues that the origin for Picasso's composition is Leonardo da Vinci's Louvre *St. Anne, Virgin, Child and Lamb*.

29 T Reff, 'Harlequins, Saltimbanques, Clowns and Fools', *Art Forum*, October 1971, pp30-43, this reference p42; and A Blunt & P Pool, *Picasso, The Formative Years*, London, 1962, caption to ill 130-33.

30 Picasso painted a *Clown and Monkey* (Z.I.57) in 1901. There was in fact a monkey circus in Paris at the time. Reff, *op. cit.*, p37.

31 G Apollinaire, 'Young Artists: Picasso the Painter', *La Plume*, Paris 15th May 1905; transl. in M Mccully, *A Picasso Anthology*, London, 1981, pp52-53.

32 *Histoire naturelle du Comte de Buffon avec des eaux-fortes de Picasso*, Paris, 1942, 'le singe', pp87-90, this quotation p88 [author's transl.].

33 J Sabartés, *Picasso: portraits et souvenirs*, Paris, 1946, p202.

34 G Cumont, *Picasso animalier*, Alfort, 1956, p18, claims that Picasso bargained with a sailor for a monkey when in Marsaille, but gives no date. Brassaï similarly mentions in passing a pet monkey during Picasso's period in the Bateau Lavoir, Brassaï, *Picasso & Co*, London, 1967, p196. G Laporte describes how Picasso and Fernande Olivier gave away a troublesome chimpanzee to gypsies whilst staying in Ceret in 1911, G Laporte, *Sunshine at Midnight*, 1973, London, 1975, (transl. D Cooper), pp39-40.

35 R Penrose, *Picasso, Life and Art*, London, 1958, p280-81.

36 'Suite de 180 dessins de Picasso' *Verve*, Vol VIII, Nos.29-30, Paris, 1954.

37 eg J Berger, *The Success and Failure of Picasso*, London, 1966, pp186-202.

38 J Richardson, *A Life of Picasso: Vol 1 1881-1906*, London, p339.

39 Brassaï, op,cit, p197.

40 eg K Kleinfelder, *The Artist, His Model, Her Image, His Gaze: Picasso's Pursuit of the Model*, Chicago, 1993, esp. Chapter Three.

41 H Parmelin, *Picasso Plain*, London, 1963, p48.

42 M Leiris, 'Picasso et la comédie humaine ou; les avatars de gros pied', repr. *Un génie sans piedestal*, Paris, 1992, pp43-64.

Chapter Nine: Monsters

1 Keith Thomas, *Man and the Natural World. Changing Attitudes in England 1500-1800*, Harmondsworth, 1984, p134.

2 S Peter Dance, *The Art of Natural History*, New York, 1978, p38.

3 For these creatures, White, pp49-53; Barber, pp61-64.

4 Edward Topsell, *The Historie of Foure-footed Beastes*, facs., The English Experience, no. 561, Amsterdam, New York, 1973, p442.

5 White p255.

6 *op. cit.*, p251.

7 *op. cit.*, p253.

8 Michael Camille, *Image on the Edge. The Margins of Medieval Art*, London, 1992, p81.

9 E Mâle, *The Gothic Image. Religious Art in France of the Thirteenth Century*, Dora Nussey (transl.), New York, 1958; 1972, pp47ff.

10 Francis Klingender, *Animals in Art and Thought to the End of the Middle Ages*, London, 1971, pp328ff.

11 Barber, p183.

12 *op. cit.*, p50.

13 Beryl Rowland, *Animals with Human Faces. A Guide to Animal Symbolism*, Knoxville, 1973; London, 1974, p81.

14 Ovid: *Metamorphoses* VI: 110-12.

15 Erwin Panofsky, *The Life and Art of Albrecht Dürer*, Princeton, 1943; repr. 1971, p87.

16 Topsell, *op. cit.*, p12.

17 *op. cit.*, p16.

18 James Hall, *Hall's Dictionary of Subjects and Symbols in Art*, rev. ed., London, 1989, p228.

19 Rowland, *op. cit.*, p149.

20 JA Phillips, *Eve. The History of an Idea*, San Francisco, 1984, p41.

21 Rowland, *op. cit.*, pp142-43.

22 Phillips, *op. cit.*, p64.

23 *ibid.*

24 Rowland, *op. cit.*, p144.

25 *op. cit.*, p140.

26 *ibid.*

27 Barber, p192.

28 White, p134. cf. the account of Bishop Theobaldus in Alan Wood Rendell (ed. & transl.), *Physiologus: A Metrical Bestiary of Twelve Chapters by Bishop Theobald*, London, 1928, pp35-37.

29 White, *loc. cit.*

30 Rendell, *op. cit.*, p36.

31 *ibid.*

32 Rowland, *op. cit.*, p53.

33 Shakespeare, *King Lear* IV, vi 124-29.

34 James Hall, *op. cit.*, rev. ed., London, 1989, p61.

35 Keith Thomas, *Man and the Natural World. Changing Attitudes in England 1500-1800*, Harmondsworth, 1984, pp134-35.

36 JG Frazer, *The Golden Bough. A Study in Magic and Religion*, abridged ed., London & Basingstoke, 1922, pp280-81.

37 Rowland, *op. cit.*, p44.

38 Frazer, *op. cit.*, p280; for the practice in general, pp274ff; see also Robert Graves, *The Greek Myths* 2 vols, Harmondsworth, 1955; rev. ed. 1984, I 91.4 p311.

39 Graves, *loc. cit.*

40 *Metamorphoses* VIII, 155-56.

41 Hall, *op. cit.*, p234.

42 *Metamorphoses* VIII: 173-74.

43 Thomas H Carpenter, *Art and Myth in Ancient Greece: a Handbook*, London, 1991; repr. 1992, p163.

44 Hall, *op. cit.*, p300.

45 P Eluard, 'Fin d'un monstre', [End of a Monster] in *A Pablo Picasso*, London/ Geneva/Paris, 1947, p78, transl. in R Penrose 'Beauty and the Monster', in J Golding & R Penrose (eds.), *Picasso 1881-1973*, Ware, 1988 [1973], p178.

46 The vexed question of the relationship between Nietzsche and Picasso continues to be a topic of research. See M Rosenthal, 'The Nietzschean Character of Picasso's Early Development', *Arts Magazine*, LV, October 1980, pp87-91; R Johnson, 'The 'Demoiselles d'Avignon' and Dionysian Destruction', *Arts Magazine* LV, October 1980, pp94-101; JM Nash, 'The Nature of Cubism, A study of conflicting explanations', *Art History*, Vol 3, No 4, December 1980, pp435-47; and J Finlay, *Violence and Destruction in the Collages and Papiers Collés of Pablo Picasso: 1926 and 1912-14*, unpublished MA Report, Courtauld Institute of Art, 1992.

47 See F Nietzsche, *The Birth of Tragedy Out of the Spirit of Music*, 1872, (transl.) W Kauffman, New York, 1968, *passim*.

48 *ibid.*, p37.

49 Nietzsche laments the loss of the spirit of the satyr in sentimental representations of him as a tender shepherd. Nietzsche's satyr, by contrast, is the 'offspring of a longing for the primitive and natural … the embodiment of man's highest and most intense emotions, the ecstatic reveler enraptured by the proximity of his god, the sympathetic companion in whom the suffering of the god is repeated, one who proclaims wisdom from the very heart of nature, a symbol of the sexual omnipotence of nature which the Greeks used

to contemplate with reverent wonder.' *ibid.*, p61. Picasso seems to have reserved this kind of existential meaning for the Minotaur.

50 *ibid.*, section eight.

51 DD Duncan, *Picasso's Picassos: The Treasures of La Californie*, London, 1961, pp141-43.

52 Interpretations as to the time of day vary. Baer argues that it changes in the various states of the print, B Baer, *Picasso The Printmaker*, Dallas, 1983, p98.

53 Picasso added three portraits of Vollard on 4th March 1937, to bring the number of prints up to a hundred. *ibid.*, p74.

54 FC Serraller, 'Revueltas Modernas del Clasicismo', in G Tinterow (ed.) *Picasso clasico*, Malaga, 1992, pp27-67, this reference p51 & p55.

55 Baer, *op. cit.*, p99. See also L Steinberg, 'Picasso's Sleepwatchers', *Other Criteria*, Oxford, 1972, pp93-114.

56 See G Schiff, 'Picasso's Suite 347; or Painting as an Act of Love', *Art News Annual*, no 38, 1972, pp238-53; and R Wollheim, 'Painting, Omnipotence and the Gaze', *Painting as an Art*, London, 1987, Chap V.

57 L Steinberg, 'Picasso's Sleepwatchers', *op. cit.*

58 A number of writers, most recently Brigitte Baer, have seen in this faun a maturity and sensitivity which ranks him alongside Picasso's Minotaur. See B Baer, 'Créativité, mythes et métamorphoses dans les annés trente', *Picasso Clasico, op. cit.*, p353.

59 Gilot reports these descriptions of the Minotaurs in *The Vollard Suite* after a delay of over twenty years. Their degree of reliability must be questioned. However, the spirit of Picasso's speech, if not the letter, seems plausible. F Gilot & C Lake, *Life with Picasso*, London, 1965, p42.

60 Surrealism had an equally strong political dimension. See, for example, HS Gershman, *The Surrealist Revolution in France*, Michigan, 1974, Ch IV.

61 For a more sophisticated account see D Ades, 'Freud and Surrealist Painting', *Freud: The Man, His Work, His Influence*, London, 1972, pp138-49.

62 Minotaur 1/1/28, Musée National d'Art Moderne, Centre Georges Pompidou.

63 The links and differences between Picasso and the Surrealists are discussed in J Golding, 'Picasso and Surrealism', in Golding & Penrose, *op. cit.*, pp77-121; E Cowling, ''Proudly We Claim Him as One of Us'': Breton, Picasso and the Surrealist Movement', *Art History* 8, No.1, March 1985, pp82-104.

64 Georges Bataille, together with the surrealist artist, André Masson, suggested the title 'Minotaure' for the periodical. According to Masson, he was to do the first cover, but gave way to Picasso at the publisher's request. See M Ries, 'Picasso and the Myth of the Minotaur', *Art Journal* 32, No.2, Winter 1972-73, pp142-45, this reference p142.

65 For a detailed discussion of this see AC Costello, *Picasso's 'Vollard Suite'*, New York, 1979, pp181-94, which makes some reference to Nietzsche's categories.

66 GK Fiero, 'Picasso's Minotaur', *Art International* 26, No.5, November-December 1983, pp20-30, this reference p21.

67 G Schiff, *Picasso at Work at Home*, Miami, 1985, p129.

68 Suite Vollard [SV], nos. 57, 58, 59, 60, 62, 63, 64, 65, 66, 68, 89, 90, 91, 92, 94.

69 SV 89-92.

70 B Baer, *Picasso the Printmaker, op. cit.*, p81, makes this point, although I do not agree with the degree of emphasis which she gives to the affair with Marie-Thérèse Walter in the re-interpretation of the Minotaur prints. I am nevertheless indebted to her extremely perceptive and scholarly analysis of the cycle.

71 SV 94.

72 Costello, *op. cit.*, p302 notes that Ariadne wears a wreath in certain versions of the myth. She also points out that in three of the print versions of the composition the bouquet is transformed into a dove, p311.

73 SV 95; 96; 97.

74 S Freud, *The Interpretation of Dreams*, 1900, (transl. J Strachey), London, 1954, Chapter VI.

75 Undoubtedly the *Minotauromachia* is the Picasso equivalent of Rembrandt's 'Hundred Guilder' Print.

76 See Costello, op. cit., p313 for references.

77 Reproduced in R Penrose, *Picasso: His Life and Work*, London, 1958, opposite p96.

78 Picasso's first text dates from 18th April 1935.

79 Translated in R Penrose, *op. cit.*, p335.

80 Penrose, 'Beauty and the Monster', *op. cit.*, p189.

81 'The Second Coming', *Collected Poems of WB Yeats*, London, 1978 (2nd ed.), p211.

82 The cancelled plates still exist, MT Ocaña et al, *Picasso: The Ludwig Collection*, Munich, 1992, no. 164.

83 See P Failing, 'Picasso's "Cries of Children… Cries of Stones"', *Art News* 75, No.7 (September 1977), pp55-64.

84 *ibid.*, *passim*, for extensive analysis.

85 JL Sert, the architect of the Barcelona Pavilion which would house Picasso's *Guernica* in 1937, during a symposium on Guernica held in New York in 1947, quoted in *ibid.*, p56.

86 Translated in AH Barr, *Picasso: Fifty Years of his Art*, New York, 1946, p196, emphases added.

Illustrations

Picasso, Barcelona (MPB 110.933) (p65).

The Donkey and the She-Ass, La Coruña, 1891, pencil on paper, 20.7 x 13cm, Museu Picasso, Barcelona, (MPB 110.927, p178) (p22).

Donkey/Ass, 1940, ink on paper, 13.5 x 21cm, Picasso Estate (Inv 4112; Z.X.554) (p65).

Dove, 14/10/53, ceramic, 15 x 21 x 13cm, MAM Ceret Coll., Musée d'Art Moderne, Ceret (p81).

The Dragonfly [La Libellule], *Histoire naturelle du Comte de Buffon*, Spring 1936, sugar lift aquatint, 36 x 28cm, Victoria & Albert Museum, London (B 354) (p156).

Dream and Lie of Franco I, 8/1/37 with aquatint added 25/5/37, etching and aquatint on paper, 31.7 x 42.2cm, British Museum, London (B 297) (p191).

Dream and Lie of Franco II, 8/1/37 with aquatint added 25/5/37 and final four panels added 7/6/37, etching and aquatint on paper, 31.8 x 42.2cm, British Museum, London (B 298) (p191).

Eel, Big Fish, Octopuses, Sea Urchins, 28/10/46, oil on plywood, 90 x 127.5cm, Musée Picasso, Antibes (Z.XIV.325) (p140).

The Elephant Trainer, 1905, China ink on paper, 30 x 41.5cm, Picasso Estate, (Inv 828; Z.XXII.191) (p27).

The Face of Peace, Vallauris, September 1951, pencil on paper, 51 x 66cm, Musée Picasso, Paris (MP 1416) (p79).

Fauns and Goat, 1959, colour linocut, 53 x 64cm, (B 934) (p182).

Faun unveiling a Woman, 12/6/36, aquatint, 31.7 x 41.7cm, Tate Gallery, London (B 230) (p177).

Flayed Head of a Sheep, Royan 4/10/39, oil on canvas, 50 x 61cm, Musée des Beaux-Arts, Lyon (MP.1990-20; Z.IX.351) (p132).

The Flea [La Puce], *Histoire naturelle du Comte de Buffon*, Spring 1936, sugar lift aquatint, 36 x 28cm, Victoria & Albert Museum, London (B 359) (p152).

Flowers and Insects, 17/6/56 (IV), China ink on paper, 66 x 50.5cm, Picasso Estate (Inv 5687; Z.XVII.126) (p156).

The Goat, 1946, oil and ripolin on fibrocement, 120 x 150cm, Musée Picasso, Antibes (Z.XIV.241) (p131).

The Goat, 1950, original plaster, 120.5 x 72 x 144cm, Musée Picasso, Paris (MP 339; S.409.I) (p132).

Goat's Skull, Bottle and Candle, 1951-53, painted bronze, 78.8 x 95.3 x 54.5, Museum of Modern Art, New York (S.410.IIb) (p133).

Guernica, May-June 1937, oil on canvas, 349 x 777cm, Museo Nacional de Arte Reina Sofia, Madrid. On permanent loan from the Museo del Prado (Z.IX.65) (p13).

Head of a Bull, Boisgeloup, 1931-32, bronze (unique cast), 35 x 55 x 53cm, (MP 296; S.127 (II)) (p38).

Head of a Bull (Minotaur), Cannes, 1958, wood, sawn and painted, 126.5 x 97cm, Private Collection, Thomas Ammann Fine Art, Zurich (S.546a) (p188).

Head of a Cat, La Coruña, 1892, pencil on paper, 16.4 x 20.2cm, Museu Picasso, Barcelona (MPB 110.998) (p104).

Head of a Horse, 3,4/11/62, oil on canvas, 73 x 59.5cm, Sprengel Museum, Hannover (Z.XXIII.66) (p64).

The Horse [Le Cheval], *Histoire naturelle du Comte de Buffon*, Spring 1936, sugar lift aquatint, 36 x 28cm, Victoria & Albert Museum, London (B 328) (p59).

Horse and Bull, 21/1/34, oil on canvas, 65 x 54cm, Picasso Estate (Inv 12677; Z.VIII.225) (p43).

Horse Lying Down, Juan-les-Pins, 5/9/30, Indian ink on a postcard of the moon, 8.8 x 14cm, Musée Picasso, Paris (MP 1034) (p62).

Little Girl with a Horse and Doll, 22/1/38, oil on canvas, 73 x 60cm, Picasso Estate (Inv 12834; Z.IX.101) (p63).

Lobster and Bottle, 26/12/48, oil on canvas, 50 x 61, Private Collection, Thomas Amman Fine Art, Zurich (Z.XV.114) (p147).

Man with a Lamb, Watermelon Eater and Flautist, 3/2/67, bistre crayon on paper, 48 x 63.5, Thomas Ammann Fine Art, Zurich

(Z.XXVII.436) (p131).

Man with a Sheep, 1943, bronze, 222.5 x 78 x 78cm, Musée Picasso, Paris (MP 331; S.280.II) (p128).

Man with a Sheep, Paris 27-29/3/43, China ink and scraping, 65 x 50.5cm, Musée Picasso, Antibes (MP 1990-75; Z.XII.297) (p128).

Man with a Wolf, 1914-15, pencil on paper, 32.5 x 23.5cm, Coll. Marina Picasso, Geneva (Inv 1719; Z.XXIX.107) (p107).

Maquette for the cover of Minotaure, Paris, May 1933, collage: pencil on paper, corrugated cardboard, silver foil, ribbon, wallpaper painted with gold paint and gouache, paper doily, burnt linen leaves, tacks, and charcoal on wood, 48.5 x 41cm, Museum of Modern Art, New York (p188).

Matt Owl, 1955, rectangular dish: authentic replica white earthenware clay, decoration in engobes engraved by knife, glaze underside, black, white, blue, 32 x 39cm, Musée de la Ville de Vallauris (AR 284; R 726) (p83).

Minotaur and Horse, Boisgeloup, 15/4/35, pencil on paper, 17.5 x 25.5cm, Musée Picasso, Paris, (MP 1144; Z.VIII.244) (p59).

Minotaur with a Glass, 29/4/58-31/5/58, oil on canvas, 146 x 114cm, Picasso Estate (Inv 13345; Z.XVIII.98) (p186).

Minotauromachia, VIIth state, Paris, 23/3/35, etching and scraper, 49.5 x 69.3cm, Fitzwilliam Museum, Cambridge (Geiser/Baer III, 573) (p189).

Monkey [Le singe], *Histoire naturelle du Comte de Buffon*, 9/2/36, sugar lift aquatint, 36 x 28cm, Victoria & Albert Museum, London, (B 339) (p167).

Monkey with a Car-Head: Study for Ape and Young, c1951, crayon on paper, Picasso Estate (Inv 6351r) (p169).

Naked Woman and Satyrs, 1905-1906, sepia wash, 21.2 x 13.5cm, Picasso Estate (Inv 577; Z.VI.803) (p193).

Night Fishing in Antibes, August 1939, oil on canvas, 205.8 x 345.4cm, The Museum of Modern Art, New York (Z.IX.316) (p148).

Octopus Plate, Vallauris, 29/10/47 (IV), rectangular plate in terracotta; painted in black, blue, green and red dots on enameled white ground; engraved lines white, 32 x 38cm, Coll. Marina Picasso, Geneva (Inv 57217) (p144).

Owl attacking a Cat, Golfe-Juan, 3/8/46, pencil and charcoal on paper, 66 x 50.5cm, Musée Picasso, Paris (MP 1376; Z.XIV.199) (p109).

The Owl Cage, 21/3/47, oil on panel, 80 x 100cm, Picasso Estate (Inv 13129) (p84).

The Pall-Bearers, August 1952, crayon on paper, 21 x 27cm, Picasso Estate, (Inv 5315) (p27).

The Perched Pigeons (Landscape with Pigeons), 2/4/60, oil on canvas, 50 x 61cm, Thomas Ammann Fine Art, Zurich (Z.XIX.199) (p78).

The Piano, Cannes, 17/10/57, oil on canvas, 130 x 96cm, Museu Picasso, Barcelona (MPB 70.472; Z.XVII,404) (p114).

Picasso par lui-même: Self-Caricature and Other Sketches, 1/1/1903, pen on paper, 11.8 x 10.7cm, Museu Picasso, Barcelona (MPB 110.440) (p168).

Portrait of a Bearded Man [Ambroise Vollard] with a Cat, c1937, oil on canvas, 61 x 46cm, Picasso Estate (Inv 12902) (p104).

The Ram [Le Belier], *Histoire naturelle du Comte de Buffon*, Spring 1936, sugar lift aquatint, 36 x 28cm, Victoria & Albert Museum, London (B 332) (p127).

The Ram's Head, 1925, oil on canvas, 83.2 x 101.65cm, Norton-Simon Museum, Pasadena (Z.V.443) (p134).

Seated Man and Young Girl with Monkey and Apple, Vallauris 26/1/54, watercolour on paper, 24 x 32cm, Private Collection (Z.XVI.229) (p170).

Seated Woman with a Dog, 1914, pencil on paper, 36 x 24.5cm, Coll. Marina Picasso, Geneva (Inv 1720; Z.XXIX.109) (p107).

Self-portrait with a Dog, Paris, 1902, pen on paper, 11.5 x 13cm,

Museu Picasso, Barcelona (MPB 110.443; not in Z) (p97).

Skull [Head] of a Sheep, Vallauris, 1951, charcoal on paper, 50.5 x 65.5cm, Coll. Marina Picasso, Geneva (Inv 05727) (p133).

The Spanish Bull [Le Toro Espagnol], Histoire naturelle du Comte de Buffon, Spring 1936, sugar lift aquatint, 36 x 28cm, Victoria & Albert Museum, London (B 331) (p36).

Sport of Pages, Vallauris, 24/2/51, oil on wood, 54 x 65cm, Musée Picasso, Paris (MP 204; Z.XV.184) (p54).

Square Tile with Donkey and Flute Player, 27/2/61, faience, engobe painting beneath glaze, 25.5 x 25.5cm, Ludwig Collection, Aachen (p67).

Still-life with Cat and Lobster, Mougins, 23/10-1/11/62, oil on canvas, 130 x 162cm, Hakone Open-Air Museum, (Z.XX.356) (p149).

Still-life with Bull's Head, Cannes, 25/5-9/6/58, oil on canvas, 162.5 x 130cm, Musée Picasso, Paris (MP.213; Z.XVII.237) (p31).

Still-life with Owl and Three Urchins, 6/11/46, oil on wood, 81.5 x 79cm, Musée Picasso, Antibes, (Z.XIV.255) (p76).

Still-life with Tuna; 18/3/37, oil on canvas, 21.5 x 27cm, Picasso Estate (Inv 12768) (p146).

Studies for illustration of Le bestiaire ou cortège d'Orphée *by Apollinaire*, 1907, ink on paper, 26 x 20.7cm, Musée Picasso, [MP 1989-1] (p21).

Studies of a woman with striped stockings; black cat; caricatures, 1902, China ink on paper, 20 x 31.5cm, Picasso Estate (Inv 224) (p95).

Study for a Manager and a Pig, 1916-17, pencil on paper, 27 x 22.5cm, Musée Picasso (MP 1613; Z.II*.957) (p26).

Study for Cat eating a Pigeon [bird], 22/4/39, China ink on paper, 23 x 29cm, Picasso Estate (Inv 4075; Z.IX.295) (p108).

Study for the American Manager and the Horse's Head, 1916-17, gouache and pencil on paper, 20.5 x 28cm, Musée Picasso, Paris (MP 1598; Z.II*.956) (p63).

Terrine: Pigeon with Peas, Cannes, 8.3.61, mixed media, 7.4 x 19.5 x 12.9cm, Private Collection, Paris (S.577A) (p81).

Three Sheep's Heads, Paris, 17/10.39, oil on canvas, 65 x 89cm, Coll. Marina Picasso, Geneva (Inv 12961; Z.IX.349) (p122).

Untitled [Man, Woman, Girl and Dog], 7/3/71 (I), etching, 15 x 21cm, Galerie Louise Leiris, Paris (B 1924) (p115).

Untitled [Naked Man and Woman with a Dog], 22/6/68 (I), etching, 12.5 x 9cm, Galerie Louise Leiris, Paris (B 1658) (p99).

Untitled (Serenading Man, Naked Woman, and Owl), 11/5/70 (IV), etching, 27.5 x 35cm, Galerie Louise Leiris, Paris (B 1901) (p72).

Vase with Goats, 6/6/52, original print: white earthenware clay, deep engraving filled with oxidised paraffin, dipped in white enamel, brown, green, 19 x 23cm, Private Collection, Roxburghshire (AR 156; R 399) (p129).

The Vauvenargues Buffet and a Blue and White Spotty Dog, 21/6/59 (I), oil on canvas, 55 x 46cm, Picasso Estate (Inv 13377) (p112).

The Winged Horse, 1948, watercolour and ink on paper, 46 x 38cm, Picasso Estate (Inv 5056) (p190).

The Wolf [Le Loup], Histoire naturelle du Comte de Buffon, Spring 1936, sugar lift aquatint, 36 x 28cm, Victoria & Albert Museum, London (B 337) (p111).

The Woman and the Monkey, 6/7/66 (I), pencil on paper, 51 x 60cm, Picasso Estate Inv 6264) (p168).

Woman playing with a Dog, 8/3/53, ripolin on plywood, 81 x 100cm, Picasso-Museum, Lucerne, Galerie Rosengart (Z.XV.246) (p98).

Woman playing with a Kitten, 7-9/5/64, oil on canvas, Picasso Estate (Inv 13484; Z.XXIV.140) (p113).

Woman sacrificing a Goat, Paris 1938, pencil on paper, 24.2 x

45.5cm, Musée Picasso, Paris (MP 1205v; Z.IX.116) (p127).

Woman with a Cat, Mougins, 30/8/37, oil on canvas, 81 x 65cm, ex collection Dr Henri Laugier, Paris, present whereabouts unknown, (Z.VIII.373) (p110).

Woman with a Cat, 1964, oil on canvas, 97 x 195cm, Private Collection (p111).

Woman with a Cock, Paris 15/2/38, oil on canvas, 142 x 120cm, Private Collection, on loan to the Kunsthaus, Zürich (Z.IX.109) (p72).

Woman with a Dog, 31/5-7/6/62, oil on canvas, 146 x 114cm, Picasso Estate (Inv 13439; Z.XX.244) (p100).

Woman with a Green Hairbun and a Bird on her Shoulder, 14/1/70, oil on canvas, 100 x 81cm, Picasso Estate (Inv 13670) (p74).

Woman with a Veil, China ink and watercolour, 6/5/36, 25.5 x 34cm, Picasso Estate (Inv 3817) (p55).

Young Female Nude and Nude Child with a Goat, Gosol 1906, oil on canvas, 146 x 114cm, Barnes Foundation, Merion Penn. (Z.I.249) (p126).

Manuscript Illuminations
University Library, Cambridge
MS I.i.4.26, Bestiary, in Latin, mid 12th century, f. 42v: *Cock*, (p70).

Koninklijke Bibliotheek, The Hague
MS 78 D40 Missal 1323 by Petrus de Raimbeaucourt, f. 124r: *Apes Mocking Writing* (p164).

British Library, London
MS Add. 49622, f. 133: *Procession: Funeral of a Dog* (p27).
MS Harley 3244, Bestiary in Latin, c1255, f. 47: *Boar, Ox, Bull* (p29); f. 45: *Dog* (p96).
MS Harley 4751, Bestiary in Latin, c1230-40, f. 11: *Ape* (p163); f. 47: *Owl* (p85)
MS Royal 12 C xix, Bestiary in Latin, c1200-10, f. 31v: *Goat* (p119).
MS Royal 12F xiii, Bestiary in French, c1230, f. 42v: *Horses*, (p50).
MS Sloane 278, Dicta Chrysostomi in Latin, mid-13th century, f. 57: *Dragon* (p174).

Bodleian Library, Oxford
MS Ashmole 1511, Bestiary in Latin, early 13th century, f. 9r: *Adam Naming the Animals* (p9); f. 86r: *Fish* (p137); f. 44r: *Turtle Dove*, (p69).
MS Bodley 764, Bestiary in Latin, c1250, f. 46r: *Horses* (p49); f. 17v: *Satyr* (p173); f. 51 *Cat* (p89).
MS Douce 219-220, Master of Mary of Burgundy: 'The Book of Hours of Englebert of Nassau', f. 171r: *Coronation of the Virgin* (p151).
MS Laud Misc. 247, Bestiary in Latin, n.d., f. 147r: *Siren & Onocentaur* (p180).

Bibliothèque Nationale, Paris
MS lat. 16169, Albert the Great: *De animalibus*, 14th century, French, f. 84v: *Copulating Animals* (p23).

Painting and Drawing
Aertsen, Pieter: *The Butcher's Shop*, 1551, oil on panel, 124 x 129cm, Universitäta Kunstammlung, Uppsala (p31).
Anon. Dutch or German: *Vanitas*, 17th century, oil on panel, 54.2 x 40.4cm, Coll. Granville, Musée des Beaux-Arts, Dijon (p76).
Anon. Palaeolithic: *Bison, fallen hunter and duck decoy*, 'Shaft of the Dead Man', Lascaux caves, 18,000-13/12,000 BC (p8).
Beyeren, Abraham van: *Still-life with Turkey*, 17th century, oil on

panel, 74 x 59cm, Musée du Louvre, Paris (p85).

Bosch, Hieronymus: *Superbia* from the *Tabletop of the Seven Deadly Sins*, 1490, oil on panel whole, 120 x 150cm, Museo del Prado, Madrid (p92).

Botticelli, Sandro: *Pallas and the Centaur*, early 1480s, oil on canvas, 207 x 148cm, Uffizi Florence (p181).

Boucle, Pieter van: *Butcher's Table with Cat and Dog*, 1651, 113 x 149cm, Musée du Louvre, Paris (p120).

Carracci, Annibale: *The Butcher's Shop*, c1582-83, oil on canvas, 185 x 266cm, Christ Church Picture Gallery, Oxford (p120).

Chardin, Jean-Baptiste-Siméon: *The Ape Artist*, n.d., oil on canvas, 73 x 59.5cm, Musée du Louvre, Paris (p166); *The Ray*, 1728, oil on canvas, 114.5 x 146cm, Musée du Louvre, Paris (p143).

Clark, James: *The Thorney Prize Ox*, 1858, oil on canvas, 56 x 66cm, Museum of English Rural Life, Reading (p33).

Cornelis, van Haarlem: *The Fall of Man*, 1529, 273 x 220cm, oil on canvas, Rijksmuseum, Amsterdam (p164).

Dou, Gerrit: *Woman holding a Cock at her Window* ('La Ménagère hollandaise'), 1650, oil on panel, 26.5 x 20.5cm, Musée du Louvre, Paris (p73).

Dyck, Sir Anthony van: *Jupiter and Antiope*, first half 17th century, oil on canvas, 150 x 206cm, Museum voor Schone Kunsten, Ghent (p177).

Eyck, Jan van: *The Arnolfini Portrait*, 1434, oil on panel, 82 x 59.5cm, National Gallery, London (p99).

Fragonard, Jean Honoré: *Girl and Dog* ('La Gimblette'), c1770, oil on canvas, 89 x 70cm, Alte Pinakothek, Munich (p98).

Gainsborough, Thomas: *Gainsborough's Daughters, Margaret and Mary Chasing a Butterfly*, c1756, oil on canvas, 113.7 x 104.8cm, National Gallery, London (p155).

Géricault, Jean Louis André Théodore: *Race of Wild Horses at Rome*, 1817, paper on canvas, 45 x 60cm, Musée du Louvre, Paris (p54); *The Derby at Epsom*, 1821, oil on canvas, 92 x 123cm, Musée du Louvre, Paris (p58).

Goes, Hugo van der: *The Fall*, c1470, 32.3 x 21.9cm, Kunshistorisches Museum, Vienna (p180).

Greuze, Jean-Baptiste: *Girl with Doves* ('L'Innocence tenant deux pigeons'), Salon, 1800, oil on panel, 70 x 58.8cm, Wallace Collection, London (p71); *Girl with a Dead Canary*, 1765, oil on canvas, 52 x 45.7cm, National Gallery of Scotland, Edinburgh (p74).

Hogarth, William: *The Painter and his Pug*, 1745, oil on canvas, 90 x 69.9cm, Tate Gallery, London (p102).

Hone, Nathaniel: *Kitty Fisher*, 1765, oil on canvas, 74.93 x 62.23cm, National Portrait Gallery, London (p94).

Hunt, William Holman: *The Scapegoat*, 1854, oil on canvas, 33.7 x 45.9cm, Manchester City Art Gallery (p124).

Ingres, Jean Auguste Dominique: *Oedipus and the Sphinx*, c1826-28, oil on canvas, 17.8 x 13.7cm, National Gallery, London (p178); *The Martrydom of Saint Sinforiano* study, black chalk on paper, 54.8 x 41.3cm, Nelson-Atkins Museum of Art, Kansas City, Missouri (33-1401) (p55).

Kalf, Willem: *Still-life with the Drinking Horn of the Saint Sebastian Archer's Guild. Lobster and Glasses*, c1653, 86.4 x 102.2cm, oil on canvas, National Gallery, London (p140).

Landseer, Sir Edwin: *The Old Shepherd's Chief Mourner*, oil on panel, Victoria & Albert Museum, London (p102).

La Tour, Georges de: *Woman with the Flea*, n.d., canvas, 120 x 90cm, Musée Historique Lorraine, Nancy (p153).

Manet, Édouard: *Bullfight*, 1865-66, oil on canvas, 90 x 110cm, Musée d'Orsay, Paris (p37); *Still-life, Red Mullet and Eel*, 1864, 38 x 46cm, Musée D'Orsay, Paris. (p141); *Woman with a Cat*, c1882-83, oil on canvas, 92 x 73cm, Tate Gallery, London (p94).

Marseus van Schriek, Otto: *Serpents and Butterflies*, 1670, 70 x 55cm, oil on panel, Louvre, Paris (RF 3711) (p154).

Master of the Procession of the Ram: *The Procession of the Fatted Ox*, 108 x 166cm, Musée Picasso, Paris (p32).

Pontormo, Jacopo Carucci: *Portrait of a Woman*, Städelsches Kunstinstitut, Frankfurt am Main (p100).

Reynolds, Sir Joshua: *Woman tying her Garter*, 1752, leaf from a sketchbook, British Museum, London, (201a 10, f. 15) (p93).

Rubens, Sir Peter Paul: detail from *The Feast of Venus Verticordia*, mid-1630s, oil on canvas, 217 x 350cm, Kunshistorisches Museum, Vienna (p176).

Snyders, Frans: *Still-life with a Swan*, c1615-20, oil on canvas, Pushkin Museum of Fine Arts, Moscow (p103).

Steen, Jan Havicksz: *The Drunken Couple*, n.d., oil on panel, 52.5 x 64cm, Rijksmuseum, Amsterdam (p93).

Stubbs, George: *Horse attacked by a Lion*, oil on panel, 24.1 x 28.2cm, Tate Gallery, London (p55).

Ubertini, Francesco: *Portrait of a Lady*, n.d., present whereabouts unknown. (p110)

Uccello, Paolo: *The Rout of San Romano*, early 1450s, oil on panel, 183 x 319.5cm, National Gallery, London (p54).

Velázquez, Diego: *Baltasar Carlos on Horseback*, 1635, oil on canvas, 209 x 173cm, Museo del Prado, Madrid (p52); *Las Meninas*, 1656, oil on canvas, 318 x 276cm, Museo del Prado, Madrid (p115); *Il Cardinale l'Infante Fernando Cacciatore*, 1635, oil on canvas, 191 x 107cm, Museo del Prado, Madrid (p97).

Watts, George Frederic: *Minotaur*, 1878, oil on canvas, 118.1 x 94.5cm, Tate Gallery, London (p186).

Sculpture

Anon.: *Christ on a Donkey*, late 16th century, polychrome wood, Musée d'Unterlinden, Colmar (p52).

Anon.: *Faun carrying a Kid*, Museo del Prado (p128).

Anon.: *Saga Ram Mask*, Mali, Musée Picasso, Paris (MP 3641) (p133).

Anon. Cretan: *Bull and Acrobat*, bronze, 16 BC, height 11.1cm, British Museum, London (p35).

Anon. French: *Carnival of Animals*, South Transept Portal, Church of Saint-Pierre, Aulnay-de-Saintonge, France, 12th century (p17).

Anon. Greek: *Moskophorus* (Man with a Sacrificial Calf), 7 BC, marble, Acropolis Museum, Athens (p128).

Anon. Roman: *Mithraic Altar*, AD 2, San Clemente, Rome (p30).

Cecioni, Adriano: *Defecating Dog*, c1880, plaster, 3.5ins, coll. Aldo Gonelli, Florence (p101).

Book Illustration

Apollinaire, Guillaume: *Le bestiaire ou cortège d'Orphée: Le Boeuf*, woodcut by Raoul Dufy, RV 29.323 (p20).

Bewick, Thomas: *General History of Quadrupeds* (1792): *Dromedary*, wood engraving (p19).

Brant, Sebastian: *Das Narrenschiff*, 1494: *On Adultery*, woodcut (p92).

Cats, Jacob: *Sinne- en Minnebeelden*, 1700: Emblem IV, 'Amor formae condimentum' (p163).

Dapper, Olfert: *Description de l'Afrique*, 1686: *African Scene* (p18).

Johnston, Johann: *Historiae Naturalis, De Insectis*, 1657: Frontispiece, copper engraving designed by Matthaeus Merian the Younger (p154).

Khunrath, Heinrich: *Amphiteatrum sapientiae aeternae*, 1602: vignette 'Wat helffen fakeln licht oder brillen...' (p77).

Topsell, Edward: *The Histoire of Foure-footed Beasts*, 1607, Bodleian (M.3.14 Th.): *Aegopithecus* (p178); *Dromedary* (p19); *Satyr* (p179); *Sphinga* or *Sphinx* (p179).

Prints

Agostino Veneziano de' Musi (after Raphael): *Rape of Lucretia*, 1534, engraving, 253 x 401cm, Albertina, Vienna (**p101**).

Bonnard, Pierre: *Portrait of Ambroise Vollard*, c1924, etching on heavy laid paper, plate 34.6 x 22.8cm, sheet 45 x 33.9cm, Brooklyn Museum, New York (**p104**).

Bruegel, Pieter the Elder: *Big Fish eat Little Fish*, 1556-57, engraving, Bibliothèque Royal Albert Ier, Brussels (**p139**).

Dürer, Albrecht: *Adam and Eve*, 1504, engraving, 25.2 x 19.4cm, British Museum, London (**p14**); *Virgin and Child with Monkey*, n.d., c1498-99, engraving, 19.1 x 12.4cm, The Metropolitan Museum of Art, New York (**p165**); *Satyr Family*, 1505, engraving, 11.5 x 7cm, Clarence Buckingham Coll., Art Institute, Chicago (**p175**).

Genelli, Bonaventura: *Who will buy Love-Gods ('Wer kauft Liebesgötter'?)*, c1875, location unknown (**p73**).

Goltzius, Hendrick: *Luxuria*, n.d., 13.8 x 10.7cm, Bibliothèque Royal Albert Ier, Brussels (**p123**); *Taste* from the Series of the *Five Senses*, 1578, engraving by Philip Galle, 14 x 8.8cm, Rijksprentenkabinet, Amsterdam (**p171**); *The Holy Family with Saint John*, from the *Life of the Virgin* series, 1593, engraving, 46 x 35cm (**p91**).

Goya y Lucientes, Francisco José: *Caprichos 75*: ¿No hay quien nos desate (Is there no one to untie [annul] us?), 21.5 x 15cm, etching and burnished aquatint, British Museum, London (**p77**); *Tauromaquia 32* (dos grupos de picadores arrollados de sequida por un solo toro – Two groups of picadors put to rout, one after the other, by a single bull), 1816, working proof etching, burnished aquatint, drypoint and burin, British Museum, London (**p42**).

Meckenem, Israhel von: *Children Playing*, engraving, 10.9 x 13.9cm, Albertina, Vienna (Inv 1926, 1244) (**p52**).

Other Media

Anon. Cretan: Marine-style flat 'pilgrim flask' from Palaikastro 1500-1450 BC, height 28cm, Archaeological Museum, Heraklion (**p144**).

Anon. Greek: *Proitos, Bellerophon and Pegasos*, Apulian, early 4th century BC, red-figure stamnos, Museum of Fine Arts, Boston (00.349) (**p62**).

Anon. Greek: *Theseus and the Minotaur*, Attic black-figure amphora (Group E) from Vulci, British Museum, London (B 205, ABV 136.55) (**p182**).

Anon. Pompeian: *Cat Stealing a Bird*, AD 1, mosaic, 51 x 51cm Pompeii, Museo Archelogico Nazionale, Naples (**p90**).

Anon. Pompeian: *Fish and Crustaceans*, mosaic, 1 BC, Pompeii, Museo Archelogico Nazionale, Naples (**p138**).

Huet, Christophe: singerie, door panel, 1735, Musée Conde, Chantilly (**p165**).